India's Fight Against Corruption

J.P. Mittal

ATLANTIC
PUBLISHERS & DISTRIBUTORS (P) LTD

Published by

ATLANTIC

PUBLISHERS & DISTRIBUTORS (P) LTD

7/22, Ansari Road, Darya Ganj,
New Delhi-110002
Phones : +91-11-40775252, 23273880, 23275880, 23280451
Fax : +91-11-23285873
Web : www.atlanticbooks.com
E-mail : orders@atlanticbooks.com

Branch Office
5, Nallathambi Street, Wallajah Road,
Chennai-600002
Phones : +91-44-64611085, 32413319
E-mail : chennai@atlanticbooks.com

Printed in India at Glorious Printers, A-13, D.S.I.D.C., Jhilmil Industrial Area, Delhi-110095

Dedicated to Anna Hazare

Today Anna Hazare is a symbol of the fight against corruption, of which virtually every citizen in this country is a victim. Anna has touched the nerve of the people. The middle class is motivated to come out in the street. Hazare's campaign is a channel through which people are giving vent to their feelings. He should now free India from corruption with undivided attention, which is still a Herculean task. He may be called the father of anti-corruption in India as Mahatma Gandhi is called the father of the nation.

Preface

So long as there are human beings, there will be human weaknesses and human desires. One of the human weaknesses is the greed for money. Greed is the cause of many evils. One of the evils is to earn more and more money and to own unlimited property by any means, whether legal or illegal.

Government servants also try to earn as much money as possible, adopting evil means. The job of the government servant is to do his duty honestly and sincerely. But when a government servant starts taking bribes for doing his duty, it becomes an evil. Due to more greed sometimes he helps undeserving people, causing loss to the public exchequer. Both of these evils are called corruption. He generally invests illegal money in property, both movable and immovable.

Corruption strikes at the root of good governance. It is an impediment to faster growth. It dilutes, if not negates, the efforts at social inclusion. It becomes the cause of many more evils like rise in prices, adulteration, failure of law and order, absence of justice, etc.

There are different ways to eradicate corruption, depending upon the different forms of government like monarchy, socialism, communism, democracy, and republic. We have selected democracy as the form of government in our country. We have to decide the ways and means to remove corruption through democratic means.

Every form of government does not suit a nation as the traditions, customs, culture and habits of different races and societies differ. A particular form of government may be good for a particular class of people, but it may not prove good for others. Corruption will spoil any form of government. Moreover, there are different ways to remove corruption for different forms of government. Every method may not suit every form of government. For example, in China and Russia millions of people were killed before communism became a success. In some cases the people were hanged from the nearest lamppost. In other cases only the threat of being shot worked and stringent laws were framed to eradicate or control corruption. So we can also make stringent laws and let the courts punish the guilty or we can appoint a Lokpal with draconian powers to prosecute and punish the corrupt.

In India there is Vedic culture where religion teaches us to have a control over desires. The desire is never quenched by indulgence any more than the fire is extinguished by pouring oil in it. The more you satisfy your desires the more they increase. No objects of desire—property, gold or women—nothing can ever satisfy the desire of man. But still in India there is rampant corruption and the greed has no limits.

The CBI caught a Chief Secretary of a State government holding several farmhouses, plots, flats and showrooms. He had two daughters who were married to the IAS officers. Still his greed had no limit. He could be arrested only after retirement because the Chief Minister of the State did not give permission to the CBI to prosecute him. The Chief Minister and his family have been found to hold assets worth much more than their known sources of income.

A Chief Engineer took more than 100 crore of rupees in bribe and deposited them in 67 bank accounts. From that amount he is alleged to have purchased an Engineering College.

Another Chief Minister of a poor State was arrested by the CBI for owning assets of more than 8,000 crore of rupees. The President of a government company is collecting gold bricks in bribe. Ten gold bricks were found in his possession. Trillions of dollars of Indians are deposited in foreign banks. Property and gold are the two main items in which the black money is being invested or it is being deposited in foreign banks. Cash is stashed in pillows, quilts, mattresses and commodes as well as in lockers. This has created an imbalance in society.

Corruption has affected our morals. A cartoon published in *Hindustan Times* dated 16th April 2011 depicts that we have a zero moral. Ponds in villages, towns and cities are disappearing. The water level in the wells and tube wells has gone down by more than 50 feet. Water in the rivers has become polluted due to untreated industrial waste and sewage going into the rivers. Even the water of the Ganga at Haridwar has become unfit for bathing or drinking. This is the condition when hundreds of crores of rupees have been spent in cleaning the rivers.

Milk is being adulterated with urea and shampoo. With 15 grams of shampoo 15 litres of synthetic milk is being produced. *Desi ghee* (oil) is being adulterated with the animal fat. On festival days sweets are manufactured with milk adulterated with synthetic milk. The size of the vegetables is being increased by giving them injections, which are harmful for human beings.

During a discussion in Parliament on the address of the President, no political party gave any suggestion how corruption can be eradicated or controlled. They only criticized the government for its inability to control corruption and inflation.

Prime Minister Manmohan Singh admitted on 4th February 2011 in New Delhi that the two of the biggest challenges facing his government are corruption and inflation (*HT* dated 5th February 2011). Numerous scams are taking place one after the other. Inflation is the cause of rampant corruption in the government and the scams and scandals. Public money is not being spent prudently. Due to corruption the officers of Haryana government failed to punish a police officer who molested a 14-year-old girl. The politics in Haryana is of *Aya Ram and Gaya Ram* sort. There is no ideology. Politicians change parties as people change clothes daily.

Corruption has been there in India since the Vedic times. There are stories in *Puranas* how a particular government servant was caught asking for a bribe and how the king whipped him. Indians are generally God-fearing people and remain law abiding when there is the fear of law. They indulge in corruption when they find that their neighbour is guilty of corruption and is not being punished or the punishment is less than the gain. The minute they find that the punishment for corruption is fast and severe, their desire to do corruption will evaporate.

I hope, after reading this book, the reader would feel better informed and educated about various forms of government, anti-corruption laws and how corruption can be eradicated or controlled in society.

I am thankful to Wikipedia and the newspapers without whose help this book would not have been written. I am also thankful to Professor Dr R.A. Gupta for his help in improving English and for the valuable suggestions he gave to me.

A substance of the UN Convention Against Corruption, RTI Act, 2005, Government Lokpal Bill, 2010 and Jan Lokpal Bill, 2010 have been given in the book. But neither the author nor the publisher takes any responsibility about their correctness.

J.P. Mittal

Contents

1

Forms of Government

Generally, there are four types of governments, viz. socialist, communist, democratic and monarchy. Socialism is a political and economic theory advocating that a country's land, transport, natural resources and chief industries should be owned and controlled by the whole community or by the State, and that wealth should be equally distributed (*Oxford Advanced Learner's Dictionary*). Modern socialism originated from 18th century intellectual and working class political movement that criticized the effects of industrialization and private property of society.

But nobody would like to part with his land and property willingly. How can this be implemented is debatable and peaceful ways and means are to be found to achieve the object. Generally the job is done through cooperative societies.

In socialism, the wealth should be distributed equally by peaceful means. Some political parties like the Samajwadi Party of Mulayam Singh and the Bahujan Samajwadi Party of Mayavati call themselves socialists. But are they really socialists is a million-dollar question.

Socialism does not suit the Asian and the African countries including India where the society does not accept equality among the citizens. Nobody likes to marry his daughter outside his caste or creed. Society is divided into many segments with different traditions, customs, habits and the ways of living and working.

Communism is one of the forms of government where the land and property, industry, transport and resources are owned and controlled by the State. Nobody may like to part with his lands and buildings willingly. In communism, a powerful group of people decide that communism is in the interest of the people. It is then implemented and forced down the throat of the people. They do not hesitate to kill millions of people if they have to do it, because it is again done in the interest of the people.

Communism is a social and economic system in which there is no private ownership and the means of production belong to all the members of society. It is a political doctrine or movement that aims at establishing such a society. Its system of government is by a ruling Communist Party (*Oxford Advanced Learner's Dictionary*).

In the scheme of historical materialism, communism is the idea of a free society with no division or alienation, where mankind is free from oppression and scarcity. A communist society would have no governments, countries, or class divisions. In Marxist theory, the dictatorship of the proletariat is the intermediate system between capitalism and communism, when the government is in the process of changing the means of ownership from private to collective ownership.

The exact definition of communism varies, and it is often mistakenly used interchangeably with socialism. However, Marxist theory contends that socialism is just a transitional stage on the way to communism. In modern usage, communism is often used to refer to the policies of states run by Communist parties, regardless of the type of economic system they preside over.

China is now a developing country and is also the fastest-growing economy. It is the second-largest luxury market where foreign designer stores post higher profits in upwardly mobile second and third-tier cities than Shanghai. Sanya, a fishing village in the south is becoming haven for the new Chinese millionaires.

According to Forbes magazine Chinese President Jintavo has become the strongest man in the world leaving behind US President Obama. He is said to be different from Western politicians. To estimate his power it is said that he can reverse the flow of the rivers [*Hindustan* (Hindi) dated 11/3/2011].

It would thus be seen from above that communism is nothing but a form of socialism, which is imposed on the public by force by a group of people by killing millions of them. So it does not suit the countries of Asia and Africa, which have their distinctive way of thinking and living. There is no rampant corruption in communist countries. But there is corruption in Asia and Africa. It can be eradicated by making stringent laws against corruption or by appointing a person with draconian powers.

In socialism and communism both the land and property, means of production, transport and resources are owned and controlled by the State. They are considered good for the people. But whereas in socialism it is to be done by peaceful means, in communism it is done by force, even if millions of people are put to death because it is done for the good of the country and the people.

Some argue that socialist states have contained two new distinct classes. The first are those who are in government and therefore have power and the second are those who are not in government and do not have power, i.e. the working class. This is taken to be a different form of capitalism, in which the government, as owner of the means of production, takes on the role played by the capitalist class. This arrangement is referred to as "State capitalism". These state capitalist regimes have generally followed a planned economy model without making a transition to this hypothetical final stage.

Thus the difference in socialism and communism appears to be that if the socialism is implemented in a democratic way, it is called socialism. If it is implemented by force of the Communist Party, it is called communism.

But so far nobody has been able to implement socialism fully either by democratic means or through force (the barrel of the gun) except in a family where the property is equally divided among its members irrespective of their age and social status. But then they seldom stay together and fight on trivial matters.

Democracy is a system of government by the whole people of a country, especially through representation whom they elect. It is a government that allows freedom of speech, religion, and political opinion, that uphold the rule of law and majority rule and that respect the rights of minorities (*Oxford Advanced Learner's Dictionary*).

Sir Winston Churchill said that democracy is the worst form of government except all those other forms that have been tried from time to time. That means the form of government, which suits the best to the people is the best type of government. After all the people get the government they deserve.

India emerged as the world's largest democracy and continues to be so. But it is also failing due to large-scale corruption, which the democratic government is not able to control. There are charges of corruption even against ministers, secretaries of the government, and Central Vigilance Commissioner. Democracy needs self-discipline among the people, which is not there in Asian and African countries.

Indians are divided among many castes, creeds, and religion. Every one thinks himself superior to other. There is no equality among various castes. We do not respect the rights of minorities. In fact we do not allow freedom of speech, freedom of religion, and often fight on small matters. We do not allow our daughters to marry in other religion or in other caste.

We do not give equal rights to lower castes. A lower caste bridegroom was sitting on a chair at his own wedding ceremonies and was watching the entertainment programme in Chhatarpur, Madhya Pradesh. He was beaten up by upper caste youth because he dared to sit on a chair in his presence (*HT* dated 21st May 2011).

Democracy may also not be suitable for a big country like India where coalition governments have become an order of the day unless the number of parties is restricted to two or three. Actually the parties are not formed based on ideology. So they can be named as Socialist Party, Communist Party, Democratic Party, Republican Party, etc. Moreover, democracy being a weak governance, stringent laws need to be framed for democracy to be successful in Asian and African countries.

A monarchy is a form of government in which all political power is absolutely or nominally lodged with an individual, known as a monarch (ruler), or a King or a Queen. As a political entity, the monarch is the head of state, generally until his death or abdication, and is wholly set apart from all other members of the state.

However, the main question is whether monarchy suits the countries of Asia and Africa. It has its own advantages and disadvantages. The democratic thinking is foreign to us. We always had monarchy and do not have self-discipline required for democracy. Both in Iraq and Afghanistan there was tribal culture and there was monarchy. But there was no corruption.

After the intervention of the USA it has been changed to democracy. But in both the countries it has caused rampant corruption. Thus monarchy may suit them better than the democracy unless stringent laws are made against corruption. Corruption is the major problem in the functioning of democracy in the countries of Asia and Africa.

A republic is one of the forms of government in which the people or some portion thereof retain supreme control over the government, and in which the head of government is not a monarch. The word "republic" is derived from the Latin phrase *res publica*, which can be translated as "a public affair". Both modern and ancient republics vary widely in their ideology and composition. The most common definition of a republic is a state without a monarch. In republics such as the United States and France, the executive is legitimized both by a constitution and by popular suffrage.

In the United States, James Madison defined republic in terms of representative democracy as opposed to direct democracy, and this usage is still employed by many viewing themselves as "democrats". Montesquien included both democracies, where all the people have a share in rule, and aristocracies or oligarchies, where only some of the people rule, as republican forms of governments. In modern political science, republicanism refers to a specific ideology that is based on civic virtue and is considered distinct from ideologies such as liberalism.

Most often a republic is a sovereign country, but there are also sub-national entities that are referred to as republics, or which have governments that are described as "republican" in nature. For instance constitution of the United States guarantees to every State in this Union a Republican form of Government. The Soviet Union was a single nation composed of distinct and nominally Sovereign Soviet Socialist Republics.

States of the US are required, like the federal government, to be republican in form, with final authority resting with the people. This was required because the states were intended to create and enforce most domestic laws, with the exception of areas delegated to the federal government and prohibited to the states. The founding fathers of the country intended most domestic laws to be handled by the states, although, over time, the federal government gained more and more influence over domestic law.

Requiring the states to be a republic in form was seen as protecting the citizens' rights and preventing a state from becoming a dictatorship or monarchy, and reflected unwillingness on the part of the original 13 states (all independent republics) to unite with other states that were not republics. Additionally, this requirement ensured that only other republics could join the union.

In the example of the United States, the original 13 British colonies became independent states after the American Revolution, each having a republican form of government. These independent states initially formed a loose confederation called the United States and then later formed the current United States by ratifying the current US Constitution, creating a union of sovereign states with the union or federal government also being a republic. Any state joining the union later was also required to be a republic.

Thus the people need someone to rule them. It is for the people to decide what type of government they want. Indians have decided to have democracy. But democracy is a very weak form of government for governance unless there is self-discipline among the members of the society, which is not there in India.

The next solution is that democracy should function with stringent laws against corruption or for not performing one's duty. Democracy is failing in India due to rampant corruption. Perhaps time has come to have draconian laws for punishment against corruption.

2

Anti-Corruption Laws

It is difficult to define in exact terms what corruption is. The World Bank defines corruption as the use of public office for private profit. Generally, bribery is considered as corruption. If any public servant is caught taking bribe or is found holding assets more than his known sources of income, it is called corruption. If this corruption can be eradicated or controlled it would solve most of the problems of the public.

Indian Penal Code, 1860: Corruption is a serious type of anti-social act in criminal law. The Indian Penal Code, 1860, contains a full chapter IX which deals with corruption. Mainly misconduct and abuse of power by public servants is covered under this chapter. Being governed by the traditional rules of criminal liability, the provisions in the IPC could not successfully combat corruption by public servants who constituted a powerful class which has a considerable influence for tilting the scales of justice.

Moreover, the definition of the public servant suffers from many defects as many important functionaries engaged in discharging public duties are left out of the definition of public servant. However, the redeeming feature of the period till the start of the First World War was that the people in India, by and large, were bound by moral values who abhorred corruption and not by materialistic considerations of the industrialized Western world.

The scope of bribery and corruption by public servants had considerably increased due to war conditions. Even after the Second World War opportunities for corrupt practices remained for a considerable time. Extensive schemes for post war reconstruction opened wide new avenues for corruption among public servants. However, the existing provisions of the Indian Penal Code were found to be insufficient for effective handling and controlling of corrupt public servants. Therefore, to supplement and strengthen law against corruption, the Prevention of Corruption Act was framed.

Prevention of Corruption Act, 1947: The Prevention of Corruption Act, 1947, was a social legislation which aimed at eradicating corruption. It changed the traditional rules of criminal liability. Criminal misconduct in the discharge of official duty was made an offence under section 5 of the Act. However, it neither gave a separate definition of public servant nor made any improvement in section 21 of the IPC through special amending clause. Generally, public servants are prosecuted under section 161 of the IPC read with section 5 of the Act. It deals with taking illegal gratification by public servant or reward for showing official favour. In pursuance of the recommendations of the Santhanam Committee the Act was amended in 1964.

In spite of the amendment of the Act, the situation vitiated by corrupt practices could not be redeemed. Corruption expanded its sphere of activity by engulfing the entire society. Even the elected representatives of the people who are supposed to be the repository of public faith by discharging their duties with honesty and integrity succumbed to the vagaries of corruption by sharing its booty with public servants. The efforts made for bringing political corruption within the purview of the Act did not succeed as elected representatives through whom most of the corruption is routed were not considered as public servants.

IPC Amendment Bill, 1972 contained provisions for making MPs and MLAs as public servants, but the Joint Selection Committee of the Parliament deleted the same. The Supreme Court in Nayak, R.S. v Antulay, A.R. AIR 194 SC 684 has held that an MLA is not a public servant.

The Supreme Court upheld the rule of law in the administration of criminal justice by giving free hand to the top investigation agency (CBI) in corruption cases involving top politicians, bureaucrats and public men. But the wheels of criminal justice have got stuck up in the quagmire of legal niceties. The trail procedure is hampered as the proceedings are stayed on one pretext or the other. Non-conclusion of trail proceedings in all mega scams and bribery cases is an ample proof of the tardy pace of our criminal justice system despite a constitutional mandate of speedy justice. The lurking fear of political uncertainty and clandestine operation of the powerful accused for winning over the witnesses and brow beating the prosecution are some of the reasons which make the anti-corruption laws ineffective.

Even in ordinary cases of corruption, the Act has failed to achieve its objects. Despite the fact that investigation of corruption cases is conducted by a senior police officer, the operation of criminal justice system is dismal.

Prevention of Corruption Act, 1988: The Prevention of Corruption Act, 1988, is considered as the strong arm of criminal law. But it lacks provisions for protection of whistle-blowers and witnesses. It only provides some degree of protection against prosecution. It does not afford any protection against action that may be taken by the wrongdoers or his associates.

This Act considers requirement of obtaining prior sanction of an appropriate authority before any court takes cognizance of an offence by a public servant. Past experiences have shown that these provisions have often resulted in long delays. This Act does not consist of direct provision prohibiting a private person from offering a bribe or engaging in other corrupt practices. Such a provision is required to ensure that all parties in a corruption case are dealt with adequately.

There are also inordinate delays in prosecution of public servants against whom complaints have been made. In cases of corruption, it is extremely important that prosecution takes place within a short period as delays can affect the morale of the complainant and also increases the possibility of reprisals.

The Prevention of Corruption Act does not contain any provisions to deal with the cases where Indian citizens engage in corrupt activities with a foreign public official. Such a provision is required for bringing India's anti-corruption laws in line with the mandatory requirement of UNCAC.

The provisions of the Prevention of Corruption Act regarding confiscation of property is only permitted after prosecution for the relevant offence. To effectively discourage public servants from engaging in corrupt activities, it is necessary that the very possession of properties disproportionate to known sources of income of a public servant should be an offence and such properties to be confiscated by the state even pending prosecution.

The Prevention of Corruption Act has also been reduced to the status of ineffective legislation being fractured by the powerful Mafia patronizing corruption through the influence it wields in every sphere of life because of its nexus with politicians, bureaucrats and publicmen of prominence. Various directions issued by the Supreme Court regarding successful working of the Act have been ignored. (http://www.mightylaws.in/466/adequacy-legal-regulatory-framewor)

Therefore, it is necessary to make a draconian Lokpal Bill with exemplary punishment and confiscation of the property if we really want to eradicate corruption.

UN Convention Against Corruption: The UN Convention against corruption is the first legal international anti-corruption instrument. In its 8 Chapters and 71 Articles the UNCAC makes it obligatory for its States Parties to implement a wide and detailed range of anti-corruption measures affecting their laws, institutions and practices. These measures aim to promote the prevention, criminalization and law enforcement, international cooperation, asset recovery, technical assistance and information exchange, and mechanism for implementation.

The UNCAC is the most recent development in which experts and politicians have recognized the far-reaching impact of corruption and the need to develop effective measures against it at both the domestic and international levels. International action against corruption has progressed from general consideration and declarative statements to legally binding agreements. The bribery, the definition and understanding of corruption and measures against it have been made broader. The UNCAC deals with forms of corruption that had not been covered by many of the earlier international instruments, such as trading in official influence, general abuse of power, and various acts of corruption in the private sector. Another development includes the recovery of assets, a major concern for countries that pursue the assets of former leaders and other officials accused or found to have engaged in corruption.

A conference of the States Parties to the UNCAC was formed to improve cooperation between States Parties and to promote and review its implementation. It was to achieve the objectives set forth in the convention. The first meeting of the CoSP was held from 10-14 December 2006 at the Dead Sea, Jordan. The government representatives discussed the ways and means to follow-up on the UNCAC. They committed themselves to establishing a formal monitoring system. An inter-governmental working group was established to start working on the design of such a review of implementation mechanism. A working group was set up to promote coordination of activities related to technical assistance and another was set up for asset recovery.

The second CoSP was held in Bali, Indonesia from 28th January to 1st February 2008. The States Parties decided to take into account a balanced geographical approach and to avoid any punitive or adverse elements. They further decided to establish clear guidelines for every aspect of the mechanism and to promote universal adherence to the Convention. It was also decided to establish constructive collaboration in preventive measures, asset recovery, international cooperation and other areas. CoSP also reiterated its support for the Working Group on asset recovery, requested donors and receiving countries to strengthen coordination and enhance technical assistance for the implementation of the UNCAC, and dealt with the issue of bribery of officials of public international organizations.

The UNCAC covers five major areas. They are (1) prevention, (2) criminalization and law enforcement measures, (3) international cooperation, (4) asset recovery, and (5) technical assistance and information exchange. It includes both mandatory and non-mandatory provisions.

General Provisions (Chapter I, Articles 1-4): It covers both the promotion of integrity and accountability within each country and the support of international cooperation and technical assistance between States Parties. They also include definitions of critical terms used in the instrument. The UNCAC does not provide for a definition of corruption. Article 4 of the UNCAC provides for the protection of national sovereignty of the States Parties.

Preventive Measures (Chapter II, Articles 5-14): The first conference of the States Parties recognized the importance of fighting corruption by going far beyond the measures of previous instruments in both scope and detail. The preventive measures cover both the public and private sectors. The chapter includes model preventive policies, such as the establishment of anti-corruption bodies and enhanced transparency in the financing of election campaigns and political parties. Anti-corruption bodies must be independent. The public service should be subject to safeguards that promote efficiency, transparency and recruitment based on merit. Public servant should be bound by code of conduct, requirements for financial and other disclosures, and appropriate disciplinary measures. The requirements made for the public sector also apply to the private sector. It too is expected to adopt transparent procedures and codes of conduct.

Criminalization and Law Enforcement (Chapter III, Articles 15-44): The States Parties should establish all criminal offences such as various forms of bribery and embezzlement, criminal conduct, trading in official influence and other abuse of official functions. Specific acts that States Parties must criminalize include active bribery of a national, international or foreign public official and passive bribery of a national public official and embezzlement of public funds. Other mandatory crimes include obstruction of justice and the concealment, conversion or transfer of criminal proceeds (money laundering). Sanctions are extended to those who participate in or attempt to commit corruption offences. States are encouraged to criminalize passive bribery of foreign and international public officials, trading in influence, abuse of function, illicit enrichment, private sector bribery and embezzlement, money laundering, and the concealment of illicit assets.

States Parties are required to simplify the provision of evidence of corrupt behaviour by ensuring that obstacles that may arise from the application of bank secrecy laws shall be overcome. This is especially important, as corrupt acts are very difficult to prove before a court. Particularly important is also the introduction of the liability of legal persons. In the area of law enforcement, the UNCAC calls for better cooperation between national and international bodies and civil societies. There is a provision for the protection of witnesses, victims, expert witnesses and whistle blowers to ensure that law enforcement is truly effective.

International Cooperation (Chapter IV, Articles 45-49): States Parties are obliged to assist one another in every aspect of the fight against corruption, such as prevention, investigation, and the prosecution of offenders. Particular emphasis is laid on mutual legal assistance, in gathering and transferring evidence for use in the court, and extradition of offenders. According to the Convention, the principle of dual criminality can only be insisted on where the assistance would require coercive action such as arrest or search and seizure and States Parties are encouraged to allow a wider scope of assistance without dual criminality where possible. Also, where dual criminality is required, it is sufficient that the conduct at issue constitutes a crime in both jurisdictions; the language of the laws need not coincide exactly. Cooperation in criminal matters is mandatory. In civil and administrative matters, States Parties are encouraged to do so.

Asset Recovery (Chapter V, Articles 50-59): Asset recovery is indeed a very important issue for many developing countries where high-level corruption has plundered the national wealth. Reaching an agreement on this chapter involved intensive negotiations, as the needs of countries seeking the illicit assets had to be reconciled with the legal and procedural safeguards of the countries whose assistance was sought. Chapter V of the UNCAC establishes asset recovery as a fundamental principle of the Convention. The provisions on asset recovery lay a framework, in both civil and criminal law, for tracing, freezing, forfeiting and returning funds obtained through corrupt activities. The requesting state will in most cases receive the recovered funds as long as it can prove ownership. In some cases, the funds may be returned directly to individual victims.

If no other arrangement is in place, UNCAC signatories may use the Convention itself as a legal basis for enforcing confiscation orders obtained in a foreign criminal court. Specifically, Article 54(1)(a) of the UNCAC provides that each State Party shall take such measures as may be necessary to permit its competent authorities to give effect to an order of confiscation issued by a court of another state party (United Nations Convention against Corruption Article 54 Section 1A, 2A). Indeed, Article 54(2)(a) of the UNCAC also provides for the provisional freezing or seizing of property where there are sufficient grounds for taking such actions in advance of a formal request being received. The identification of experts who can assist developing countries in this process is also included as a form of technical assistance [Article 60(5)].

Technical Assistance and Information Exchange (Chapter VI, Articles 60-62): Chapter VI of the UNCAC is dedicated to technical assistance, meaning support offered to developing and transition countries in implementing the Convention. The provisions cover training, material and human resources, research, and information sharing. The Convention also calls for cooperation through international and regional organizations, and research efforts. Cooperation is also called for the contribution of financial resources both directly to developing countries and countries with economies in transition, and to the United Nations Office on Drugs and Crime, which is the Secretariat to the Conference of the States Parties.

Mechanisms for Implementation (Chapter VII, Articles 63-64): The chapter deals with international implementation through the CoSP and the UN Secretariat.

Final Provisions (Chapter VIII, Articles 65-71): The UNCAC requirements are to be interpreted as minimum standards. States Parties are free to exceed with measures more strict or severe than those set out in the specific provisions and the two Articles governing signature, ratification and the coming into force of the Convention.

UNCAC Coalition of Civil Society Organizations: The UNCAC Coalition (http://www.uncaccoalition.org), established in 2006, is a network of more than 200 civil society organizations (CSOs) that is committed to promoting the ratification, implementation and monitoring of the UNCAC. It aims to mobilise broad civil society support for the UNCAC and to facilitate strong civil society action at national, regional and international levels in support of the Convention. The Coalition is open to all organizations and individuals committed to these goals. The breadth of UNCAC means that its framework is relevant for a wide range of CSOs, including groups working in the areas of human rights, labour rights, governance, economic development, environment and private sector accountability.

Signatures, Ratification and Entry into Force: The UNCAC was adopted by the United Nations General Assembly in Merida, Yucatan, Mexico, on 31 October 2003 by Resolution 58/4. The convention was signed by 140 countries. Ecuador became the thirtieth country to ratify the Convention on 15 September 2005, and in accordance with Article 68(1) of Resolution 58/4, it entered into force on 14 December 2005. As of 15 May 2011, the convention had been ratified, accepted, approved or acceded to by 151 countries as well as the European Union and applies to most of the world population. The countries with a population of over 1 million, that had not ratified convention till 15 May 2011 were North Korea, Chad, Guinea, Somalia, Eritrea, Oman, and Botswana.

India Ratifies UN Convention Against Corruption: India has completed the process of ratification of the United Nations Convention Against Corruption. The move will help the Manmohan Singh government blunt the opposition's charge of UPA dilly-dallying on this agreement. The government has been under pressure not just from its political opponents but also from the courts, which have cracked the whip in several cases such as the 2G scam.

Prime Minister Manmohan Singh said in a statement issued before his departure for Kabul, "The ratification of the United Nations Convention Against Corruption is a reaffirmation of our government's commitment to fight corruption and to undertake vigorously administrative and legal reforms to enable our law-enforcement agencies to recover the illicit assets stolen by corrupt practices" (*Times of India* dated 13th May 2011).

Changes in Domestic Laws: However, government has to make changes in domestic laws to have more transparency in funding election campaigns and the political parties among other crucial legislative steps to bring it at par with the international instrument. According to the UN convention, "each State Party shall also consider adopting appropriate legislative and administrative measures consistent with the objectives of this Convention and in accordance with the fundamental principles of its domestic law, to prescribe criteria concerning candidature for an election to public office".

It also prescribes disciplinary or other measures against public officials who violate the codes or standards established in accordance with this article. The convention, when ratified, makes it easier for India to repatriate billions of dollars of black money alleged to be stashed away overseas.

The laws of election need several amendments. Political corruption in India is a major concern and the criminals in politics have become a problem. About ¼th of the MPs face criminal charges. In UP elections in 2002 the candidates with criminal records won the majority of seats.

Criminals should be excluded from becoming members of political parties including the local bodies once the lower court prosecutes them. We should not wait till the higher courts finally decide their appeals. They should not be allowed to fight elections.

To finish the dynasty rule the voter of the constituency only should be allowed to fight the election. Then out of husband and wife, father and son, only one would succeed and not the entire family. The person who acquires more than 50 per cent of the votes should be declared to be elected. Otherwise there should be a re-election between the first two candidates who have got the highest votes.

The minimum qualification to fight an election on the symbol of a recognized political party should be 5 years continuous membership of the political party for MLAs and 10 years for MPs. There should be an exemplary punishment for disturbing elections. The world is changing fast. No body should be allowed to become President, Governor, Prime Minister, or Chief Minister for more than two terms or say 10 years.

In democracy it is the representatives of the public who rule and become ministers or Prime Minister or Chief Ministers. Sometimes on the death of a popular Prime Minister or Chief Minister, his wife, son or daughter is made the Prime Minister or the Chief Minister without being elected by the people. Such practices should be banned. This would end the dynasty rule.

There has never been a dearth of competent persons in any ruling party or in government to take the place of the deceased or on his retirement. Some officers are given extension in service for six months or a year. This is nothing but favouritism and corruption. It is the duty of every officer to train his juniors to take his place on his retirement or death.

At the time of elections in the State or in the Centre, the Prime Minister or the Chief Minister should not be allowed to continue as he gets certain advantages over his rivals due to his being in the chair. The President or the Governor should form a national government for the period of election.

If we want corruption free state, we have to follow international standards for forming political parties and the conduct of elections. We have yet to make a beginning.

The laws for forming political parties and the election laws must be overhauled. We are still discussing the draconian laws to put an end to the rampant corruption in the country.

3

Corruption in India

Morality in 2011
(*HT* dated 16th April 2011)

Corruption means giving or taking bribe. Bribe means money, etc. offered to a public servant to procure illegal or dishonest action in favour of the giver. Thus in corruption it is the public servant that is involved and without his connivance no corruption can take place. In the biggest scam of 2G spectrum it was the telecom minister, his secretary and his staff that were involved.

The political corruption is the abuse of public power, office, or resources by government officials or employees for personal gain by taking bribes. An illegal act by an office holder constitutes political corruption if the act is directly related to their official duties.

The forms of corruption vary. They include embezzlement, nepotism, graft, bribery, patronage, extortion, and cronyism.

The corruption helps in criminal activities like drug trafficking, money laundering, human trafficking, etc. But it is not limited to these activities.

Corruption poses a serious challenge. It undermines morality. It also undermines democracy, good governance, trust and tolerance. Corruption in government administration creates inefficiency in the services. Corruption in judiciary compromises the rule of law. Corruption in elections and in legislative bodies reduces accountability. It distorts representation in policy-making. Corruption reduces the institutional capacity of government. The procedures are disregarded and resources are siphoned off. The government offices are bought and sold.

Corruption generates distortions and inefficiency in economic development. It increases the cost of business due to illicit payments. A lot of time is wasted in negotiations with the officials due to underhand dealings. There still remains the risk of breach of agreements. To favour a contractor, the rules are either misinterpreted or ignored. The competitors are avoided. The giving or taking of bribe, both is punishable. So there remains the danger of both being caught and punished.

But the corruption is rampant in India. We have a system that allows corruption to flourish. It is a country where the people think that it is a common phenomenon of life and majority of the people are guilty of it. It is not confined to politics or the government machinery alone. It is prevalent amongst almost every section of society at every level. During the time of monarchy, strict laws and the religion controlled it by calling certain acts as sins and punishable by God.

The Constituent Assembly of India intended that the bureaucracy should be able to speak out freely, without fear of persecutions or financial insecurity as an essential element in unifying the nation. The IAS, IPS and IFS officers are recruited by the Union government on the recommendations of the UPSC and posted under various State governments. While the respective State governments have control over them, they cannot censure or take disciplinary action against them without the concurrence of the Union government and the UPSC.

While speaking to IAS, IPS and IFS and other senior bureaucrats on the Civil Service Day on 21 April 2011, Prime Minister Manmohan Singh said that he expected civil servants to be honest and fearless in advising the political leadership. This is possible only when they are provided necessary security of service.

The Indian system of administration through the IAS, IPS and judicial services is one of the best systems in the world. No body has so far been able to suggest a better system than this, although many criticize it for causing delay. Every system of administration works on the quality of its officers. Our officers are among the best brains in the country and can deliver the goods if they are not pressurized. They proved their worth several times in the past.

However, there are complaints that every thing is no longer transparent in UPSC, the recruiting agency for these officers, due to rampant corruption in the country. They do not show the marks-sheet of a candidate with the model answer format in spite of orders by the RTI Commissioner and the Delhi High Court. The MP from Hapur, district Ghaziabad, UP, raised the point in Parliament. If the UPSC does not remain transparent and fair the entire system of administration called the steel administration may collapse.

Due to rampant corruption three copies of the names of the candidates are sent by the Employment Exchange, Hyderabad, AP. After comparing all the three, the officer keeps one copy. Then two copies are again sent to the officer advising him to keep one copy out of them and return two copies including the copy earlier retained by him. This is done to avoid additional names being added in the list during the post with the connivance of the postal staff. Every day new ways are being invented to make money by unfair means.

We have not to import any thing from outside, neither the system of administration nor the officers. Every thing is available in the country. The Indians are among the intelligent and diligent races of the world. Then what is lacking that our system of administration is not delivering fast justice?

Unless we find an answer to this question, hundreds of Ruchikas would continue to commit suicide and hundreds of Rathore would go unpunished. Justice in courts would continue to be delayed and denied and bought and sold.

The answer to this question is that it is the corruption, which is eating our society and our system of administration. We have become money minded with illegal money and have stopped differentiating between just and unjust. Otherwise no body would make synthetic milk and ghee (cooking oil) by adding shampoo and urea and animal fat respectively. This is a sin in our religion.

We have become so much money minded that minor girls are being sent into flesh trade by pumping them with hormones and steroids to hasten their physical growth. The Police rescued from brothels in Mandsaur in Madhya Pradesh twenty-one abducted girls aged between one and eight. In 39 hamlets of Banchra tribe in Madhya Pradesh 869 minor girls up to the age of ten years have been found. It is reported that the members of this tribe are abducting minor girls and are sending them into flesh trade after hastening their physical growth (*HT* dated 23 and 26 March 2011).

Ten foetuses, including four of females were found in garbage in a dry pond of mortuary behind district jail in Aligarh, UP, on 19 May 2011. The foetuses were of three to six months and were reportedly thrown by hospitals and nursing homes involved in the illegal practice of aborting the foetus. This is not the first time that this has happened. In August 2006, nine foetuses were found in Nai Basti and nine female foetuses were found in March 2007 in Charakbalan. This practice of illegal abortions and killing of females is taking place due to corruption in Health Department (*HT* dated 20th May 2011).

There has never been a perfect world with honest governments and efficient civil services. Certain bad elements have always been there. Greed has been a major cause for many evils and corruption is one of them. Does the Chief Secretary of a State government need several farmhouses, showrooms, flats and residential and commercial plots? So long he is in the government service, he gets all the facilities. After retirement he needs a small bungalow/flat, a car and a servant. Then where is the necessity for him to indulge in corruption and accumulate so much property, which may send him to jail except the greed?

There is a limit for each and every thing in the world. If one crosses the limit one has to face problems. Acquisition of money and property also has a limit provided it is not earned by dubious means. Even if it is earned through honest means, a portion of it must be continuously spent on charitable purposes. Otherwise it may cause dissatisfaction and revolt among the poor who may kill you and your family, loot your property and make you unhappy on small pretext.

The chief economic consequences of corruption are the loss to the economy, an unhealthy climate for investment and an increase in the cost of government-subsidized services. The TI India study estimates the monetary value of petty corruption in 11 basic services provided by the government, like education, healthcare, judiciary, police, etc., to be around ₹ 21,068 crore ($4.6 billion). India still ranks in the bottom quartile of developing nations in terms of the ease of doing business, and compared to China and other lower developed Asian nations, the average time taken to secure the clearance for a startup or to invoke bankruptcy is much greater.

The corruption being done by officers has surpassed all limits. The said Chief Secretary of UP government did the corruption to the tune of ₹ thousands of crore. He could be booked only after retirement due to shelter from the top. He has again been booked in the scandal of ₹ 5.51 crore in the purchase of seeds for the farmers for ₹ 32 crore. Even seven of his subordinates are involved for toeing his line [*Amar Ujala* (Hindi) dated 15th and 16th January 2010].

In Madhya Pradesh an IAS Officer has been found to own 25 flats and 400 acres of land. Another is found to be having cash in washing machines, pillows, quilts, and mattresses. In the case of a government engineer, 7.8 kg of gold and ₹ 1.60 crore in cash has been found. Large amounts of money come daily to the officers, which they cannot spend. So they invest it in purchasing property and gold in their names and in the names of near and dear ones. The result is that the rates of property and gold have gone up several times. This is creating imbalance in the society.

Under economic help plan, poor persons were to be selected who do not fall under BPL category and were not taking benefit of any other scheme. Out of 216.68 lakh persons selected for the benefit, more than three lakhs were found to be UP State government employees. In some districts rich persons were identified as poor beneficiaries. The greed has no limits. This is due to no punishment or minor punishment being awarded for cheating and fraud.

In Chhattisgarh and Orissa hand pumps and tube wells have been installed without testing the sub-soil water. The doctors have confirmed that the water contains fluoride. The result is that hundreds of people have become crippled or have died. But no engineer has so far been punished for gross negligence.

There has been an increase in the number of fast speed vehicles. The road accidents have increased due to poor quality of roads. It is not that the Indian engineers and the contractors do not know how to construct good roads. It is due to high corruption that the quality of roads is poor. They wither away in one monsoon. By the side of roads the drain is seldom planned and made along with the road or it would found to be blocked. Out of 3 lakh road accidents, about one lakh people are killed and 2 lakh are injured seriously.

There is an increase of 8 per cent in road accidents. The WHO and the Indian government got a survey done. It was found that whereas the roads in other countries are becoming better and better, the roads in India are getting worse and worse day by day. Out of 10 thousand vehicles, 12.7 meet with accidents. This ratio is 9.78 in the USA, 1.00 in Britain, and 1.10 in Germany. The roads in India are considered most unsafe in the world. After the road accident, the medical aid is not easily available.

After independence DDT was used to eradicate malaria. It was a five-year plan. In the first two years it appeared as if all the mosquitoes had been killed including those in the villages. But instead of continuing the good work, only water was used in the remaining three years and the new generations of mosquitoes became used to DDT. Since then the corruption has increased many folds and so are the mosquitoes. Both are the cause of sufferings to the people.

"With the constant use of repellants and insecticides, mosquitoes are turning resistant so much that even their larva develops resistance. As such there are no desired results of fogging or repellants against them", said Dr IPE M. IPE, an expert insect scientist. The solution is that we need to break their life cycle and go for the modern technique of genetic science, which involves technique to sterilize the male mosquitoes by castration in lab and then releasing them for copulation with female mosquitoes with no further breed coming on. This technique is being successfully used in Israel (*HT* dated 27th May 2011). But in India where there is rampant corruption how many mosquitoes would be sterilized and how many would be charged for payment can be well imagined.

The Supreme Court appointed a Vigilance Committee, headed by former SC judge Justice D.P. Wadhwa. He has said that the public distribution system (PDS) is the most corrupt system of the country. The central government is spending every year ₹ 28,000 crore in subsidy to make available cheap ration to the poor. But due to corrupt officers, ration dealers, transporters and mill owners the poor hardly get any thing. The system is witnessing rampant corruption, black marketing and diversion of funds. Due to political pressure the PDS system in Rajasthan has more or less been demolished. Similar is the condition in Uttrakhand, Jharkhand, Bihar, Gujarat, Orissa and Karnataka [*HT* and *Amar Ujala* (Hindi) both dated 17th March 2010].

The UPA government's ambitious rural employment project has come under the scrutiny of the Supreme Court, which on 7th April 2010 said that there is no uniform policy and the money is not reaching the poor (*HT* dated 8th April 2010). A new World Bank study reiterates that social security funds are not reaching the poor. India spends a healthy 2 per cent of its GDP on core safety net programmes (the PDS, MGNREGS, IAY and others), much more than its South Asian neighbours and even countries like China and Indonesia. Yet, as the report says, only 40 per cent of the poor benefit from the safety net. What happens to the funds meant for the other 60 per cent is anybody's guess (*HT* dated 21st May 2011).

The standard of education is deteriorating day by day. The universities and the Boards of Education are losing their credibility. Every year question papers get leaked and sold in the market. The gangs involved in the leakage have been caught several times, but the evil has not ended because the punishment through the courts takes years before it is finally decided and the guilty is punished. The punishment being given is not commensurate with the crime.

This year the IIT Kanpur has withheld the result of 30 students after a probe revealed that some of them cheated in the IIT-JEE exam. Gyani Zail Singh Engineering College, Bhatinda, has been blacklisted and three teachers, including the centre in-charge have been debarred from participating in any administrative work of the IIT. The report said that the students were given extra time to solve the paper (*HT* dated 15th May 2011).

There are examination centres where mass copying is done. The criminals also prepare fake question papers of UP Board and sell them as original papers at ₹ 500 to 1000. The criminals who have been identified by the police include two retired senior officers of the education department, five MLAs and three MPs [*Amar Ujala* (Hindi) dated 17th March 2010].

The salary of primary school teachers in UP and Bihar has been raised to ₹ 20,000 per month. But the teachers still take no interest in teaching. The rumour is that most of them are busy in doing other jobs. Due to corruption in recruitment no preference is given to the local teachers for appointment in schools in the villages. In fact there should be separate education services for rural India. One teacher remains busy for collection, preparation and distribution of mid-day meal.

State government is spending millions and millions of rupees on mid-day meal. But the quality of mid-day meal is very poor and is not worth eating. It also wastes the time of school teachers in preparing and distributing the mid-day meal.

There are government primary schools in cities in UP where there is actually no student, but there is a headmaster, 4 teachers and a school peon on the strength of the school. There are fake names of students in the attendance registers of classes. There are private primary schools, which charge high fees. There may be one or two primary schools where there is a playground for children.

The recognition to these private schools is being given with a consideration. During inspection many of such schools have been found to have not completed the requirements necessary for running such schools. The Finance Minister of India has said that these days a fifth class student is not able to do multiplication and division. There are government aided schools where some teachers have been found to have fake degrees.

The condition in village dispensaries is no better. There is a qualified MBBS doctor with a qualified compounder on its strength. But the doctor hardly attends the dispensary, once or twice a month. He pays a regular cut to the Chief Medical Officer of the district and the head of the village and does his private practice in the city.

It was money that took chief medical officer Dr B.P. Singh's life on 2 April 2011. His predecessor Dr Vinod Atya was also murdered for the same reasons in October 2010. The CMO's murder could be the work of medical Mafia who wanted work orders and tenders under the National Rural Health Mission.

Due to corruption in recruitment no preference is being given to the local doctors for appointment in village dispensaries. In fact there should be separate medical services for rural India. Most of the medicines allotted to the dispensary are sold in the open market. The compounder gives a few for cough and cold and fever. This is how the health services in rural India are being run. After 60 years of independence the villagers still survive on herbal medicines. This happens when crores of rupees are being spent on health services in rural India.

The condition of Government hospitals in the cities is no better. There are regular complaints that the lady doctor demands money for admission to the maternity ward. In Government Hospitals, corruption is associated with non-availability of medicines, duplicate and fake medicines, getting admission and consultations with doctors and diagnostic services. There have been cases of diversion of medical supplies from government hospitals and clinics to private market as well as supply and distribution of medicines of inferior quality. Some hospitals are charging extra amounts from government pensioners and pay a cut to the government officers for reimbursement of their bills from the Health Ministry.

Although the treatment for the Tuberculosis is free in the government hospital, but fake medicines are being issued to the patients or illegal money is being demanded for issue of original medicines [*Amar Ujala* (Hindi) dated 25th March 2010].

Public Analyst Laboratory officials, Lucknow, have said that Laboratory tests have found chemicals including lead chromate, Rhodamin-B, Metanil yellow in the edibles samples. Sand and gritty matters have been found in refined flour and gram flour. Large portions of Agremone Mexicana were found in mustard oil and contents of sawdust and dye in tea and coffee samples. Vanaspati and mixture of detergent was found in desi ghee (cooking oil) and pulses were found mixed with khesari (*HT* dated 19th January 2010).

Eighty-seven people in Meerut, Bulandshahar and Muzaffarnagar, UP, fell ill after consuming food prepared from buckwheat flour (kuttu ka atta) while observing the Navratra fast on 4th April 2011. The buckwheat flour has also been mixed with some cheap poisonous substance. A day may come soon when nothing pure or original would be available in the market to eat or drink due to rampant corruption in the country (*HT* dated 6th April 2011).

According to sources, the synthetic milk trade is a well-organized business. Around 120 to 130 quintals of milk is produced every day in district Aligarh in UP. But, during the anti-adulteration drive, officials of the health department generally take samples of milk from small dairies while the big dairies, which are run by influential people, are skipped.

When *Hindustan Times* contacted a dairy owner and asked him how synthetic milk was produced, he said 60 gram shampoo or liquid detergent is taken in a drum and one kg refined oil is added to it. A white paste is made and it is diluted till it looks like milk. This helps to produce 15 litres of synthetic milk. After mixing it with some pure milk, the synthetic milk is sold at three times the cost of production (*HT* dated 16th April 2011). Stringent laws need to be made for adulteration.

The recycled plastic is being used for teacups and packing material for food items. This is creating cancer including breast cancer. It damages the kidney and the lever. It is also harmful for pregnant ladies and for the yet to be born children [*Hindustan* (Hindi) dated 29th March 2011]. Some traders adulterate pure mustard oil and are selling it with a different brand name. They are thus committing double crimes. First, they reduce the availability of pure mustard oil in the market. Secondly they indulge in adulteration.

During festivals like Holi, spurious-liquor tragedy takes place. The demand for local liquor during festivals increases many folds. In the liquor the ethanol is used. But at this time the liquor Mafia adulterates the liquor with methanol, being cheap and easily available. This is poisonous. It not only causes diarrhea, but also blindness due to optic nerve getting damaged and also the risk of death due to formation of metabolic acid oasis.

On the Holi on 1 March 2010, 4 people died in Delhi, 15 in district Bulandshahar, 22 in district Ghaziabad, UP and 15 others are in danger. Nearly half of them have lost their eyesight. The SSP of the district has suspended the SHO of Simbhavali for carelessness. This is only eyewash to keep the public satisfied. Four people have been arrested and their leader is at large [*Amar Ujala* (Hindi) dated 3rd and 4th March 2010 and *HT* dated 5th March 2010]. They are never booked for attempt to murder. Fake medicines are being sold in the market although there is paraphernalia of government drug inspectors and health officers to check adulteration.

The government money is being wasted and there is no accountability. We all know about it, but tolerate corruption by saying that it is global. But there is a difference in the corruption between Europeans and Americans on one side and the Asians and Africans on the other side. There is a self-disciple in European and American societies. In Asia and Africa the discipline is to be maintained by the fear of law by providing stringent punishment. Therefore the framing of stringent laws against corruption in Asia and Africa is a must. Those who are working against the human beings have no right to talk about human rights.

Pilgrims come to have a dip in the river Ganga on the occasion of Kumbh Mela. They bathe in polluted water and get skin diseases. The water does not meet the standard for outdoor bathing set by the Central Pollution Control Board. All rivers are losing the purity of their water. For cleaning the Ganga, its tributaries are not being cleaned simultaneously. Then how the Ganga would get cleaned is a million-dollar question (*HT* dated 19th January 2010). No industry should be allowed without a treatment plant for their industrial waste. Similarly the first priority should be given to the sewage treatment plant for all municipalities whose sewage is falling into the river.

A research has revealed that heavy water pollution in Ramganga river and its tributaries is spelling doom on fish species especially magur or singi, most commonly consumed by people. Prof Neelima Gupta of Bareilly, UP, said that these fish has less haemoglobin and are anaemic (*HT* dated 15th May 2011).

Yamuna Action Plan (YAP) has become a source of making money. The first YAP was prepared in 1993 at the cost of ₹ 682 crore. In this action plan the planners ignored to make the Yamuna water of standard quality. After the failure of YAP-1, YAP-2 was made at a cost of ₹ 624 crore in 2004. This plan is not yet complete and YAP-3 has been made at the cost of ₹ 1749.40 crore. The object of this plan is that the sewage of 17 main drains be allowed to fall in Yamuna after treatment only, which should have been the aim in 1993 itself. The result is that after spending more than ₹ 1300 crore the condition of Yamuna is the same what it was in 1993 [*Dainik Jagran* (Hindi) dated 4th April 2011].

It is not only the rivers, which are getting polluted, but also the sea, which is being polluted due to discharge of the industrial waste into the sea. This pollution is now spoiling the underground water. The skin diseases are on the increase in addition to cancer and Asthma. Vapi City in Gujarat is considered among one of the most ten polluted cities of the world. The rich people are using mineral water for drinking. But the common man has to depend on the under ground water which has become polluted [*Amar Ujala* (Hindi) dated 3rd March 2010].

The procedures are being streamlined to make it transparent. But new ways are being discovered to sabotage it. The punishment has been made and is being made harsher day by day, but there is delay and denial of justice. Even in criminal cases it takes years before the Supreme Court decides the final appeal. The government thinks that it is the judges who are responsible for the delay.

A Bill is being brought in the Parliament to fix responsibility on the judges for the delay [*Amar Ujala* (Hindi) dated 4th March 2010]. But are the judges only responsible for the delay or the rampant corruption in the government machinery? Unless the government officers are given exemplary punishment for indulging in corruption the common man is not going to get justice.

The amount of corruption has gone up to rupees thousands of crore. Twenty-five years ago Shri Rajiv Gandhi, the then Prime Minister of India, said that for every rupee sent to the common man only 17 paisa reach them. Shri Manmohan Singh, the Prime Minister, told reporters in Mumbai on 11th October 2009, that the leakage of funds does exist, but it is not as big as mentioned by Rajiv Gandhi. By coincidence a day later, Planning Commission deputy chairman Montek Singh Ahluwalia told a seminar that the former PM was correct about the extent of leakage and a Plan panel study on PDS recently found that only 16 paisa out of a rupee was reaching the targeted poor. Thus there is a leakage of 84 per cent of public money (*The Times of India* dated 15th October 2009).

The people carry millions of rupees in cash in trains, busses, cars, and scooters. Are they not inviting thieves and robbers to loot them? If they are being looted who should be blamed, they or the robbers? They also cannot be blamed because the corrupt economy is going on in the country. The businessmen maintain two accounts, one for income tax and the other for their day-to-day working.

The cases of robbery and murder are on the increase. Now the bikers are looting the people who go to banks both to deposit or withdraw the money from the banks. Generally, there is no trace of the bikers. On 3 March 2010, ₹ 34,17,000 were looted by the bikers near a police station from colonel V.V. Singh, owner of Bharat Petroleum Pump, who was going to deposit the amount in the SBI Greater Noida, along with his cashier Dushyant and the Guard Suresh. On receipt of the information, the police officers arrived on the scene. But there was no trace of the robbers [*Amar Ujala* (Hindi) dated 3rd March 2010].

The regular payment of money by the shopkeepers to the local criminals has become an order of the day. Even some doctors who have a good practice have to pay monthly to the local criminals. In addition to this a big amount is being demanded now and then from those businessmen who have a roaring business. Otherwise either they are killed or their son or daughter or both are kidnapped and released for a big ransom.

Abduction or kidnapping has become an industry. There are secret organizations of criminals called the Mafia who arrange the kidnapping of children of rich families. The small criminals do the kidnapping and handover the captive to the Mafia for a small price. They then become untraceable. The Mafia then asks for a big ransom for the release of the captive. Otherwise the captive may be killed.

With the fear of the child being killed they pay the big ransom without informing the police. About two years ago a child of the CEO of a big company was kidnapped and he had to pay about ₹ 50 lakh (5 millions). The police and the media were informed that the kidnappers released the captive due to pressure of the police. From where the big amount of ₹ 50 lakh was paid no body knows. Due to corruption there is a parallel economy in the country.

The majority of politicians are rolling in wealth. There are allegations of corruption against several chief ministers and their ministers to the tune of crores of rupees. Jharkhand Chief Minister is involved in illegal transactions worth over ₹ 8,000 crore (*The Times of India* dated 3rd, 4th, 7th and 9th November 2009).

In UP a BSP leader from Kanpur purchased a plot on the moon from US-based Lunar Republic Society and gifted it to the Chief Minister. However, he did not tell the price, which he paid for it. The chief minister also did not think it proper to inquire from him about the price of the plot paid by him [*Amar Ujala* (Hindi) dated 17th January 2010].

The black money in the country is on the increase. Even the currency notes of ₹ 1,000 are in common use. On 15 March 2010, the Chief Minister of UP wore a multi-crore garland made of currency notes of ₹ 1,000 at the silver jubilee rally of the BSP in Lucknow. On 17 March 2010, she wore a garland of ₹ 18 lakh made of currency notes of the denominations of ₹ 100 and ₹ 500, with a sprinkling of notes of ₹ 1,000 at a function at the party headquarters in Lucknow. BSP general secretary said that from now on, party workers all over the country would welcome their supremo with currency garlands at BSP functions (*HT* dated 18th March 2010).

Mahatama Gandhi National Rural Employment Guarantee Scheme (MNREGS) is in a mess. A central team detected misuse of funds and other irregularities in the MNREGS. In district Sunbhadra in Orissa, a den of Maoists, the team has found justification in the allegations that firms run by people politically influential and senior government officers have been selected for supplying material for building Check Dams. It has also been reported that the labour has often not been paid. Most of the Check Dams are leaking and there was little transparency in the manner in which materials were procured (*HT* dated 16th February 2011).

The matter came up before the Supreme Court on 14th March 2011 and it was found that there was massive misappropriation of funds to the tune of 88 per cent in some districts of Orissa State. Reports of CAG as well as of National Institute of Rural Development show misappropriation of funds allegedly by officials and functionaries of the implementation agencies (*HT* dated 15th March 2011).

In police recruitment in UP thousands of constables were recruited. Later on it was discovered that there had been a large-scale corruption in recruitment involving 13 officers of the ranks of IG and DIG. Thousands of constables were removed from service. They knocked at the door of the court and many had to be taken back in service. Action is being taken against the officers through a departmental inquiry, which may take years to finalize [*Amar Ujala* (Hindi) dated 5th January 2010].

Policemen who are supposed to protect the people are now robbing the public. Seven constables posted in Mathura (UP) have been suspended for their *prima facie* involvement in loot and burglary incidents in buses and trains (*HT* dated 19th January 2010).

The police are shooting the innocent citizens in the name of encounter of hardcore criminals. Of the 2560 police encounters reported between 1993 and 2009, 1224 were found to be fake encounters, according to the National Human Rights Commission (*HT* dated 26th March 2010).

On 17 October 1998 and in the jurisdiction of Bhadohi police station the police shot dead four youths near Saroi petrol pump in the name of the gang of Mafia Dhananjaya Singh. This was a fake encounter. Thirty-three policemen were made accused. The murder charge was proved on 29 policemen in the Fast Trek Court on 20 February 2010. Thus the lower court has already taken 12 years to decide the matter. Now the appeals in the High Court and the Supreme Court will further take time to decide it finally. During this time many of the policemen may die the natural death [*Amar Ujala* (Hindi) dated 21st February 2010].

There is so much corruption and lawlessness in the country that even the judges appear to be afraid of the criminals and are finding it difficult to award punishment to them. On 19th July 1986, at 7.30 pm the dacoit (robber) Dadua looted and beat the villagers of village Ramu Purva, district Chitrakut, UP and shot dead 9 villagers. Out of them one was a woman. One of the dead was Shambhu Singh. His son Man Singh made a FIR against Dadua and his 19-20 men including Sita Ram, Dhungua, Kishore and Radhey.

After 23 years the case was decided on 16 February 2010. The court awarded the punishment of life imprisonment to five persons and three persons including Radhey, the deputy of Dadua, were let off in the absence of sufficient evidence against them. The punishment of life imprisonment only was given when they had killed 9 villagers in broad daylight. Chitrakut is a dacoit-infested area. Perhaps even the judicial officers are afraid of them [*Amar Ujala* (Hindi) dated 17th February 2010].

In another case of fake encounter in district Sonbhadra, UP, attempt has been made to murder the Additional District Judge of Fast Track Court. Shri Avanish Kumar Dwivedi, the ADJ, sentenced 14 cops, including two sub-inspectors, to life imprisonment on 4 and 5 January 2010, in connection with the fake encounter of two youths of Jharkhand in the forests of Rantola in Sonbhadra. On 19th February 2010, the armed miscreants fired two shots at the room of the judge, but he escaped unhurt. He even opened retaliatory fire from his licensed pistol, in self-defence and the miscreants ran away. A case of attempt to murder has been registered against them (*HT* dated 22nd February 2010).

There have been allegations of corruption in the judicial and higher judicial services. In Provident Fund scam case at Ghaziabad of class III and IV Employees, the prime accused Ashutosh Asthana, the treasury officer, named 36 sitting and retired judges including those of Allahabad High Court and district courts in UP, besides a Supreme Court Judge. Shri Asthana has died in mysterious circumstances (*HT* dated 20th October 2009 and *The Times of India* dated 21st October 2009).

In the case of High Court and Supreme Court Judges, even if the probe found the allegations proved the members of

Parliament let them off perhaps out of respect to the judiciary. But how long will all this go on? The judges have to show restraint (*HT* dated 6th and 16th January 2010).

There is disappointment in judiciary about the corruption in India. Justice Markendeya Katju of the Supreme Court, while hearing the case of irregularities committed in the recruitment of junior basic teachers in Haryana, said on 4 November 2009, "everybody is corrupt in India. This corruption would never end. He was mistaken that he could correct the corrupt. Now he has understood that there is no way to correct them" [*Dainik Jagran* (Hindi) dated 5th November 2009].

The special judge of district court in Delhi while announcing punishment to an Assistant Engineer of DESU remarked that corruption is spreading fast in the country. Corruption is spreading in the government departments as well as in politics. It appears that honesty is for namesake only. There is a necessity to stop it (*Amar Ujala* dated 16th January 2010).

The corruption is now infecting the army. Now and then even senior officers are getting involved in corruption. The Chief of the Army Staff, General V.K. Singh, said on 2nd April 2010 that unless our internal structure is improved, we cannot fight successfully with the foreign dangers. He gave a hint to control corruption in the army with a heavy hand.

The CBI has registered a case against six officials of the Directorate General of Quality Assurances. It includes N. Kalyan Ramakrishnan, a serving Colonel, and the Managing Director of Elca Quality Systems and Calibrations, a lab accredited by the DGQA to test and clear defence supplies. The scam is for the purchase of sub-standard anti-skid chains used in Army vehicles in snowy region and sub-standard mudguards worth over ₹ 7 crore. Ramakrishnan is accused of clearing both the mudguards and the chains (*HT* dated 19th January 2010).

Indians are famous in foreign countries for their intelligence and diligence. Now they are also becoming famous for indulging in corruption. The FBI has charged further 14 people, including two Indians and Wall Street professionals, in a widening $53 million insider trading scam, the largest ever such case in the

United States. The latest action brings the number of people who have been charged in the case to 20, including four Indians (*The Times of India* dated 7th November 2009).

The issue of corruption is being discussed off and on, on the TV and in newspapers, without coming to any permanent or long-term solution for its eradication. We have stopped finding long-term solutions. We get satisfied with short-term measures. Hang Rathore and the public would be satisfied. Shri Vir Sanghvi in his article "Don't let Ruchika's death be in vain" has mentioned that in our minds we have decided that Ruchika died because Rathore is an evil man and have concluded that if Rathore gets punished, justice will have been done (*HT* dated 17th January 2010). People would forget the 19 years delay and the sufferings of Ruchika's family. If a poor man loses his balance of mind and his cool in such cases and takes up arms to get justice, what is strange about it?

Shri Sanghvi in his article has mentioned that the members of the IAS, IPS and Judiciary succumb to pressure. They ask for protection from top. But what for do they require protection and what wrong are they doing that they have to ask for protection? They are already a protected class under the Constitution of India. Actually they need protection against punishment to corruption in which they are indulging day and night. So they have to do favours to those from whom they get favours or are likely to get favours. We hardly find an officer who can stand erect against injustice. So how can they do their duty honestly and sincerely?

Majority of the government servants is indulging in corruption. The honest officers may not be even 10 per cent. For a democracy to function smoothly, we need more than 90 per cent honest and sincere officers. A black sheep here and there can be controlled. Those who are not getting a chance to do corruption or are afraid to do corruption are also not doing their duty honestly and sincerely. In this condition who would give us justice or get us justice.

It is not that the government officers were always corrupt. During the time of old politicians the government officers were deadly honest. It is said that about 50 years ago Japanese were proposing to install 8 factories in Tamil Nadu. An Under Secretary was assisting the minister. The leader of the Japanese delegation told in the officer's ears that he would pay 12 per cent commission to him if he makes the proposal through. The officer agreed and told the minister about it. When the contract was being made, it was mentioned that the Japanese would install 9 factories and the Tamil Nadu government would pay only for 8 factories. Such was the standard of honesty even among junior officers.

Democratic system of government is an abstract system to govern the country. Shri Tiket, the late Kisan Union leader of Muzaffarnagar, UP once said that he went to Delhi, but found no government there. Everybody gave him only assurances to look into his case. This system is very tough and can punish the most powerful man in the country provided officers do their duty. It is very weak if there are pulls and pressures from top and the officers indulge in corruption.

Shri Vir Sanghvi has suggested that both Rathore and other police officials, who tortured Ashu should be punished. But will this solve our problem? Our aim is that such cases should become rare. There are hundreds of Rathores in society and there is no dearth of officers who are protecting them by not doing their duty, which includes honesty and sincerity.

The system of administration should be such that all such officers are automatically punished by the system. It should not require a Home Minister to ask the CBI to look into the case where the justice has been delayed or denied. Justice should be available as a matter of routine. The system should safeguard against delay and denials of justice by streamlining the procedures and by punishing those who tell lies in the court or try to sabotage the system.

There is a problem in some states relating to the poor tribal. This is about Jihadis and Maoists. Jihadis are the religious fanatics who think that their religion is supreme and others have no right to live unless they are converted to their religion or pay 'jaziya tax' in lieu of conversion. With their religious brothers their dispute is that the state should be ruled according to their religion. The rights and duties of the women of their religion should remain the same whatever was there in the medieval times, neither less nor more. If there is any dispute about it they would only decide and for that they should be made the ruler and the judge. Otherwise their co-religionist would also be their enemies.

In communism (socialism) every thing belongs to the government and the government provides the employment to the people. In democracy like in USA the government only governs and the people are free to do any business they feel like. India has adopted the middle way called the democratic socialism where some things are in the hands of government and some are left to the people. But there is no such thing as democratic communism. It can't work and has not worked.

West Bengal had a democratic communist government for decades. But West Bengal has become the poorest state in India. Industries were controlled in West Bengal through the unions and all major industries shifted from West Bengal due to the union problem. They implemented land reforms successfully. When West Bengal government tried to acquire land for industries they lost the power in the election. In communism all land and industries belong to the state. So there is no problem. But it cannot happen in democracy.

The problem of Maoists is a greater one. It is spreading among the poor tribal in some of the states like Andhra Pradesh, Madhya Pradesh, Chhattisgarh, Orissa, Jharkhand, Bihar, West Bengal and Assam. The tribal lives in forest and survives on forest produce. They and their women folk are exploited by the rich and the government officers posted in their areas due to both poverty and illiteracy. If they try to resist they are killed in the name of maintaining law and order. Communism breeds in poverty and in delay or denial of justice.

Some educated youths, including one or two young girls, come to their areas. They tell them about their rights and become their godfathers. They promise them safety against exploitation and injustice. They become their judges to decide the disputes among them. If the villagers do not obey their orders they kill them or even burn the whole village. In village Kasari, district Jamui, Bihar, the villagers did not cooperate with the Maoists and they killed about 12 persons and burnt the village.

Similar is the problem of dacoit (robber) infested areas in Madhya Pradesh and UP. When the police chase the dacoits, they take shelter in the villages and have their food. In return they give some money to the villagers. If the villagers do not cooperate with them, they shoot them or assault their women folk. When the police come to know that the villagers had given shelter to the dacoits, they beat the villagers for giving shelter to them and also have their food without payment. The author once went to the ravines near Gwalior in Madhya Pradesh with his uncle who was a doctor there. On inquiry about the life in the ravines, an eighteen-year-old boy told this story.

The ravines can be levelled without much effort. The River Chambal is nearby to irrigate the land. The hideout places of the dacoits will disappear. The quantity of agricultural land will increase providing employment to the villagers. The government has spent millions and millions of rupees on police to eliminate the dacoits, but do not spend money on levelling the land to make it fit for agriculture. The problem of dacoits continues.

The paramilitary soldier and policeman are mostly from poor rural families. So they get little attention in the media or in our imagination even when they die. The Indian Maoist is young, educated and is adept at guerrilla warfare, handling arms and living a life of hardship. Their game plan is to physically occupy the countryside beyond state control and surround the cities until they can force the regime to change in their favour. But this is not likely to happen in India.

The people are god fearing and loyal to the government of the day. The fights between the security forces and the Maoists go on and the children of poor rural families die in every clash between the two sides. This can be avoided if the development works are undertaken in these areas sincerely and honestly. The roads are a few and connect only the district headquarters and subdivisions.

Roads do not connect even all police posts. Untrained policemen are posted to these outer areas. The Maoists are able to attack even a police camp and kill most of the constables. In a recent attack on 15 February 2010, in West Bengal, the Maoist killed 24 constables of Eastern Frontier Rifles. Due to rampant corruption in the government machinery only 16 per cent of the allotted funds is spent on development works. So from where will the roads come? No development can take place where there are no roads.

Either the development works have not been undertaken or have been done for namesake only. Most of the money for development works has gone into the pockets of politicians, government officers and the contractors (*HT* dated 18th February 2010).

In the case of employment of illiterate persons, the proof of age is not available. Even if available, it is not given to have a benefit of getting a lower age recorded. It so happens that the younger sister retires first and the elder afterwards. Sometimes to have a driving license the children get a higher age recorded. But when in service a complaint is received about their age they have a hard time to explain the difference between their ages recorded in the driving license and the High School Certificate. Our standard of morality has become the lowest due to corruption.

Even in the case of Army Chief General V.K. Singh, it has been found that he has two different dates of birth—10 May 1950 and 10 May 1951 in various documents creating confusion regarding his date of retirement. Attorney General has opined that his date of birth should be treated as 10 May 1950, which is mentioned in his UPSC application form for the National Defence Academy (*HT* dated 21st May 2011). It is not clear why his date of birth given in his High School certificate not being accepted.

The grieving families are often asked to pay a bribe to get their loved one's Death Certificate in the offices run by the government. Officials who oversee transportation regulation, safety norms, and traffic violations engage in rent seeking activity.

A lenient treatment for an offending driver or vehicle is accompanied by expectation of a bribe.

The land in areas with short supply is awarded to private concerns at negligible rates in the name of opening schools or dispensaries for the poor children or a hostel for widows. Other examples include the award of mining leases to private companies without a levy of taxes that is proportionate to the market value of the ore. The Supreme Court had appointed Central Empowered Committee to give its report on illegal mining in Bellary district in Karnataka. On its report it restrained 19 mines from carrying out mining operations and transportation of iron ore on 29 April 2011. A special forest bench headed by chief justice also said that it would pass an order on another 68 mines, which have been indicted by the CEC for violating rules in mining operations (*HT* dated 30th April 2011).

The Indian Armed Forces are now frequently witnessing corruption involving senior armed forces' officers. Many officers have been caught for allegedly selling defence lands and stores in the black market. It has shaken public faith in the country's growing military at a time when large sums are being spent on modernizing the armed forces. A string of eye-popping fraud cases has damaged the institution in recent years.

But corruption in armed forces should not be judged separately from civil. They constitute men whose family and relations are in the civil. The infection is bound to come from civil. Due to hard training and discipline, they try to control the corruption in their ranks. The day the corruption in the civil is reduced, it is hoped that the same would be over in the armed forces.

Despite State prohibition against torture and custodial misconduct by the police, torture is widespread in police custody, which is a major reason behind deaths in custody. The police often torture innocent people until a 'confession' is obtained to save influential and wealthy offenders. G.P. Joshi, the programme coordinator of the Indian branch of the Commonwealth Human Rights Initiative in New Delhi comments that the main issue at hand concerning police violence is a lack of accountability of the police.

In India, the corruption has also crept into religious institutions. Here and there we find air-conditioned ashrams made by religious leaders containing hundreds of rooms. There are complaints of the people being murdered who do not obey their orders. Money and women are alleged to be behind those murders. To make money, some churches are selling Baptism certificates.

The States as well as Central Government have adopted the semester system of education. The system of semester is nothing else but parrot tests, attendance, and practical test and marks awarded to the students. For awarding marks, teachers collect money from students. Some students, though they are poor, give the money for the fear that otherwise they will get poor marks.

The absentee students or poor performed students find this type of shortcut way to get more marks from the teacher. They may come forward to pay the money to the teacher and may succeed. Though it is shameful on the part of teachers, but many teachers are doing it. It is due to corruption being done by the majority and every where, even though it is against their ethics. The rumour is that instead of guiding and supervising the work of students, the Ph.Ds are being bought and sold ranging from ₹ 50,000 to 1,00,000. So the research in the Indian universities is only for namesake.

The corruption in India is not merely limited to bribes, kickbacks, commissions, cuts, etc. It is also there due to non-recovery of revenue by the government officers. The CAG in his UP Finance Audit Report ending 31 March 2009 has mentioned that ₹ 15,731 crore, and 74 lakh have not been recovered. When they asked since when this recovery is pending, except Trade Tax and Entertainment Tax Departments, no other department replied. The Trade Tax and Entertainment Tax departments had not recovered ₹ 9,214 crore, and 86 lakh for the last 5 years or more.

The Trade Tax department had not been able to recover ₹ 230 crore, and 25 lakh from government and semi-government departments. Even after issue of recovery certificate to the collector of the district, the balance still remained is ₹ 11,223 crore, and 37 lakh.

The government and the courts stayed a recovery of ₹ 2,211 crore, and 44 lakh. Leaving this aside, even then the recovery of ₹ 13,520 crore, and 30 lakh still remains. With this amount several development projects could have been completed. Thus we are not only failing in spending money like a prudent taxpayer, but are also failing in recovering the government dues like a moneylender. Something, therefore, needs to be done immediately [*Amar Ujala* (Hindi) dated 27th February 2011].

The Right to Information Act, 2005, and equivalent acts in the states, that require government officials to furnish information requested by citizens or face punitive action, computerization of services and various central and state government acts that established vigilance commissions should have considerably reduced corruption. Or at least it should have opened up avenues to redress grievances.

But this has remained on paper only. The procedure of getting information is so lengthy, expensive and time consuming that majority of applicants drop it in mid-way. Except in one or two cases, no punishment is being awarded. The information being supplied is incomplete. Had the above measures been effective, there would not have been any more scams. But scams are coming to light almost off and on.

The Lokayukta is an anti-corruption organization in the states. These institutions are based on the Ombudsman in Scandinavian countries. An amendment to the Constitution has been proposed to implement the Lokayukta uniformly across States as a three-member body, headed by a retired Supreme Court Judge or high court Chief Justice, and is to comprise of the state vigilance commissioner and a jurist or an eminent administrator as other member. But they do not have the powers to look into any complaint on their own and punish the guilty. It would be a showpiece only. When at central level the vigilance commissioners have not been able to do much to eradicate corruption, anything will happen at state level is only a hope against hope.

Bhoomi is a project jointly funded by the Government of India and the Karnataka local government to digitize the paper land records and create a software mechanism to control changes to the land registry in Karnataka. The project was designed to eliminate the long-standing problem of inefficiency and corruption. Smart cards for vehicle registration, drivers' licenses by Karnataka Regional Transport Organization and enforcement of automation of traffic violations by Bangalore Traffic Police were introduced.

All these schemes looked good on paper. But sub-standard quality computers were purchased. They go out of order now and then. Repairs are being done through local engineers who use local parts for repairs and charge for original parts. The result is that the computers are going out of order off and on. Even in the banks in small stations the condition is the same. So long there is corruption in the country nothing much can be done and even the best schemes would prove to be a failure.

Whistleblowers play a major role in the fight against corruption. India does not have a law to protect whistleblowers, which was highlighted by the assassination of Satyendra Dubey. There is no need to protect every whistleblower. The need is to provide exemplary punishment in the anti-corruption law to the corrupt officials of the government so that it may create a fear among other officials and the public.

There are enough laws, courts and agencies to punish the corrupt officials of the government. There are fast track courts to decide the cases. But even the Supreme Court judges are finding themselves helpless to punish the guilty suitably in the absence of a law providing exemplary punishment. The punishment provided in the law is not commensurate with the quantum of corruption. Still the Prime Minister is giving assurances that the guilty would be given severe and exemplary punishment after the Commonwealth Games.

The Kerala State airport has become notorious for theft of valuables from bags on incoming flights. One can imagine the condition of passengers from whose bags valuable things are found missing. The authorities are turning a blind eye to the theft when a complaint is received. Perhaps thefts are taking place in connivance with the authorities.

A 2005 study done by Transparency International in India found that more than 50 per cent of the people had first-hand experience of paying bribe or peddling influence to get a job done in a public office. Taxes and bribes are common between state borders. Transparency International estimates that truckers pay annually $5 billion in bribes.

No corrupt nation çan progress beyond certain limits. Its progress would get stalled. The difference between the rich and the poor would go on increasing, and it may cause bloodshed. Law and order and justice would be the first casualty.

Political corruption in India is a major concern and the criminals in politics have become a problem. About ¼th of the MPs face criminal charges. In UP elections in 2002 the candidates with criminal records won the majority of seats. On the illicit flight of money, India has been drained of $462 billion between 1948 and 2008. The criminal network is virtually running a parallel government. The criminal gangs are enjoying the patronage of politicians and the protection of government functionaries.

4

Corruption in Haryana Government (Ruchika molestation case)

Ruchika

Shri Vir Sanghvi, in his article in *Hindustan Times* "Rathore is not the only guilty man around" has mentioned about the sexual molestation of Ruchika, a 14-year-old girl of Panchkula (Chandigarh), in 1990 by Rathore, the then Inspector General of Police in Haryana. When she made a complaint to the Director General of Police, Haryana, Rathore got her out of her school and also harassed her and her family to the extent that she had to commit suicide in 1993.

It took 19 years for the police and the judiciary to punish Rathore in December 2009, when he had already retired as Director General of Police Haryana with a President's Police medal. Moreover, the court awarded him a minor punishment of six months' imprisonment and a fine of ₹ 1000 only, when the guilt had been proved to the hilt (*HT* dated 27th December 2009). Rathore still had a chance to file appeals in the High Court and the Supreme Court, which may take years to decide and by which time he may die without going through the punishment awarded by the court.

The question is who is responsible for the delay and denial of justice to Ruchika and her family? Is Rathore alone is guilty or are there other officers who are also guilty? Will the punishment to Rathore be a deterrent to others and the case of Ruchika would become one of the rare cases or would it continue like this? If it continues like this what is the solution that it may not happen again?

The story of Ruchika as reported by newspapers and the Internet (*Wikipedia,* the free encyclopedia) appears to be like this:

> Ruchika was a student of class X at the Sacred Heart School for Girls in Chandigarh. She was a fourteen-year-old girl and was a tennis player. Her father, S.C. Girhotra, was a manager with UCO Bank. Her mother died when she was ten years old. She had one younger brother, Ashu. Ruchika, along with her friend Aradhana Prakash, was enrolled as a trainee at the Haryana Lawn Tennis Association (HLTA). She used to practice at the State Tennis Association Courts.

S.P.S. Rathore

Shri S.P.S. Rathore was an Indian Police Service officer of 1966—Batch of Haryana Cadre. He was on deputation to Bhakra Beas Management Board as Director, Vigilance and Security. He was the founding President of the Haryana Lawn Tennis Association. He had his office in his garage at 469, Sector 6, Panchkula. He was of the rank of Inspector General of Police and had been awarded President's Police Medal.

Ruchika was a promising tennis player. On 11 August 1990, Rathore visited Ruchika's house and met her father S.C. Girhotra. As head of the Haryana Lawn Tennis Association, he promised to get special training for Ruchika. He asked Ruchika to meet him the following day in this connection.

On 12 August (Sunday), Ruchika, along with her friend, Aradhana Prakash, went to play at the lawn tennis court and met Rathore in his office in the garage of his house. On seeing both of them, Rathore asked Aradhana to call Mr. Thomas the tennis coach in his room. Aradhana left, and Rathore was alone with Ruchika. He immediately grabbed her hand and waist and pressed his body against hers. Ruchika tried to push him away, but he continued molesting her. Aradhana returned and witnessed what was going on. On seeing her, Rathore released Ruchika and fell back in his chair.

Rathore then asked Aradhana to go out of his room and personally bring the coach with her. When she refused, Rathore rebuked Aradhana loudly, asking her to bring the coach. He insisted that Ruchika stayed in his room, but she managed to run out. Rathore was about 49 at that time.

Ruchika told Aradhana what happened with her. First, both the girls did not tell anything to anybody. The next day, they did not go to play tennis. The following day on 14 August, they changed the time of practice to avoid Rathore, and played till 6:30 pm. However, as they were leaving, the ball picker, Patloo, told them that Rathore had called them to his office.

It was at this point that the girls decided to tell their parents about the incident. Following this, Panchkula residents, mostly parents of tennis players, gathered at the residence of Anand Prakash, father of Ruchika's friend Aradhana, and decided that some strong action must be taken to bring up the matter to the notice of higher authorities.

They could not contact either Chief Minister Hukum Singh or Home Minister Sampat Singh, but met Home Secretary J.K. Duggal, who, on 17 August 1990, discussed the matter with the Home Minister and asked DGP Ram Rakshpal Singh to investigate it. Rathore allegedly paid money to some residents of Rajiv Colony (a slum) in Panchkula and also garnered the support of people from his community in Naraingarh, Ambala district. They staged dharnas outside the office and home of R.R. Singh the DGP.

On 3 September 1990, the inquiry report submitted by R.R. Singh to Home Secretary J.K. Duggal indicted Rathore. It recommended that an FIR be filed immediately against Rathore. Home Secretary Duggal forwarded the report to the Home Minister Sampat Singh, who did not forward it to the Chief Minister for necessary action. The Home Secretary who replaced Duggal never took any action on the report.

The report also revealed that an ex-MLA, Jagjeet Singh Tikka and ex-MP from Moradabad Chandravijay Singh who is also related to Rathore, organised a large group of men to shout slogans in front of Ruchika's house and harass her family. Rathore enjoyed the patronage of both Hukam Singh and Om Prakash Chautala.

Instead of filing an FIR as recommended by Home secretary the government preferred departmental action, and, on 28 May 1991, issued a chargesheet against Rathore. However, the government's legal remembrancer, R.K. Nehru, suggested in 1992 that state government was not competent to issue the chargesheet and insisted that an FIR be registered. Then, the CM Bhajan Lal's office referred the case to chief secretary for advice. Eventually, no action was taken.

On 20 September 1990, two weeks after the inquiry indicted Rathore, Ruchika was expelled from her school. Ruchika had studied there from Class I. The school actively plotted against Ruchika. The official reason for her expulsion was non-payment of fees. The school had actually refused to accept her fees. No notice was given to Ruchika for non-payment of fees, as is the normal procedure. The school brochure states that non-payment of fees can only lead to being disallowed to take exams. It is no ground for expulsion.

A magisterial inquiry has found that there were 135 similar cases of non-payment of fees at Sacred Hearts, but Ruchika was the only student ever expelled on this ground. Of the 17 cases of late fees in 1990, at least 8 students paid their fees later than Ruchika did, but no action was taken against them. Ironically, the defaulters included Rathore's daughter Priyanjali.

The principal of the school, Sister Sebastina, who still occupies the office, admitted before the magisterial inquiry that she personally issued instructions for the removal of Ruchika's name from school register. Ruchika's expulsion from school was later used by Rathore's lawyers to question her character. It has been alleged that Ruchika was expelled to avoid embarrassment to Rathore's daughter Priyanjali, who was her classmate.

The school tried to stall the magisterial inquiry into Ruchika's dismissal. Sister Sebastina only appeared before the inquiry after five days. The Chandigarh authorities threatened the school with legal action if they continued to stall the investigation. After her expulsion, Ruchika confined herself to her home. Whenever she went out she was followed and abused by Rathore's henchmen. Rathore deployed policemen in plainclothes in front of Ruchika's house to keep an eye on the family.

False cases of theft, murder and civil defamation were filed against Ruchika's father and her 10-year-old younger brother Ashu. Five theft cases against Ashu were registered by Sub-Inspector Prem Dutt and one case by Assistant Sub-Inspector Sewa Singh. The cases were filed when K.P. Singh was the Superintendent of Police, Ambala. K.P. Singh has been named in an FIR filed by Ashu. K.P. Singh later provided Rathore's advocates with a statement absolving Rathore. K.P. Singh is now the Inspector General of Police (Training) in Haryana and works at the Chandigarh Head Office.

Cases were filed against Anand Prakash, his wife Madhu, and their minor daughter Aradhana. Anand Prakash worked as

Chief Engineer in the Haryana State Agriculture Marketing Board and had a spotless record until this incident. Rathore then filed more than 20 complaints against him. He was suspended from his job for some time and demoted to Superintendent Engineer. He was eventually given premature retirement. He, however, did challenge the government orders and was given relief by the court and was cleared of all the complaints.

Aradhana, who is the sole witness in the molestation case, had ten civil cases filed against her by Rathore. She received abusive and threatening calls for months until she got married and left for Australia. Pankaj Bhardwaj, the lawyer, who took up Ruchika's case, was slapped with two court cases by Rathore—a defamation case and a case for compensation. When Rathore was heading the vigilance team in the Haryana State Electricity Board (HSEB), he sent special teams from Bhiwani to raid houses of several of his complainants. Rathore also filed two cases against each of the journalists who had reported the matter—one criminal and another civil—demanding compensation of ₹ 1 crore each.

On 23 September 1993, Ruchika's then 13-year-old brother, Ashu, was picked up in the market place near his house by police in plain clothes. They drove him in a jeep to the Crime Investigation Agency (CIA) Staff Office in Mansa Devi. There, he was tortured by Sub-Inspector Prem Dutt and Assistant Sub-Inspectors Sewa Singh and Jai Narayan. His hands were tied to his back and he was made to bend. His feet were tied with a weight. He was kept in this uncomfortable position for a long period of time. After some time, Rathore also arrived there. Ashu was then tortured further. A roller, referred to by the police as "Mussal", was rolled on his legs and thighs after four constables boarded the roller.

While still in illegal confinement, Ashu was taken to his house and beaten mercilessly in front of Ruchika by Rathore. Rathore then threatened her, saying that if she did not take back the complaint, her father, and then she herself, would face the same fate. Ashu was paraded in handcuffs in his neighbourhood. Ashu was picked up again on 11 November 1993.

Ashu was tortured again and was unable to walk due to the beatings. He was not given food and water for days at a stretch and was beaten mercilessly. He was repeatedly told to convince his sister to withdraw her complaint. He was allegedly forced to sign on blank papers, which were used by the police to show his "confessions" that he had stolen 11 cars. He would not be released until after his sister's suicide. No charges were ever framed in any of these cases filed against Ashu.

The Panchkula Chief Judicial Magistrate exonerated Ashu in 1997, saying he had "no hesitation to pinpoint that nothing is on record to *prima facie* indict the accused" and that the disclosure statement made by the main accused, Gajinder Singh, was "just wastepaper". Gajinder Singh, a resident of Bihar, had been arrested by the Panchkula Police for a car theft and police claimed he had named Ashu as his accomplice. Gajinder Singh later absconded and was named a proclaimed offender.

Gajendra Singh was arrested by a team of Haryana Police assisted by their Pune counterparts on 9 January 2010 from the Baner Road area, where he was running a dhaba. The Girhotra's one-kanal bungalow in Sector 6, Panchkula was forcibly sold to a lawyer working for Rathore. Ruchika's father was suspended from his job as bank manager, on charges of alleged corruption, after coercion from Rathore. They moved to the outskirts of Shimla, and had to take up earth filling to make a living.

On 28 December 1993, days after Ashu was paraded in handcuffs in his locality, Ruchika consumed poison. She died the next day. Rathore threw a party that night to celebrate his victory. Rathore refused to release Ruchika's body to her father Subhash unless he signed blank sheets of paper. The blank papers were later used by the police to establish that the family had accepted Ruchika's forged autopsy report. Rathore also threatened to kill Ashu, who was still in illegal police custody.

At this time, Ashu was allegedly unconscious in CIA lock-up. He had been stripped naked and beaten the previous night by drunk policemen. He was brought back to his house, still unconscious, after Ruchika's last rites were over. In the inquest and the postmortem report, the name Ruchika was replaced with her nickname Ruby, and her father's name was changed to Subhash Chander Khatri. This was to ensure that anyone reading the report would not know that it pertains to Ruchika. The government closed the case filed against Rathore less than a week after her death. Unable to bear the harassment, her family moved out of Chandigarh.

Just a few months later, Rathore was promoted to additional DGP in November 1994, when Bhajan Lal was the chief minister of Haryana. No action was taken on the inquiry report. He was even awarded President's Police medal on 15 August 1995 for meritorious services. Birbal Das Dhalia, who, was then Home Secretary, defended the decision, saying that there was no chargesheet against Rathore. Anand Prakash tried to get a copy of the report. After 3 years, he finally obtained it in 1997, and in November, moved the Punjab and Haryana High Court. On 21 August 1998, the High Court directed the CBI to conduct an inquiry. In October 1999, the Haryana government led by Om Prakash Chautala made Rathore the police chief (DGP) of the state.

Shanta Kumar, who was then vice-president of the BJP, in 2000, wrote a letter to Om Prakash Chautala, urging him to take strict action against Rathore in the case of Ruchika. However, instead of acting on the letter, Chautala complained to then Prime Minister Atal Bihari Vajpayee about it. Shanta Kumar was the Minister for Consumer Affairs in the NDA government at that time. Chautala's Indian National Lok Dal was a coalition partner.

Ashu's case reached before the High Court following *suo moto* cognizance taken of a media report highlighting his plight, by justice Mehtab Singh Gill on 12 December 2000. The then chief justice had referred the matter to a division bench comprising justice N.K. Sodhi and justice N.K. Sood. While deposing before the division bench, Ashu stated that he had undergone inhuman treatment at the instance of Rathore and the Panchkula police. This was his first statement since the family was forced to leave Panchkula. At the time of making the statement, the family was living in Sector-2, New Shimla.

On 13 December 2000, the division bench voiced support for compensation to Ashu for the harassment caused to him at the hands of Panchkula police. Rathore filed an affidavit in 2001 denying the allegations. The HC then referred the inquiry to sessions judge Patiala. On 3 September 2002, Ashu detailed the torture he was put through to a Patiala Sessions Court. But Rathore approached the Supreme Court and got the High Court order quashed on technical grounds.

On 21 August 1998, the Punjab and Haryana High Court directed the CBI to conduct an inquiry. The High Court had ordered completion of investigation of the case and filing of chargesheet expeditiously, "preferably within six months". However, more than a year passed before the CBI filed a chargesheet. On 16 November 2000, the CBI filed a chargesheet against Rathore. Despite the CBI filing the chargesheet, the Chautala government allowed Rathore to continue as police chief. The case was put to hearing in the CBI special court in Ambala from November 17. The hearings in Ambala continued till May 2006. The chargesheet was filed only under Section 354 (molestation). Abetment to suicide was inexplicably not included in the chargesheet.

On 8 October 2001, counsel for Anand Prakash moved an application demanding the addition of abetment to suicide (306 of IPC) against Rathore. Rathore argued that Prakash had no standing to move the court. However, in a scathing judgment on 23 October 2001, Special CBI Judge Jagdev Singh Dhanjal demanded that the offence be added. In his 21-page judgment, the CBI Judge underlined witness statements, including those of Ruchika's father, Anand Prakash, friend Aradhana and others in adding Section 306 (abetment) of IPC against Rathore.

The CBI Judge Dhanjal was forced to take premature retirement two years later. However, in February 2002, Justice K.C. Kathuria of the Punjab and Haryana High Court dismissed the CBI court's decision to register an FIR against Rathore for abetment to suicide, claiming the lack of a complaint regarding harassment.

Justice Kathuria was a neighbour of the Girhotras, with whom he was engaged in a property dispute. In another glaring conflict of interest, he was also a close relative of O.P. Kathuria who was an associate of Rathore and had served as secretary of the Haryana Lawn Tennis Association which was floated by Rathore. Justice Kathuria is now the President of the Haryana State Consumer Disputes Redressal Commission.

Incredibly, after filing the chargesheet in 2000, the CBI took 7 years to record evidence from 16 prosecution witnesses. On the other hand, the defence counsel took nine months to complete examination of 13 out of the total 17 witnesses. Rathore tried to use his influence also with the CBI. R.M. Singh, who was CBI Joint Director in 1998 and retired in 2001, said that Rathore was tracking the case.

Once the file arrived at R.M. Singh's desk, he started getting frequent visits by Rathore to his officers. Rathore visited several times in 1998, trying to influence the CBI to clear him on all charges. Rathore had learnt that R.M. Singh was constructing a house in Gurgaon, and offered to provide building materials and other assistance. R.M. Singh also found out that Rathore had also approaced the Investigating Officer, Rajesh Ranjan, CBI's Deputy Superintendent of Police for the case. When he failed to influence the officers, Rathore had the case transferred. Rathore enjoyed access to all the levels of the CBI since he was the DGP, Haryana.

Ruchika's case was one of the few cases which were heard in three subordinate courts of three different states: Haryana, Punjab and Chandigarh—apart from one in high court and the Supreme Court. Around 15 applications were accepted in Punjab and Haryana High Court on behalf of Rathore, a strategy meant to delay the case. For example, on 23 January 2006, Rathore moved an application demanding transfer of trial from Ambala CBI Special Magistrate Ritu Garg to any other court.

The application was moved when evidence of two prosecution witnesses was only to be recorded. The ground was that Rathore knew Ritu's father and that Rathore's son Rahul was friendly with Ritu. Surprisingly, the CBI didn't object to it. In the reply filed in February 2006, S.S. Lakra, the then Additional Superintendent of Police, New Delhi, said that he did not object to the transfer, so that the case would "conclude expeditiously". The case was then transferred to Patiala.

Again when the case was at the last stage, Rathore accused the then Special CBI Judge, Patiala, Rakesh Kumar Gupta of overawing the defence witnesses and scolding Rathore. This time also the CBI did not object to the transfer of the case to Chandigarh. Rathore also used other technical grounds like demanding that the trial be videographed to cause more delays. Ironically, he later claimed that the long delays were grounds for a reduced sentence, which he got.

On 5 November 2009, the case was transferred from the Ambala court to CBI Chandigarh. In December, the court closed all final arguments. On 21 December 2009, it found Rathore guilty. But in spite of the guilt being proved fully, the special judge J.S. Sidhu pronounced only a six-month jail sentence and a fine of ₹ 1000 to Rathore. The sentence was suspended upto 20 January 2010 for filing an appeal. He was granted bail minutes after the sentencing, after furnishing a bail bond of ₹ 10,000. The court mentioned in its judgement about the application of abetment to suicide being rejected by the High Court and the Supreme Court.

This is all nothing but delay and denial of justice to Ruchika and her family. Perhaps everybody in the hierarchy was protecting Rathore who was a high-ranking police officer in Haryana government. Had the punishment in this case been given to Rathore within a year or two in 1990-91, it might have been sufficient. Rathore would have lost his job as Inspector General of Police and would have lost both his prestige and reputation. But in 2009 he had retired about seven years before as the Director General of Police, Haryana, with a President's Police medal.

When the court announced the punishment and was given a bail immediately after filing an appeal in the higher court, he came out of the court smirking instead of feeling ashamed of his behaviour of molesting a 14-year-old girl of the age of his daughter. He is about 68 years old now. He perhaps might have been thinking that it would take several years before the High Court and the Supreme Court finally take decision on his appeal. He may either be let off honourably on some technical grounds in the case or due to old age with a minimum punishment or he may die before the appeal is finally decided.

Even the Punjab and Haryana High Court has accepted the delay in Ruchika's case and has further said that the blame of the delay in this case has to be shared by all concerned, including the justice delivery system. The hon'ble High Court asked the administration in Punjab, Haryana and Chandigarh to submit the details of all pending criminal cases against "highly connected people" pending against them by 10 January 2010.

In his order, Justice Ranjit Singh has asked the Home Secretariats to give the information about cases pending against officers of the rank of Superintendent of Police and above besides those against IAS and PCS officers, as the court did not want to be blamed for delaying justice (*HT* dated 5th January 2010). But how long this tempo can be maintained is a matter to be seen. Judicial process takes years to complete. Every other day there is a Ruchika who is committing suicide due to molestation or rape and for being pressurized by the accused to withdraw her complaint by harassing her and her family.

Ruchika's father Girhotra was shown on the TV with the grief and helplessness on his face. The culprit must at least be behind bars and must be awarded the maximum punishment, if found guilty. A powerful police officer molested Ruchika, his daughter, and she committed suicide due to harassment to her and her family. Girhotra lost nearly everything and he could do nothing much in the past nineteen years due to protection been provided to the culprit by all in the ladder. The molester was still not behind bars and was roaming around smirking. What more grief and helplessness could have been there on his face?

The case was brought up for debate in Parliament. "After 19 years, the criminal has been found guilty but all he got as punishment was 6 months in prison. Within 10 minutes of conviction, he was out on bail. Is it not a shame for all of us?" asked CPI(M) leader Brinda Karat.

Now under mounting public pressure the Central Government woke up. First it appeared in the newspapers that owing to his bad conduct the Home Ministry was planning to issue a notice to Rathore for withdrawing his President's Police medal and to stop his pension. The notice of stoppage of pension was issued to him. The Central Government began withdrawing the medal from all police officers that have been convicted by the court including Rathore. But why not from everybody who has been awarded a medal and has been convicted by a court? Let the medal at least ensure a good conduct on the part of its receiver [*HT* and *Amar Ujala* (Hindi) both dated 5th January 2010]. However, the President is said to have issued the orders for withdrawal of Rathore's Police medal on 11 March 2010 (*Amar Ujala* dated 2nd April 2010).

The CBI was ordered to take over the fresh case of abetment to suicide against Rathore without going through the records of the case. The High Court and the Supreme Court have already rejected this matter. However, on the complaint of Ashu, the brother of Ruchika, the third FIR for abetment to suicide was registered against Rathore. K.P. Singh, the then SP Ambala, Prem Dutt, SI, SHO Police station, Panchkula, and Jainarayan and Sewa Singh, both ASI in the said Police station were made the co-accused. It was entrusted to the Special Investigation Team of Haryana Government for inquiry.

However, Haryana Government recommended that the CBI might take over this case. The CBI has taken it over and has registered the case against Rathore under section 306 (abetment to suicide) of the Indian Penal code. The Haryana police that were trying to save itself from arresting Rathore heaved a sigh of relief (*Amar Ujala* dated 10th January 2010). The officers are now hesitating to do their duty. Why?

Haryana Police disbanded the STF on 14-3-2010 following reports of the involvement of the personnel in extortion. The STF was constituted to look into serious and organized crimes in the state. Two cases of extortion came to light on March 10 in which the STF men were allegedly involved. The district police detained on 15-3-2010 the 8 policemen, including the ASP, of the disbanded STF, to investigate allegations of extortion reported from Panipat Industrial Township (*HT* dated 15th March 2010).

The state police having become unreliable, how much load the CBI can take over especially when the corruption and other criminal cases being given to the CBI are on the increase. There is a marked delay in investigations and trials due to shortage of officers and prosecutors in the agency. The CBI has vacancies ranging from 10 to 60 per cent at different ranks of its primary investigating wing (*HT* dated 15th March 2010).

In a case of abetment to suicide, a bench of the Supreme Court said that an accused could be convicted if he or she is guilty of abetting the suicide or has committed an act that pushed the deceased to take the extreme step. There is no set formula for convicting an accused because each person's pattern of suicide is different from others. Each person has his own idea of self-esteem and self-respect (*HT* dated 6th January 2010). On 8 January 2010, the district court refused anticipatory bail to Rathore and Sewa Singh ASI (*HT* dated 9th January 2010).

During arguments Abha, the advocate and the wife of Rathore, had made a complaint to the court that the police were acting under media pressure and the media has assumed the role of prosecutor and the judge. They want to hang Rathore publicly. The session's court took note of her argument and held that the importance of the media could not be denied or undermined. Sometimes the media oversteps its limit and becomes extreme in highlighting the things without going to the root of the merits thereof. But at the same time as a fourth pillar of democracy, the role and importance of the media cannot be denied or undermined. In certain other cases the media has come to forefront to aid and help the most deprived and downtrodden segments of the society in a bid to save/protect them from the atrocities and highhandedness of the system of the country and in order to secure justice for them.

However, at the same time it is also relevant to observe that the judicial system of the country and the courts of law established thereunder in the past have not been swayed by any media hype nor they would be swayed in future by any media consideration.

The courts of law would keep on discharging their duties in accordance with law strictly on the merits of each and every case. The session's court however gave bail to Rathore up to 8 February 2010 (*HT* dated 9th January 2010).

The Punjab and Haryana High Court on 15 February 2010, adjourned to April 5 the hearing in the two FIRs levelling serious criminal charges against Rathore in the Ruchika molestation case after the CBI sought more time in the investigations. The CBI registered the two more FIRs on the basis of complaints by Ruchika's father Girhotra and brother Ashu. They accused Rathore of committing serious offences including attempt to murder, wrongful confinement, giving false evidence and doctoring the post-mortem report of Ruchika, who committed suicide three years after being molested by Rathore on 12 August, 1990 (*HT* dated 16th February 2010).

On 8 February 2010, a student posing as a journalist stabbed Rathore thrice in the face. The assailant, Utsav Sharma, resident of Varanasi, UP is pursuing a post-graduate diploma course in animation and film design at the National Institute of Design, Ahmedabad. He appears to be psychologically unbalanced. Rathore (68) had just stepped out of the local court after morning proceedings when he was attacked. Sharma, standing with the media persons, lunged forward, caught Rathore by his neck and stabbed him thrice on his right cheek with a pocketknife. He also punched Rathore in the face. A shaken Rathore came back to court for the post-lunch session with a bandage on his right cheek and a walking stick (*HT* dated 9th February 2010).

Tough measures and mandatory registration of FIR are being proposed for molestation and sexual offences (*HT* dated 29th December 2009 and 1st and 2nd January 2010).

As regards the compulsory registration of all the FIRs, the Delhi Police say that it would create more problems than it would solve. It might be misused, leading to substantial harassment of law abiding and innocent citizens. There are numerous possibilities of harassment, which could be caused by mere registration of an FIR and the same becomes relevant specially where there are political enmities, rivalries and matrimonial disputes. Delhi Police said that preliminary inquiry is required before registering an FIR in cases pertaining to property disputes, will and power of attorneys, economic offences and dowry harassment.

After an FIR has been registered, till such time the case remains pending, the individual against whom the FIR has been filed, cannot get an employment in a government department. A criminal proceeding is a bar to obtain passport under section 6(2) of the Passport Act, 1967 and a government officer cannot get promotion (*HT* dated 3rd January 2010).

Ruchika's father and her brother have filed three fresh FIRs after 16 years of the crime. They would certainly keep the sword of justice hanging on the neck of Rathore.

But can all these measures bring back Ruchika to life and the status of her family, which has been ruined by Rathore? Can they punish all those officers of Haryana government who delayed the matter and obstructed justice? They include the then Home Secretary, the then Director General of Police, Haryana, the then SP Ambala, the then SHO Police station, Panchkula and his subordinates, the two ASI. Sewa Singh, one of the two ASI, is currently the Assistant Station House Officer of Pinjore police station. He has not reported for work since the sentencing of Rathore created national headlines. The then Home secretary and the then Director General of Police have said that they could not take action in this case due to pressure from the top (*HT* dated 27th December 2009).

The punishment to Rathore or to the officers of Haryana government is not the main question in this case. The main question is why no officer of Haryana government could stand erect against injustice being done to Ruchika and her family. We have one of the best forms of government in the country, i.e. democracy which is a government of the people, by the people and for the people and looks after the interest of the weaker section of the society and the steel administration to punish the guilty. Then in Ruchika's case why no action was taken for 19 years by the officers of Haryana government and why the people have come to believe that only public pressure would bring the guilty to book?

Ruchika's case is an example that the Central and State governments woke up only after public pressure was exerted on them. Now both the governments are trying their best that Rathore gets the maximum punishment including the then SP Ambala, SHO Police Station, Panchkula and his two ASIs who helped Rathore in harassing Ruchika's family to get the complaint against Rathore withdrawn by her (*HT* dated 6th January 2010).

But is all this sufficient? Will it bring back Ruchika to life? What happens to her honour and the sufferings to her family? If not, then what should we do that our officers do their duty in spite of pressure from the top for which they are already protected under the Constitution of India?

5

Scams and Scandals in India

Corruption has increased many folds. Now the assets of corrupt officials are in thousands of crores. It is no longer limited to bribes, kickbacks, cuts, commission, etc. Now there are scandals and scams (dishonest schemes) which causes the public exchequer loss of crores of rupees. Indians are creating history in all fields. They are also creating history in corruption through scams.

The major scams and scandals in India are: (1) Jeep Scandal, (2) Haridas Mundhra Scandal, (3) K.D. Malaviya Sirajuddin Oil Scandal, (4) 1971 Nagarwala Scandal, (5) National Games Scam, (6) Sukhna Land Scandal, (7) Oil for Food Programme Scam, (8) Barak Missile Scandal, (9) Palmolein Oil Scam, (10) IPO Scam, (11) Mining Scam, (12) Bitumen Scam, (13) Cement Scandal, (14) IPL Scam, (15) Animal Husbandry Scam, (16) Satyam Software Services Scam, (17) Tansi Land Scam, (18) ULIP Insurance Scam, (19) Cash for Votes Scandal, (20) RBG Resources Scam, (21) Bangalore-Mysore Infrastructure Corridor Fraud, (22) Bofors Scam, (23) Haji Scam, (24) Animal Fodder Scam, (25) Churhat Lottery Scam, (26) Telgi Stamp Papers Scam, (27) Urea Scam, (28) St Kitts Forgery, (29) Anantnag Transport Subsidy Scam, (30) Yugoslav Dinar Scam, (31) Kargil and Coffin Scam, (32) Uday Goyal Arrow Global Agrotech Scam, (33) Emaar Scam, (34) HDW Submarine Scandal, (35) Land Acquisition Scams on name of SEZ with false harassment cases, (36) Provident Fund Scam with current corrupt Judges in both Supreme Court and High Court, (37) Ketan Parek Stock Market Scam, (38) Bansal Scam, (39) Cobbler and Shoes Scam, (40) Nagarjuna Finance Scam, (41) Dalmia DSQ Software Scam, (42) UTI Scam, (43) Uday

Goyal Scam, (44) Letter of Credit (LOC) Scam, (45) Sanjay Agarwal Home Trade Scam, (46) LIC Insurance Scam, (47) Harshad Mehta Stock Market Scam, (48) Suflam Sujalam Rice Scam, (49) Madhavpura Mercantile Cooperative Bank (MMCB) Scam, (50) Hawala Transaction Scams, (51) Global Trust Bank Scam and Bankruptcy, (52) Charminar Cooperative Urban Bank (CCUB) Scam and Bankruptcy, (53) Vasavi Bank Scam and Bankruptcy, (54) Krushi Cooperative Urban Bank (KCUB) Scam, (55) Prudential Bank Scam and Bankruptcy Nagpur, (56) District Central Cooperative Bank (NDCCB) Scam, (57) 2010 Housing Loan Scam, (58) Sugar import Scam, (59) Preferential Allotment Scam, (60) Meghalaya Forest Scam, (61) Fertilizer import Scam, (62) Telecom Scam SNC, (63) Lavalin Power Project Scam, (64) Teak Plantation Swindle Scam, (65) Scorpene Submarine Scam, (66) Taj Corridor Scam, (67) Army Ration Pilferage Scam, (68) State Bank of Saurashtra Scam, (69) Flood Relief Scam, (70) Rice Export Scam, (71) Bulletproof Jackets Scam (MCD), (72) Pension Scam, (73) AICTE Scam, (74) Medical Council of India (MCI) Scam, (75) Rail Recruitment Scam, (76) NREGA Scam, (77) Siachen Scam, (78) J&K Milk Scam, (79) Gorshkov Scam, (80) MPLAD Scam, (81) Public Distribution System (PDS) Scam, (82) Rajya Sabha Vote Scam, (83) Cash for Questions in Parliament Scam, (84) Commonwealth Games Scam, (85) Adarsh Housing Society Scam, and (86) 2G Spectrum Scam.

The list of scams is growing larger and larger day by day. Some people say that the disease of corruption in our democracy has become incurable. But it is not so. The Indians are God fearing and are afraid of exemplary punishment provided in the law. We have only to change our form of government or have to frame stringent laws with exemplary punishment and the corruption can still be eliminated or controlled to a large extent.

One of India's biggest corruption cases that tarnished the image of late Prime Minister Rajiv Gandhi in the 1980s returned to haunt the ruling Congress Party on 5 January 2011 amid new charges of kickbacks and graft. Shri Rajiv Gandhi was voted out of office in 1989 largely over the Bofors gun deal. The Swedish group AB Bofors was accused of paying bribes of $1.3 billion to secure the sale of 400 howitzers, though the company and all those accused have always pleaded their innocence.

India's Income Tax Department has now concluded in a 98-page report on the case that illegal commissions of 410 million rupees were paid to the Italian businessman Ottavio Quattrocchi and an Indian arms dealer, Win Chadha, in the 1986 Bofors gun deal. Since Mr Quattrocchi and Shri Chadha had received payment, they should have paid income tax in India on this income.

It said that inaction in this regard may lead to a non-existent, undesirable and detrimental notion that India is a soft state and one can meddle with its tax laws with impunity. It also cited a Swedish investigation into Mr. Quattrocchi, which concluded that he had no experience in guns or defence equipment and was a chartered accountant by profession.

The Income Tax Tribunal's order has confirmed that there had been a pay-off. The CBI dropped the charges against Mr. Quattrocchi last year and he has withdrawn the money from the bank. It led to claims from the opposition in Parliament that the ruling Congress Party was trying to bury the embarrassing episode.

In India with its culture and past, corpses can only be cremated and not buried. If they were buried, they would be exhumed from time to time to haunt those connected with the controversy (*HT* dated 31st January 2011).

The Adarsh Housing Society was originally meant to be a six-storied building to house Kargil war heroes and their kith and kin. It was a prime defence land and was constructed in alleged violation of rules. Its height was made 97 meters and was further increased to 107 meters to accommodate unauthorized allottees. The CBI is investigating the case where many VIPs are involved. The CBI carried out searches at the premises of Bombay Municipal Commissioner. He holds properties in three different cities in Delhi, Mumbai and Pune. The officer appears to have amassed wealth due to rampant corruption in the country. His son owns apartment in Adarsh Housing Society meant for Kargil war heroes and their kith and kin.

The 2010 Commonwealth Games, officially known as the XIX Commonwealth Games were held in Delhi from 3 to 14 October 2010. A total of 6,081 athletes from 71 Commonwealth nations and dependencies competed in 21 sports and 272 events. It was the largest international multi-sport event to be staged in Delhi, eclipsing the Asian Games in 1951 and 1982.

Several objections were raised over the preparations of the Games. These included excessive budget overruns, infrastructure compromise, poor living conditions at the Commonwealth Games Village, delays in construction of the main Games venues, and widespread corruption by officials of the Games Organizing Committee. Mani Shankar Aiyar, former Indian Minister for Youth Affairs and Sports criticized the 2010 Commonwealth Games in Delhi.

The Indian media alleged that Games' Organizing Committee officials were involved in serious corruption and these allegations included acceptance of bribe during the process of awarding construction contracts for the Games venues.

Weeks before the start of the Games, Indian media outlets highlighted the poor construction standards at several of the main Games venues. In late September 2010, the president of the Commonwealth Games Federation remarked that the Games village were far from completion and needed a "deep clean". The concerns came to media attention in late September 2010 after media outlets began reporting on "filthy and unlivable conditions" and they took photos of paan stains and excrement in living quarters at the Games village.

Just a day after these remarks, a footbridge under construction near the Nehru Stadium collapsed, injuring 27 persons and seriously injuring five. On 22 September 2010, some tiles at the wrestling stadium's false ceiling caved in. However, there were no reported injuries. After the start of the games, a large scoreboard at the rugby stadium toppled over, though before any competitions had started in the stadium.

Suresh Kalmadi

Suresh Kalmadi was the chairman of the Commonwealth Games Organising Committee. He was the Congress MP from Pune. In the opening ceremony, he faced further embarrassment when the Indian spectators at the start of his welcome speech booed him. Reports of locally filled bottles with tap water, sealing them and then selling the bottled water as purified water have come out of Delhi. The negative pre-event publicity and heavy security presence played in part in low spectator attendance during the initial events. However, the number picked up as the Games progressed.

In Commonwealth Games initially, a tentative estimate of ₹ 400 crore was made. Subsequently, the estimate was revised to ₹ 948.52 crore. This was brought down to ₹ 687.86 crore. The Organizing Committee rented equipment at ₹ 42.34 crore against the actual cost of ₹ 2.80 crore. This is in addition to the double payment and inferior quality of items.

In one such case, 72 golf carts were hired for ₹ 4.23 lakh each, when they could be purchased for ₹ 1.84 lakh each. The generators were hired for ₹ 1.5 lakh each, when they could be purchased for ₹ 50,000 each (*HT* dated 14th March 2011).

The day after the conclusion of the Games, the Indian government announced the formation of a special committee to probe the allegations of corruption and mismanagement. The probe committee was led by former CAG of India. This probe was in addition to the investigations by the CBI, Enforcement Directorate and CVC. This shows that large-scale corruption had taken place in conducting Commonwealth Games (CWG).

Shunglu committee looked into the irregularities in the CWG. They found procedural violations by Delhi Lt. Governor, the chairman of the DDA, and Delhi Chief Minister in executing CWG projects. The committee put at ₹ 900 crore the cost of delay in the infrastructures projects and ₹ 300 crore loss to DDA in construction of residential facilities.

Taking a serious view of Shunglu committee findings, the Prime Minister's Office suggested to sports ministry a probe by the CBI and Enforcement Directorate into irregularities listed by the panel in the contracts executed by the Commonwealth Games Organizing Committee (*HT* dated 9th May 2011).

The Prime Minister Manmohan Singh promised in mid-August, 2010 when reports of the bungling first surfaced, that corrupt officials would be given severe and exemplary punishment after the Games. This shows that severe and exemplary punishment is needed to eradicate corruption. But the exemplary punishment is not provided in the Prevention of Corruption Act, 1988. So from where he would give them exemplary punishment is a million-dollar question.

On 5 August 2010 the Commonwealth Games Organizing Committee suspended T.S. Darbari Joint Director, and Sanjay Mahendroo DDG, following the report of the three-member panel which was probing the financial irregularities related to the Queen's Baton Relay. Anil Khanna treasurer resigned from the post in the wake of allegations that his son's firm had secured a contract for laying synthetic courts at a tennis stadium.

Due to serious irregularities committed in the projects for the Commonwealth Games, its Organizing Committee chairman Suresh Kalmadi was sacked. He was arrested on 25 April 2011 by the CBI along with several other officers for allegedly awarding a Games contract to a Swiss company to install a Timing-Scoring-Result (TSR) system at an exorbitant cost and had paid it ₹ 158 crore. Another French company had offered to do the same job for ₹ 62 crore. Thus Suresh Kalmadi caused a loss of ₹ 96 crore to the exchequer in a pre-planned manner.

It is alleged that officials of the CWG Organizing Committee had conspired with the representatives of the private firm in Switzerland and contract for TSR was awarded by wrongfully restricting and eliminating competition from other suppliers in a pre-meditated and planned manner (*HT* dated 26th April and 21st May 2011).

Kalmadi, 66, was walking to the court when a man Kapil Thakur, tried to break the police cordon. When he failed, he chucked a slipper. Kalmadi looked a bit taken aback, but was rushed into the courtroom. Kapil Thakur is unemployed and belongs to Madhya Pradesh. Shri Kalmadi would have remembered his own days when he similarly threw a slipper in 1977 at the car of Morarji Desai the then Prime Minister of India near Tilak Memorial temple in Pune. We have to suffer for our bad deeds. It only remains a question of time (*HT* dated 27th April 2011).

Enforcement Directorate registered the case against Kalmadi under the Prevention of Money Laundering Act as he had a role in all financial dealing of the organizing committee by virtue of being its chairman. The agency has asked Kalmadi to furnish details of his bank accounts, movable and immovable properties, instances of foreign travel before the Games held last year (*HT* dated 20th May 2011).

Adding to the list of CWG scams the Central Vigilance Commission has found serious deficiencies in the major projects carried out by the Games Organizing Committee including an expenditure of over ₹ 27 crore on "image and look" which it said was "highly inflated".

The CVC said that the Suresh Kalmadi-led OC has wrongfully moulded eligibility criteria in tenders to pave the way for certain private firms to help them make profit out of the projects worth ₹ 718.33 crore that included ticketing, accreditation card work, purchase of fitness equipment and overlays (*HT* dated 28th April 2011).

The Prime Minister ordered a CBI probe into alleged graft in the 214 crore Games Telecast Scam. In the dock are B.S. Lali, head of Prasar Bharati, and Aruna Sharma, DG Doordarshan (*Times of India* dated 20th February 2011).

Mr. A. Raja, Telecommunication minister, faces allegations of corruption over the licensing and allocation of second-generation 2-G telecom spectrum services in 2008 on a first come, first served process. It netted India only 1658 crore rupees and awarded licenses to ineligible participants. They in turn sold their stakes at a premium. According to audit report, the government lost 1.76 lakh crore in potential revenue.

The CBI is investigating the case and has arrested Ex-Telecom minister A. Raja, his secretary Siddharth Behura, and his private secretary R.K. Chandolia on 2 February 2011. It is alleged that the minister received ₹ 3,000 crore in bribes, a part of which he deposited in his wife's bank account in Mauritius. The companies who benefited from this scam are also being questioned.

Sadiq Batcha, trusted aide of the Minister, was turning to become an approver. He is said to have committed suicide in Chennai on 16 March 2011. The CBI informed the Supreme Court on 1st April 2011 that it was willing to take over the probe into the mysterious death of Sadiq Batcha. The central government has to issue the necessary orders (*HT* dated 17th March 2011 and 2nd April 2011).

The family of the Chief Minister of Tamil Nadu is understood to be involved in this case with ₹ 206 crore. The CBI was allowed by a Delhi court on 30 March 2011 to interrogate Asif Balwa and Rajeev Agarwal, arrested for their alleged role in the 2-G spectrum allocation scam for transferring ₹ 206 crore to Kalaignar TV Ltd., in its custody for two days. Special CBI Judge O.P. Saini allowed CBI's plea saying that as per the allegations against both the accused, they were "instrumental in transferring ₹ 206 crore in accounts of Kalaignar TV Pvt. Ltd.".

Tamil Nadu chief minister M. Karunanidhi's daughter and DMK MP Kanimozhi, her mother Dayaluammal and Sharad Kumar, MD of Kalaignar TV Pvt. Ltd., have 20 per cent, 60 per cent, and 20 per cent equity in the company. It is alleged that

₹ 206 crore investment has been made by subsidiary of Shahid Usman Balwa's company D.B. Realty in Kalaignar TV during 2008-10. The CBI has already arrested him in this case.

Agarwal has 50 per cent equity along with Balwa's cousin Asif Balwa in company's subsidiary—Kusegaon Fruits and Vegetables Pvt. Ltd. But from where the money had moved to Cineyug Films Pvt. Ltd. and subsequently to Kalaignar TV has not been explained. They did not produce the agreement dated 19 December 2008, if any, for such a deal (*HT* dated 31st March 2011).

The CBI on 25 April 2011 named Kanimozhi and four others as co-accused in the 2-G spectrum scam. She has been charged under the Prevention of Corruption Act dealing with alleged acceptance of gratification. The CBI has accused her of entering into a criminal conspiracy with prime accused and former telecom minister A. Raja (*HT* dated 26th and 27th April 2011). She has been arrested by the CBI on 20th May 2011 and the court has declined to give her the bail on the plea that she was present in the meeting where the decision to take 206 crore for Kalaignar TV was taken (*HT* dated 21st May 2011).

A. Raja, King of Scams

But in spite of such a large scam there was no body in the UPA government to have the courage to point out the wrong doings of Raja. The new telecom minister and the DMK Party in Tamil Nadu were even defending Raja. Perhaps corruption and the party politics have eroded our morals.

Shri A. Raja, ex-Telecom minister, is behind bars for corruption in 2-G spectrum scam of ₹ 1.76 lakh crore. The bad deeds had their effects. Elections were held in Tamil Nadu in May 2011 where due to corruption in 2-G spectrum the DMK lost power to AIADMK. According to allegations that led to A. Raja resigning as Telecom minister, he had presided over the under-pricing of bandwidth to mobile companies, apparently in return for bribes. Some estimate that it may have cost the Indian government around $7 billion (*HT* dated 20th May 2011).

After 17 months of investigation into the 2-G spectrum allocation scam, the CBI filed its first chargesheet on 2nd April 2011 indicting former Telecom Minister A. Raja and others for causing a loss of around ₹ 31,000 crore to the exchequer. The chargesheet consists of 80,000 pages. But no money has been recovered so far from the accused. The result is the rise in prices due to scandals and seams.

The chronology of events of 2nd November 2007 show that the PM wrote to Raja directing him to ensure that 2-G spectrum is allocated in a fair and transparent manner and to ensure that licence fee was properly revised. Raja wrote back to PM allegedly rejecting many of his recommendations. Ministry of Finance wrote to Department of Telecom on 22 November 2007 raising concerns over the procedure adopted. But the demand for review was rejected. It is not clear why the PM and the Finance Minister did not bring this matter to the kind notice of the Cabinet instead of allowing the loss to take place (*HT* dated 3rd April 2011).

The public accounts committee (PAC) of Parliament has, in a draft report on the 2-G spectrum scam, strongly indicted former telecom minister A. Raja and come down heavily on the prime minister's office for not taking corrective action. It has not spared Prime Minister Manmohan Singh too over some unfortunate omissions. The report circulated by PAC chairman M.M. Joshi is understood to have attacked the then finance minister P. Chidambaram for recommending to the PM to treat the matter as closed.

It says that Mr. Manmohan Singh kept his office at arm's length of the 2-G spectrum allocation thereby giving Raja an indirect green signal to execute his unfair arbitrary and dubious designs. It says that the PMO either failed to see the foreboding or was rendered a mute spectator. "Raja's assurance to the PM that he was not deviating from the existing procedures was a blatant lie as he deformed the first-come, first serve policy", the draft report says (*HT* dated 28th April 2011).

The 2-G scam is ranked second in the all-time Top 10 Abuses of Power list, next only to ex-American President Richard Nixon. Raja beat some tough contenders and is ahead of Libyan strongman Muammar Gaddafi, North Korean autocratic leader Kim Jong-II and *skirt-chasing* Italian premier Silvio Berlusconi.

The Time write-up on the telecom scandal says that in recent months, India's ruling coalition government has been rocked by an epic corruption scandal that has challenged its once unbreakable grip on power. Following the 2008 elections, the telecom ministry was awarded to Raja, a relatively green lawmaker from a regional party who won his post as a result of India's usual parliamentary political horse-trading. The 2-G spectrum hands down the largest episode of graft in Indian history. Raja languishes in jail as the snail-paced Indian judicial system inches the case forward (*HT* dated 20th May 2011).

The world's second-fastest growing economy of India ranks 87th on graft watchdog 'Transparency International' list based on perceived corruption, a worse rating than rival China. Investors have so far shrugged off these issues, attracted by one of the world's fastest growing economies. But they say that the glacial pace of economic reforms, such as opening up the market to foreign investment and boosting the rule of law, could drag on India's ambitions to expand its economy at China's pace.

The Congress in alliance with other smaller parties, retained power in the 2009 polls, but is seen as struggling amid a raft of scandals including October's over-budget Commonwealth Games, at which investigators found suspect contracts and substandard public works. Congress leaders have been linked to graft during the Commonwealth Games in seizing prime property.

The Kerala government asked for sanction for prosecuting the officer Shri P.J. Thomas. The Home Ministry neither sanctioned nor rejected the request and the case has been pending in the criminal court against the officer for the last 20 years. The Prime Minister approved the appointment of Shri P.J. Thomas as the Central Vigilance Commissioner, against whom the charges of corruption are still pending and in spite of the objection by the leader of the opposition. The Supreme Court set aside the said appointment.

But no body has asked the Secretary, Ministry of Home Affairs, so far why the request of Kerala government is still pending in his Ministry and why he did not put up a note before the Appointment Committee about this case.

For obtaining Pilot's licence one has to clear three subjects—Aviation Meteorology, Radio aids and Instruments and Air Navigation. Abhishek Kaushik and many others allegedly obtained pilot's licence by producing forged documents to the Director General Civil Aviation (DGCA). Four officials of the DGCA have been arrested. The DGCA is scrutinizing the licences of 3000-4000 pilots in the wake of the scam.

India is a Sovereign Socialist Secular Democratic Republic. In Socialism the wealth should be equally distributed. This can be done through the Cooperative Societies. But they have failed in India because those who made money by foul means were not given exemplary punishment. They were let off by taking bribe.

Socialism has also failed in India due to the leaders making money by foul means. Although several cases are pending in courts against the politicians for holding assets more than their known sources of income, but none of them has so far been punished. Instead of deciding their cases fast, the courts are giving long date of adjournments to while away the time. Thus socialism in India is a failure.

Even Communism has failed in West Bengal and Kerala due to corruption. Those who were supposed to administer it failed to check/control corruption. In Calcutta Corporation there were hundreds of workers who came on payday only to get their salary. Garbage and rubbish were lying in the centre of roads. Discipline became the first casualty. The officers could not check workers for coming late or for not doing work. If anybody checked the worker, he would go out of the office and shout slogans against the officer for harassing the workers.

The Communist Party of India failed to check the rot in West Bengal and lost power to Trinamool Congress in May 2011 elections after 34 years of rule. Even its Chief Minister lost his seat to the ex-Chief Secretary of the state who was also a candidate of Trinamool Congress. Perhaps there is no such thing as democratic communism.

The CPI (M) in West Bengal executed land reforms successfully, but lost industries due to the interference by the unions. When the CPI (M) tried to acquire land for industries, the people did not like it and they lost power to Trinamool Congress. In communism there is no necessity to acquire land as both the land and industries belong to the state. This was not done by the CPI (M).

India has become truly a democratic country with very weak administration. The Departments and the Ministries of Government of India do not even acknowledge a registered letter. They do not pass a reasoned order. Unless they are bribed they would reject the claim saying "not admissible under the rules". They would not even name the rules under which it is inadmissible. For every information and every decision they force a citizen to go to the RTI Commissioner or the court which is time consuming and costly. Even if one wins in the court no officer is punished for not passing the reasoned order. The Ministry of Defence is no exception to it.

Democracy in India is weak due to corruption. There is no discipline anywhere in the society. Everybody is free to do what he likes. There is no law and order. The moneyed people can purchase justice. Power of money and the might have become the order of the day.

The economy of India was under socialist-inspired policies from the 1950s until the late 1980s. The economy was subject to extensive regulations, protection, and public ownership, leading to pervasive corruption and slow growth. License Raj was often at the core of corruption.

According to Jitendra Singh, "in the bad old days, particularly pre-1991, when the License Raj held sway, and by design, all kinds of free market mechanism were hobbled or stymied. Corruption emerged almost as an illegitimate price mechanism, a shadowy quasi-market, such that scarce resources could still be allocated within the economy and decisions could get made. There were large distortions created by the politico-economic regime.

Liberalization has further increased corruption. But is License Raj responsible for corruption or the liberalization or something else? One of the major problems and obstacles to development that many developing countries face is corruption by greedy and power-hungry politicians. But then how to control them?

Officials often steal state property. In Bihar, more than 80 per cent of the subsidized food aid to the poor is stolen. In cities and villages throughout India, Mafia Raj, consisting of government officials, politicians, judicial officers, real estate developers, and law enforcement officials, acquire, develop and sell land in illegal ways.

Government officials having discretionary powers in awarding contracts, engage in preferential treatment for selected bidders, and display negligence in quality control processes. Many state-funded construction activities in India, such as road building, are dominated by construction Mafia, which are groupings of corrupt public works officials, material suppliers, politicians, and construction contractors. Shoddy construction and material, substitution like mixing sand in cement while submitting expenses for cement result in roads and highways being dangerous, and sometimes simply get washed away when India's heavy monsoon season arrives.

Due to corruption law and order has become the biggest casualty. Even the children have learnt how to extort money. A 16-year-old class XI student of St Paul's Church School, Agra, has been arrested for bullying and extorting money amounting to around ₹ 30 lakh from his 11-year-old junior Kushagra Nagwani.

Kushagra Nagwani's father, in his complaint to the police, said that his son, a class VII student, had been demanding large sums of money for the past two years and that some valuables had gone missing from the house too. Suspecting something amiss, Kushagra's parents confronted him and he confessed that his senior was forcing him to get the money.

When the older boy called Kushagra again, the father, a local jeweller, managed to get the call recorded and handed the evidence to the police. They then laid a trap for him on 25 March 2011 and when he came to collect the money, policemen in plain clothes nabbed him.

The police said that the senior boy, the 16-year-old son of a banker, had confessed to the crime, though he told them that he received only ₹ 5-6 lakh. The police further said that the accused also confessed to having squandered the money in five-star hotels and restaurants.

Kushagra's father said that the complaints to the school went unheeded and that the "bully" had a full-fledged gang operating in the school. The school authorities perhaps have forgotten that it is one of their duties to give moral training to children.

Several new initiatives have come up in the private sector to raise awareness about corruption related issues and to build anti-corruption platforms. These methods work where there is awareness. Corruption is not considered bad or a sin by the Indian society and the majority are guilty of it. The rich are respected in India without caring how they have earned money.

When they go to select a bridegroom for their daughter, they not only inquire about his salary, but also the money he earns by other means. In Andhra Pradesh an inspector is said to be preferred as a son-in-law against an officer if he has good income over and above his salary. They do not advise their brothers and sons not to indulge in corruption. In fact they love and respect him more than the other brothers and sons if he earns and supports the family.

The housewife never advises her husband and her children not to indulge in corruption. On the other hand she gives examples of those who are earning by all means. But Indians do advise outsiders to be honest in their dealings and to be sincere in their duties and give examples of those that remained honest and spent a hard life. They even go to listen to lectures on honesty and sincerity, but remember it for being acted upon by others.

The politicians promise to punish every wrong doer by exemplary punishment fully knowing that it is not provided in the Prevention of Corruption Act. They would also say that the law would take its own course fully knowing that it would take more than twenty years before the case is finally decided and by that time the culprit may die.

Even the culprit would say that he has all the faith in the law of the land. But in spite of every citizen having all the faith in the anti-corruption law, there is rampant corruption in India. The reason may be that the punishment for corruption provided in the law is not at all sufficient to the quantum of corruption and there is unexplainable delay in awarding the punishment.

The corruption is not there for public servants and politicians only. While abuse of office in the government or public sector by politicians or bureaucrats is commonly called political corruption, the role that the private sector plays in influencing it is often not in public focus. As the nation watches a well-supported hunger strike by social activist Anna Hazare to usher in a Jan Lokpal Bill (ombudsman) to fight corruption, the public and private sectors are both reflecting on the need to cleanse the system.

Private sector corruption has two aspects—one in which profit seeking companies influence policymakers, politicians or bureaucrats, and the other in which they—or their employees—may be evading tax or be involved in irregularities hurting the interests of their shareholders, customers or employees.

India has been rocked by five major corruption scandals over the past 12 months. Complex official procedures and several approvals needed to get projects going are linked to efforts by private firms to bribe their way through the system to get clearance.

A recent study by a research firm Marketing and Development Research Associates showed that 9 out of 10 employees working in private firms feel that corruption or fraud is a common phenomenon in corporate India. Apparently irked by the 2-G spectrum scandal that brought to the forefront the questionable role of corporate lobbyists, some corporate leaders issued a joint letter to the government to crack down on corruption.

The letter, signed by Deepak Parekh, Azim Premji and Keshub Mahindra among others said that lack of governance has affected every sphere of national activity, and decisions were increasingly driven by unwanted influences. The lack of an auction mechanism (no transparency and a large dose of discretionary power) brought forth the 2-G spectrum.

The national executive committee of industry chamber last December passed a resolution that said, "corruption in high places is denting India's image and that both parties involved in corrupt transactions should be swiftly and severely punished". FICCI has offered support to create a Jan Lokpal (Ombudsman). A study by consulting firm said that those large investments, complex processes and huge projects give immense opportunity for corruption in sectors such as telecom and real estate.

That is significant given that an estimated $1 trillion (about ₹ 45 lakh crore) will be spent over the next six years on infrastructure and will involve private-public partnerships. KPMG said that new firms had crowded the scene and some were using unfair means to compete. "Regulations in India tend to focus on the bribe taken rather than the bribe payer and hence corporate do not shy away from adopting corrupt practices", said Deepankar Sanwalka Head-Risk & Compliance, KPMG, in India.

A survey says that 10.50 per cent bribe is given by companies to tax authorities, 4.80 per cent by employees to employees, 12.30 per cent by company to employees, 12.70 per cent by company to customers, 19.70 per cent by company to company and 40.00 per cent by company to government.

The Common Corporate corruption practices are the under-invoicing of bills by issuing bills for less than what is paid and thus evading the taxes by the firms. Another is by creating Black money by tax evasion or illegal income and often parking in property deals and loans given to friends or interlinked firms to show losses and thus evading taxes.

But is the government interested in eradicating corruption? This is what the Supreme Court said. The Supreme Court on 28 March 2011 criticized the government for not probing specific sources of black money stashed in banks abroad and asked the Central government to apprise it of its investigation into the threat to national security posed by it.

The court also expressed dismay that the probe was focused only on the case involving Pune businessman Hasan Ali Khan and no name of any other person involved in stashing funds abroad had come out. "No further information is coming out. Only one individual is there. What about others", a bench of Justices B. Sudershan Reddy and S.S. Nijjar asked solicitor general Gopal Subramanium, who submitted to the bench, in a sealed cover, the Enforcement Directorate's (ED) status report of its probe.

After going through the report, the bench criticized the steps taken by the government in the investigation of the matter, including that relating to the case against Khan for allegedly acquiring a passport on fake documents. "It is very difficult to be calm and quiet after seeing the status report," the court remarked. "Why have all these agencies been sleeping since 2008? Why did it move only when we stepped in? If a writ petition had not been filed, nothing would have happened."

The court was hearing a PIL, filed by former Law minister Ram Jethmalani, seeking retrieval of black money stashed by Indian citizens in tax havens abroad. The court reiterated its idea of setting up a special investigation team (SIT) comprising officers of the Intelligence Bureau, Research and Analysis Wing, CBI and ED to probe the entire issue. The solicitor general, for his part, said the investigation has revealed the involvement of a "power broker" and assured the court that substantial progress has been made into the investigation against Khan. He said the case wasn't simply a case of forgery of passport, but had far more serious implications.

At the last hearing on 18 March 2011, the court had toyed with the idea of forming a SIT to probe the black money issue and had asked the Central government to come up with its possible composition (*HT* dated 29th March 2011).

WikiLeaks founder Julian Assange has said that there are Indian names in the Swiss bank data list and will be made public. There were more Indian deposits in Swiss banks than any other country, he added (*HT* dated 27th April 2011).

This is how the Central government is dealing with the cases of corruption. No one has so far paid any attention to the fact that the punishment provided in the Anti-corruption law is not at all sufficient. It has to be made exemplary if the corruption is to be rooted out of India. The amendment in the law needs to be speeded up.

Geeta Bhadoriya from Vrindavan, UP, says that although corruption has become a major problem in India, but to take bribe has become one of the rules for the government servants. The people do not think it bad to take a bribe. Those who resist it are presumed to be fools. You may believe it or not, but you cannot prove it to be wrong.

Recently a number of names have been published who were found involved in corruption. They were mostly on high posts in one organization or the other. When she looked at their names she felt angry with them and also felt hurt. The anger she shows because the society contributed for them to rise high. But when they reach high positions they forget about society and think about themselves only. They only exercise their rights and forget to perform their duties.

They now do not bother about the problems of the common man. They only see wealth, honour and the chair. We feel hurt because we are not able to think what they will do with this money. If they purchase many palaces, in which palace will they live? By purchasing many plots of lands how will they enjoy them? The money, which should have been used for development and prosperity for the country, is lying idle with them. Neither they use it nor do they allow it to be used by others. They are least bothered even if the public may die of starvation.

In five star hotels they hold the costliest parties. We elect such type of selfish people and they suck our blood. We may talk of any department or any region; there is corruption all over. She wants to ask them only one question. How much money is required by them to fill their belly? [*Amar Ujala* (Hindi) dated 25th February 2011].

The answer is that there is no limit to corruption. Akhand Pratap Singh, the Chief Secretary of UP government, was found to be having several farmhouses, showrooms, flats and plots before the CBI arrested him. The CBI arrested Arun Misra, Chief Engineer, UP State Industrial Development Corporation, for holding property worth more than ₹ 100 crore in Lucknow, Kanpur, Noida, Dehradun, Kolkata and Delhi. He is holding 67 bank accounts in different banks. He is running an Engineering College.

In Madhya Pradesh one IAS Officer has been found to be having 25 flats and 400 acres of land. Another is found to be having cash in washing machines, pillows, quilts, and mattresses. In the case of a government engineer, 7.8 kg of gold and ₹ 1.6 crore in cash has been found. Even the woman officers are not lagging behind in this field.

Shri Madhu Koda, the Chief Minister of Jharkhand, is found to be involved in a corruption case of ₹ 8,000 crore. Shri A. Raja, Ex-Telecommunication Minister, is alleged to be involved in a scam of ₹ 1.76 lakh crore. The list of new financial terminology is "100 crore make one Koda, 100 Koda make one Kalmadi, 100 Kalmadi make one Raja and 100 Rajas make one Rani".

Thus there is no limit of money within which the belly of a corrupt man gets filled or his desires are satisfied. They may learn some lesson if what Pandit Jawaharlal Nehru said is done—hang them by the nearest lamppost.

The Allahabad High Court on 20th May 2011 directed the Enforcement Directorate to probe charges of money laundering against former Samajwadi Party general secretary Amar Singh. The charges pertain to awarding of government contracts worth thousands of crores when Singh was the Uttar Pradesh Development Council chairman in 2003-07. Singh had allegedly misused his official position and awarded contracts to companies owned and controlled by him and also received kickbacks (*HT* dated 21st May 2011).

Election Commission officials counting the cash seized from suspected DMK workers in April 2011

The big scams have started showing their effects. During elections in May 2011 in Tamil Nadu, cash seizures made regular news, but the one by assistant returning officer from the rooftop of a private bus in Tiruchy made the world sit up—she had stumbled upon ₹ 5.11 crore of unclaimed cash. Investigations revealed links to people close to the local DMK leaders. In all, a sum of ₹ 60 crore in cash was recovered and seized by election commission officials (*HT* dated 15th May 2011).

The above details of corruption and scams show that corruption is widespread in Indian society from top to bottom. In such a situation no individual or class of individuals or caste or creed or region can be blamed for it. The present law is not sufficient to deal with corruption.

Then how to remove corruption from Indian society, which is eating our economy and the progress of our nation? There appears to be one and only one solution and that is to provide such an exemplary punishment with no mercy that even the soul of an individual may start shivering before thinking of corruption.

It does not look nice when early morning we read in the newspapers about the arrest of ministers and secretaries by the police. In old good days such officers used to commit suicide instead of getting arrested. But now they have all become shameless. They come out of court smirking when punished for molestation with six months imprisonment. Even withdrawal of pension and medals has no effect on them. They are no longer human beings. For money they have made the life of a common man miserable. We can only say that they deserve maximum punishment that can be awarded and no mercy.

6

Corruption in Asian and African Countries

Asia is well known, publicized and often criticized, as one of the regions of the world where corruption has taken deep roots. It has become a part of daily life everywhere. This is considered an evil thing, which must be put to an end outright. No doubt power tends to corrupt, and absolute power corrupts absolutely, but even then those who are indulging in corruption never justify it.

One of the reasons for corruption in Asian and African countries is the increase in population. In the good old days there was no way to control the childbirth. But now the childbirth can be controlled. The diseases like malaria, plague, smallpox, which annually used to have a heavy death toll, have been controlled. But still no family planning is being adopted for various reasons including the religious objection. So the population is bound to increase.

No new resources are developed and the existing resources go on decreasing reducing the per capita income. The result is that there is always a tendency to earn more and more money by any means, whether legal or illegal. Hence, there is an urgent need to adopt family planning in all countries. Populous countries like India should adopt the Chinese policy of one child. Its population has already increased to 1.21 billion, an increase of over 181 million in the last decade. It is 17.50 per cent of world's population.

In spite of having money in one's pocket, one does not get pure water, milk, butter or butter oil, and medicines. Everybody curse adulterators. In fact those who are corrupt have a strange psychology. They think that they only can indulge in corruption while others should be honest. At least in India even the corrupt praise those who are honest. Of course for them honesty is not the best policy.

In corruption it is not only the honest man that gets harassed, but the corrupt also feels the pinch here and there. That is why all religions advise us to be honest, otherwise everybody in the society would feel its harmful effects. Corruption being a bad deed, God punishes those who are guilty of corruption. Suddenly we find someone behind bars whereas others similarly involved are roaming free. But they may also suffer when their time comes. Why this difference takes place is a mystery. How He punishes man, please read the book *God made Man and Man made God* by the author and published by Atlantic Publishers and Distributors (P) Ltd.

It may be surprising to many if they see the results of a recent survey of government transparency and corruption in the government departments by Transparency International. In 2009, New Zealand and Denmark are in the top positions. There is a little corruption in Singapore, Hong Kong, and Japan, which share 17th place with the UK. Next is the US in 18th position.

Bangladesh: Corruption is not new to Bangladesh. A general impression conveyed by the media and by popular discourse is that among ordinary people in Bangladesh, corruption is viewed quite clearly as 'a way of life'. A recent survey carried out by the Bangladesh Unnayan Parishad reinforces this impression.

The survey found, among other significant data, that 95 per cent of respondents believed that the police were the most corrupt department in the land, followed very closely by the customs, the department of excise and taxation, the bureaucracy, and the judiciary. A solid 62 per cent of respondents believed that the primary responsibility for corruption in Bangladesh lay in the hands of government officials.

The extent to which corruption has become acceptable as 'a way of life' in Bangladesh is challenging in its implications. A recently published feature on corruption in a leading weekend magazine, entitled 'Corruption of Politics and Politics of Corruption' consisted of a virtual litany (prayers to God) of dubious deals, underhand agreements and blatantly corrupt acts by political leaders and parties in Bangladesh, from the infamous regime of H.M. Ershad, to the present leadership as well.

But surprisingly, both the media report and the research conducted by the Bangladesh Unnayan Parishad, upon which it was partly based, appear to have generated little reaction. Certainly, there were no reports of a public outcry, not even a barrage of letters or telephone calls in response to these successive and extremely challenging expressions of public opinion and media analysis.

Does this mean that the people of Bangladesh are unmoved by the all-pervasive level of corruption in their government? Or have they become so immune to its horrors, so cynical about what they perceive to be the unhappy reality of their lives that they have ceased to care? Whatever may be the reasons, people appear to believe that nothing can be done to eradicate corruption.

Perhaps this is one reason for a marked absence of objective and analytical literature on corruption as a social exchange or process. There are, of course, other reasons. But generally speaking, there is a tendency to focus on the enormity of the problem, on the normative aspects of corruption, on the negative impact of corruption and to perpetuate the notion that corruption is its own culprit.

The media report mentioned above, for instance, states at the outset that 'Corruption', in our view, lies at the root of the overall degeneration of politics and of a section of our politicians that we see today. Thus, corruption is seen both as the root and as the effect of a situation, with the result that its salient features are often masked and its behavioural patterns difficult to discern.

Indeed, as far as Bangladesh is concerned, little is known about the manner in which corruption occurs, the process by which it grows and flourishes, the conditions which are conductive to its existence and the structure which support its survival. Little is known about corruption as a process, as practice and as structural outcome. It can be said, therefore, that there is inconsequential independent appraisal of corruption as a social phenomenon in this country.

Whatever independent or neutral discussion has been generated tends to focus mainly on the political or economic aspects of corruption. Certainly, very few academic works have been devoted towards obtaining empirically sound, theoretically analyses of the subject from a sociological perspective with special reference to Bangladesh.

A major aim of this Study has been to seek out with a sociological perspective of corruption in Bangladesh. As the Study will bear out, the search has been disappointing in the sense that only a few works of specific relevance have been found. Consequently, the challenge has been to identify and analyze the literature available, from a sociological perspective. Many works on the political or economic aspects of Bangladesh do contain data on social issues in general and corruption in particular and hence, such works have been included as sources on corruption.

Pakistan: Corruption in Pakistan is a well-established phenomenon. It has had a consistently poor ranking in the Corruption Perceptions Index, being 143rd with a score of 2.3 in 2010 (with 10 being clean and 0 being totally corrupt).

Pakistan was created as a result of the partition of India and the British left behind a strong bureaucracy and army. The country was divided again when Eastern Pakistan seceded to form Bangladesh. A factor in this division was that Bengal's elite and ruling class had been Hindus who were displaced by the partition, while the Punjab's rich land-owning class were Muslims and so had retained power.

As of 2002, during survey 96 per cent of individuals reported corruption issues in electricity department officials during the past year. The most common types of corruption were related to billing of electricity consumed. Some consumers admitted to have illegally got reduced their electricity bills, while others reported being harassed with inflated electricity bills intended to solicit bribes. Out of the pool of corruption-affirmative respondents, 71 per cent reported that money was "demanded directly by the official whom they approached".

According to the 2002 study, 99 per cent of 256 respondents reported facing corruption of taxation. Furthermore, 32 per cent of respondents reported paying bribes to have their tax assessment lowered, and nearly 14 per cent reported receiving fictitious tax assessments until a bribe was paid.

In 2010, 69 per cent of those surveyed reported that they or someone in their household was subjected to an act of corruption when interacting with the judicial system. Of 339 affirmative respondents asked to identify the officials involved in corruption, 119 said that the court employees, 84 said a public prosecutor, 50 said a witness, 44 said a judge, 29 said an opponent lawyer, 16 said the magistrates, and 12 said the others.

As of 2010, 24 per cent of those surveyed reported that they themselves or a family member received admission to educational institutions through illegal means. This was most commonly reported to be through an influential relative, followed by "additional money to be paid other than donation", by means of political influence, through a private tutor or faculty member, or by donation. 32 per cent reported facing corruption after admission, which was most commonly done by a teacher, a member of the management committee, or an invigilator.

In 2010, 42 per cent of surveyed individuals reported gaining access to hospital services by a method other than normal admission, and 48 per cent reported either having to pay additional costs for essential services or being forced to utilize the services of a designated affiliate. Of the respondents who were asked to identify which parties helped in the corrupt acts, 61 per cent reported hospital staff, 25 per cent reported doctors, and 13 per cent reported nurses.

According to documents released by WikiLeaks in the 2010 Afghan War Inter-Service Intelligence played a role in aiding insurgents during the War in Afghanistan.

According to 2002, 2006, 2009 and 2010 surveys, the majority of respondents consistently view the police as being the most corrupt sector of Pakistan government. In the 2010 survey, 31 per cent of 4,224 respondents reported paying bribes to the police. In 2005, Prime Minister ordered an investigation into a claim by a 23-year-old woman who alleged that, in retaliation for attempting to reveal police corruption, police falsely detained her for 15 days and raped her.

Since the US provides enormous aid to the country as a frontline power in the war against terrorism, the government seems to be taking active steps to combat corruption. But it's working in only a spotty fashion. Early this year, President Pervez Musharraf, suddenly suspended and detained the nation's chief justice, apparently because of his failure to sanction illegal detentions of terror suspects and overturning corrupt privatization of steel mills. Corruption remains rife in the judiciary, financial markets and civil service.

Afghanistan: Corruption is a very important and quite likely a growing problem in Afghanistan. Based on available indicators, Afghanistan appears to fall near the bottom among all the countries in terms of the seriousness of its corruption problem. The very large opium economy is widely considered to be the most important source of corruption in the country.

However, other illicit activities as well as the unprecedented large inflows of international assistance and the pressures to spend money quickly, carry the associated factors responsible to corruption. Other, normal sources and forms of corruption, related to government roles in service delivery and regulation, appear to be increasing as state activities and capacity are increasing.

As the political system is progressively developed, there is a serious risk of political corruption. There are important issues about the definition and scope of corruption in Afghanistan, and Afghan perceptions must be taken into account in designing and implementing an effective anti-corruption strategy that is suited to the country. It may also be possible that the form of government may be changed to another form, which suits best to Afghanistan and not necessarily to the best form in the world.

Corruption has multiple and severe adverse effects on Afghanistan. The direct financial costs of corruption are higher costs of contracts and public services and loss of public funds due to theft or misuse of government facilities and assets. There are substantial costs related to time devoted to corrupt practices. In the case of the security it is the human costs of threats, intimidation, and victimization by security forces.

Widespread corruption deters and distorts private investment. Perhaps most important are the adverse implications of corruption and popular perceptions for the effective functioning, credibility, and legitimacy of the state.

By all indications corruption, defined as "the abuse of public position for private gain", is a very important and quite likely a growing problem in Afghanistan. Corruption is generally considered to be a symptom and outcome of weak government. Afghanistan reflects in large part the legacy of a quarter-century of conflict and erosion of state institutions, irregular financing of the conflict from various sources, worsening tensions among ethnic and tribal groups, and the growth of illicit economic activities.

Hence in Afghanistan corruption has been intimately linked with the development and destruction of the state. Since 2001 the drug economy combined with unintended adverse side effects of counter-narcotics efforts and large inflows of aid have greatly increased opportunities for corruption. It includes, to some extent, the revival of the economy due to regulations and red tape, which provide scope for corrupt activities.

The US spent more than $1.2 billion last year on reconstruction and relief in Afghanistan and Iraq. The funds were paid to local contractors, often in cash, at the discretion of officers in the war zones. But due to corruption several projects have remained incomplete.

Corruption has multiple and severe adverse effects on Afghanistan. It has direct financial effects due to corruption. There is an increase in the cost of contracts and public services and loss of public funds due to theft or misuse of government facilities and assets. There are substantial costs related to time devoted to corrupt practices by government officials.

In fact democracy does not suit the Asians where there is no self-discipline and respect for other's rights. Therefore it is the limited monarchy or democracy with stringent laws against corruption, which may suit them and to their customs and traditions, habits and behaviours, and to their way of living.

Iraq: Iraq's political parties used the relative stability created by the surge to enrich and empower themselves by stealing from government projects, big and small. Iraq is now considered one of the most corrupt nations on earth. The political parties, still mostly based on sectarian lines, are unpopular among most Iraqis. But the question is whether the change from monarchy to democracy is useful to Iraq or it has only spoiled its administration.

The US combat troops left Iraq in August 2010. American forces are scheduled to withdraw from Iraq by the end of 2011. But what will happen to Iraq, when US troops leave, is a million-dollar question? Iraq certainly has a new reality today deeper than it did under Saddam Hussein. A dictatorship has been replaced by a corrupt political system called democracy.

Under Saddam, Iraq had a callous and at times evil government, but the state was firmly part of the Arab world and had a clear national and secular identity. What has been created in its place is a country of power-hungry political parties based on ethnic and religious divides, and a nation much more in the orbit of non-Arab Iran.

Although Iraq has frequent elections, there is very little true democracy because most of the parties do not believe in democratic principles. Elections are merely tools, which the parties have accepted as a means to determine which self-interested group gets the biggest piece of the pie. If the political parties begin fighting each other, Iraq's civil war might return.

Do Iraqis have a stable government that the people in Baghdad believe would bring them out of what has been a dark and tumultuous period? Iraq now faces a similar threat as that of Lebanese. If Iraq is lucky, its political parties would mature and

Iraq would skip the civil war Lebanon went through. But the chances are bleak. Asians do not learn any lesson from the mistakes of others.

If Iraq is unlucky, however, the battles among the political parties in Baghdad may easily become violent and Iraq may be involved in civil war of short duration or of long duration depending upon how soon the political parties realize their folly. How Iraq's civil war develops and American legacy in the country remains to be seen.

The US spent more than $1.2 billion last year on reconstruction and relief in Afghanistan and Iraq. The corruption has plagued Iraq reconstruction. Hundreds of projects may never be finished, including repairs to the country's oil pipelines and electricity system. Congress gave more than $30 billion to rebuild Iraq. According to a government audit, at least $8.8 billion of it has disappeared. Will Iraq be able to come out of its problems or it will require a change of government? If it requires a change of government, should the form of government be changed to limited monarchy or to the democracy with stringent laws against corruption?

Myanmar: In Myanmar corruption is perceived as widespread. This is vicious dictatorship run with an iron hand by a strong-willed clique of military leaders. They persist in repression of civil society at every level. Illicit facilitation payments and informal fees are required to access to most basic government services.

Vietnam: Vietnam is in a phase of transition from centrally planned economy to a market economy with socialist orientation. Vietnam's efforts to attract foreign investment have led the ruling party to seek to improve the business climate for foreign investors. This involves attempts to combat corruption, which is rampant throughout the country and permeates the activities of the many state companies that still dominate the economy's strategic sectors. Yet, corruption is still cited as one of the most problematic factors for doing business in the country.

In Vietnam its light-fingered bureaucrats cream off at least 20 per cent of infrastructure spending. Corruption has been identified as one of the government's main challenges. Vietnamese are now battling corruption at all levels.

Thailand: Corruption has always been a parasite of society. From the absolute monarchy regime till the present period, Thailand has passed many sequences of bureaucratic reform, especially during the reign of King Rama V in which ministries, departments and other public agencies were established.

Ever since 1932, the year the democratic system has been laid down in Thailand, all Thais have always depended on bureaucrats in every activities of their life. Let's say from womb to tomb, it is inevitable that corruption exists not only receiving a small bribe by base echelon officials but also gaining huge sums of money from abusing power in mega project by politicians.

While huge amounts of money will be lost during the implementation of projects due to corruption, more will be lost while trying to fight against it and stop it. Thailand's ex-Prime Minister Thaksin Shinawatra has used very rough methods to control the media, which is one of the most powerful watchdogs against corruption.

Cambodia: Corruption is pervasive in all levels of society in this country where two-thirds of the population earns less than $2 a month and one-third earns less than $1. No one has ever been prosecuted under a skeleton anti-corruption law. The International groups have charged that judges in the trial of top former Khmer Rouge leaders had bought their positions.

International aid donors have warned of diversion of large chunks of the $500 million or more provided to this nation as aid. The system of illicit facilitation payments by businesses and individuals may only intensify as oil found off the coast replaces donor aid, removing even today's rudimentary control on use of public revenues.

Malaysia: When we say money politics, people don't get the real picture. It is nothing but bribery and corruption. It is buying votes to get elected to the leadership of UMNO, the dominant party in the Barisan National that rules the nation.

Indonesia: Indonesia has been categorized as the number 5 of the 96 most corrupt nations in the world. In the past two years, Indonesia has lost more than $2 billion due to corruption. Former President Suharto, as the most corrupt political leader in the world in the past 20 years, has ruled this country with an iron fist for more than three decades. All the leading candidates have made fighting corruption a central theme of their campaigns but none have been clear on how they will solve the problem.

Bribes by firms in Indonesia arise principally from regulations, viz. the licenses and levies imposed by local government officials. Regulations generate direct revenues for local governments plus indirect revenues in the form of bribes for its officials. This is to compensate public officials for the low salaries given by the local governments.

Insufficient revenues from formal tax and transfer sources to pay salaries plus fund for public services hamper localities in Indonesia. The local taxes rates capped by the centre and inter-governmental transfers are limited. Thus the direct and indirect revenues from local regulations are not at all sufficient.

The paper model estimates the key aspects of corruption, viz. the relationship between bribes, time spent with local officials, and different forms of regulations. The paper model estimates a large reduction in regulation in better funded localities. The findings are directly relevant to Indonesia where corruption is high and the country is in the struggle of major decentralization and local democratization.

Philippines: The republic of Philippines is a weak postcolonial state. The public sector is basically subservient to the dominant social classes and deeply entrenched special interests. The reasons can be traced back to the historical evolution of the political system and modes of governance.

Both Spain and America created bureaucracies based on their own models. Indeed, the Philippine State owes little to indigenous Filipino norms or culture. The whole apparatus was externally imposed. Part of the problem was that the Americans were conflicted about the unaccustomed role of colonialist power. Lacking the long history of colonial rule of the Spanish or British, the Americans were never quite comfortable as authoritarian rulers, and never solved the dilemma of how to "save the little brown brothers" while still protecting their strategic interests in Asia.

The American administration imposed colonial-style rule albeit with a Filipino-staffed bureaucracy while simultaneously encouraging grassroots democracy. They introduced local elections in 1901, then legislative elections in 1907, and eventually presidential elections in 1935. Powerful clans in the provinces dominated the domestic political process.

From the beginning, electoral competition did not revolve around class differences. Instead, politics was a game played within the elite classes, which manipulated and controlled the political process. They were a homogeneous group, and there were few substantive differences in politics or political philosophy. Everybody was a conservative. One consequence was that the political and electoral process was based more on personality than on substance.

Expatriate businessmen in Asia perceive the Philippines as the most corrupt country in the region. Nearly two billion dollars, or roughly 13 per cent of the Philippines' annual budget, is lost due to corruption in the country each year, according to the United Nations Development Programme.

Its judicial system is believed to be ineffective at prosecuting and punishing individuals for corruption when abuses are uncovered. Local corruption monitors confirm that graft and bribery in the Philippines remain rampant. Corruption has penetrated every level of government, from the Bureau of Customs down to the traffic police officers who pull over motorist to demand bribes.

Taiwan: Taiwan's problem lies in its own history. Taiwan was a notoriously violent and lawless frontier society. Since the government could not control its tough citizens, it granted them official titles to sustain the fiction of central control. Local government by gangsters was vastly preferable in the eyes of the Taiwanese to no government at all. Here we have local muscle power being used to gain access to political and economic spoils, which are used to legitimize community standing.

Korea: Power corrupts and absolute power corrupts absolutely and South Korea is no exception. The five men they elected to successive five-year terms as president under the 1987 democratic constitution had absolute powers. The power allegedly corrupted every one of them.

The tale of presidential corruption, or corruption committed by president's wives or elder brothers or sons or daughters or in-laws, are so common that it's possible to shrug off the headlines of the newspapers before turning to the sports pages. Like rhetoric from North Korea, corruption stories provide fodder for the media, but are hardly perceived as being important for the average Korean.

The investigation into the assets of the family of Roh Moo-hyun, who had a Mr. Clean reputation as president from 2003 to 2008, is being done. The figure being talked about is $6 million, but now the prosecutors say that it is much more. Since the financial crisis of 1997, Korea's image has radically changed from a model development state with good governance to a country with rampant corruption and cronyism.

Singapore: The Prevention of Corruption Act provides extensive powers to Corrupt Practices Investigation Bureau in the investigation of corruption. It gives the power to investigate corruption in the public and private sectors. It is incorporated within the Prime Minister's Office. There is no undue interference in its investigation.

It investigates not just the suspect, but also the suspect's family or agents and to examine their financial and other records, the power to require the attendance of witnesses for interview, it has the power to investigate any other sizable offence which is disclosed in the course of investigation into corruption. The result is that the corruption in Singapore is completely under control.

Japan: Japan is the Asia's 3rd least corrupt country. Since the years of the bubble economy and the ensuing economic and political turmoil after the bubble burst, political corruption in Japan has become a major concern for the general public. The most recent case is Abe cabinet's scandals.

China: Corruption in China became increasingly serious during the early period of its social transition, resulting in severe economic losses and huge challenges to China's government institution as well as gradually becoming socially widespread.

Bribery has become the main accusation of corruption against China's senior officials. It was found that the spouse (usually the wife) and the child played an important role in senior officials' acts of corruption. Also corruption cases have shown that having a "love affair" often coincided with the first steps of corruption.

African Countries: African nations have made marginal progress in the core areas of governance over the last four years, according to a new United Nation's report of 16th October 2009, which has expressed concern over a rise in corruption in the continent's authorities in the same period. The second edition of the African Governance Report, an overview of the state of governance in 35 African countries, highlighted a 3 per cent decline in the corruption control index.

UN Economic Commission for Africa (ECA) recently released its report. It said that the corruption remains the single most important challenge to the eradication of poverty, the creation of predictable and favourable investment environment and general socio-economic development in Africa.

A key finding of the report shows that although elections in Africa are more regular, they are still flawed and in many countries the quality of the elections remains suspect, with incumbent parties remaining hostile to the opposition which is unable to be competitive.

Despite a negative performance on issues involving corruption, there has been a 2 per cent increase on governance indices overall, including in areas of human rights, the rule of law, the effectiveness of the legislature, the executive and the judiciary as well as independence of civil society organizations and the media.

Positive trends in the continent's economies and the role of women in public life were also spotlighted in the report. The indices indicated a 6 per cent rise in pro-investment policies, up to 3 per cent increase in efficient economic management and tax systems, and more women represented in national parliament than anywhere else did in the world.

South Africa: Corruption in South Africa includes the private use of public resources, bribery, electoral fraud, and improper favouritism. The Department of Public Service and Administration coordinate government initiatives against corruption.

Notable incidents of fraud and corruption are the South African Arms Deal, finalized in 1999, which became mostly known for the bribery that was used to gain the contracts. The presence of Advance-fee fraud in South Africa is another example of corruption.

Egypt: In 2010, Transparency International's Corruption Perceptions Index report assessed Egypt with a CPI score of 3.1, based on perceptions of the degree of corruption from business people and country analysts (with 10 being clean and 0 being totally corrupt). Corruption costs Egypt about $6 billion and a total of $57.2 billion from 2000 to 2008, according to a report by Global Financial Integrity. Much of this money, the Washington based watch dog group notes, was driven out by personal tax evasion, in addition to corruption and crime (*HT* dated 12th February 2011).

Political corruption in the Hosni Mubarak's administration has risen dramatically, due to the increased power over the institutional system necessary to prolong the presidency. The rise to power of powerful businessmen in the NDP in the government and the People's Assembly led to massive waves of anger during the years of Prime Minister Ahmed Nazif's government. An example of that is Ahmed Ezz monopolizing the steel industry in Egypt by holding more than 60 per cent of the market share.

Hosni Mubarak had to resign under pressure from the public. He is reported to be ailing with cancer. He is the richest man in the world with his wealth about $70 billion including $474 million in Swiss Bank accounts. He is reported to have moved his family assets from European banks to institutions in Gulf countries after Swiss authorities took steps to freeze his accounts (*The Times of India* dated 15th February and 7th

March 2011). Egyptian prosecutors detained Hosni Mubarak, on 13 April 2011 with his two sons to face investigation on charges of corruption and abuse of power (*HT* dated 14th April 2011).

The people are happy that they removed Mubarak. But would Mubarak's fall really make a difference? Can democracy alone eradicate corruption and financial and political instability from the land of pyramids? Can democracy wipe out the corruption that exists in every corner and every government institutions is still a million-dollar question?

Democracy only creates conditions, which will ensure equality of citizens before the law of the country. But for proper functioning of democracy citizens have to know their duties and their rights. Enforce the duties with a heavy hand and the rights would flow. After all we get the government we deserve.

The democracy needs self-discipline in the public not to encroach on other's rights. This is not there in Asian and African countries. It is there in Europe and America and they would support all the efforts to form a democratic government in Egypt.

Today there is rampant corruption in Egypt. So they must ensure that stringent laws are made against corruption and the anti-corruption institutions must be independent having all the powers to prosecute the suspected corrupts. There should be fast track courts to deal with corruption. The punishment for corruption must be very severe like confiscation of all property and the death penalty.

Libya: Libya is in North Africa. It is bordering Egypt and Mediterranean Sea. Colonel Muammar Gaddafi has been ruling the country for the last 40 years. He got power in 1968 by a military coup. Now he is all the time afraid of being assassinated. So he keeps himself surrounded by women battalion commanded by a Major General. The people revolted against his rule on 15th February 2011. Swiss authorities announced that he is holding assets worth $416 million in their accounts.

The scope of his control is whittling away as major Libyan cities and towns closer to the capital Benghazi fell to the rebels on 23rd February 2011. In the east the rebels vowed to liberate Tripoli, a stronghold of Gaddafi. There is a rebellion in Airforce personnel. They are not bombing a rebel held city and allowing the warplane to crash after parachuting out of it.

Colonel Gaddafi has kept the regular army in a poor condition and is depending on paramilitary units. Foreign mercenaries are managing these units. The fighting is going on. Gaddafi has tens of billions in cash secretly hidden in Libyan Central Bank and other banks around Tripoli (*HT* dated 11th March 2011).

Morocco: Morocco is in North Africa bordering Algeria. It is curious as to why the Jasmine revolution which has consumed neighbouring Tunisia, Egypt and Libya, has not reached Morocco in any significant measure despite the odd protest or two. King Mohammed is the ruler.

The King is a lot smarter than the dictators in the region are. To counter the excesses of his father's rule, he set up the Arab world's only Truth and Reconciliation Commission, encouraging the growth of human rights bodies. He has also slowly created more space for the opposition, for a robust press and for civil society. This is quite a change from Gaddafi or Mubarak who have insatiable appetite for acquiring real estate in Europe and bulging Swiss Bank accounts.

The royal family in Morocco has, by and large, kept their noses out of political maneuverings. Much like the Thai king, this has given them the power to intervene in times of crisis as King Mohammed VI is doing now.

As in all countries of this region, corruption is an issue, which exercises young people. But given the numerous anti-corruption institutions, which exist, they have recourse for redress of their grievances, which keeps them off the streets. Thus King Mohammed of Morocco by his far sight has created democratic institutions to redress the grievances of the public. He has already given them democracy by not interfering in politics except in emergency. He has proved his honesty by not acquiring property in foreign countries and by not keeping any balance in a foreign bank.

In fact if this could happen in all countries of Asia and Africa ruled by monarchs and dictators, then there would not remain any problem of having democracy only. All democratic institutions for getting justice can be provided even under monarchy like that of Morocco.

7

Object, Reasons and Provisions of RTI Act, 2005

Introduction: Democracy is the government of the people, by the people and for the people. The MPs and the MLAs rule in the Centre and in the States respectively as public representatives. For their guidance the public has given them a Constitution. They have also given them an Indian Administrative Service called the Steel Administration of India to advise the ministers and to execute their orders with full protection under the Constitution to work without fear or favour. Then there is the Supreme Court, which ensures that the rule of law is maintained.

The public representatives are human beings and are not above greed. Power corrupts a man and absolute power corrupts absolutely. Therefore it is necessary that a watch be kept over their working. This is possible only when the working is transparent and you get the information whenever and wherever you have a doubt.

For this purpose the government of India resolved that in order to ensure greater and more effective access to information, it is required that the Freedom of Information Act, 2002 must be made more progressive, participatory and meaningful.

On this issue National Advisory Council suggested certain important changes to be incorporated in the said Act to ensure smoother and greater access to information.

After examining the suggestions of the National Advisory Council and others the Government decided to make number of changes in the law.

In view of the significant changes proposed by the National Advisory Council and others, it was decided to repeal the Freedom of Information Act, 2002 and enact another law for providing a framework for effecting the right of information recognized under Article 19 of the Constitution of India. To achieve this object, the Right to Information Bill was introduced in the Parliament.

Object and Reasons: In order to ensure greater and more effective access to information, the Government resolved that the Freedom of Information Act, 2002, enacted by the Parliament needs to be made more progressive, participatory and meaningful. The National Advisory Council deliberated on the issue and suggested certain important changes to be incorporated in the existing Act to ensure smoother and greater access to information. The Government examined the suggestions made by the National Advisory Council and others and decided to make a number of changes in the law.

The important changes proposed to be incorporated, *inter alia*, include establishment of an appellate machinery with investigating powers to review decisions of the Public Information Officers; penal provisions for failure to provide information as per law; provisions to ensure maximum disclosure and minimum exemptions, consistent with the constitutional provisions, and effective mechanism for access to information and disclosure by authorities, etc.

In view of significant changes proposed in the existing Act, the Government also decided to repeal the Freedom of Information Act, 2002. The proposed legislation will provide a framework for effecting the right of information recognized under Article 19 of the Constitution of India.

The Bill seeks to achieve the above objects.

Act, 2005: The Right to information Bill, 2005 was passed by the Lok Sabha on 11th May, 2005 and by the Rajya Sabha on 12th May, 2005 and it received the assent of the President of India on 15th June, 2005.

Right to Information: Information means any material in any form, including records, documents, memos, e-mails, opinions, advice, press releases, circulars, orders, logbooks, contracts, reports, papers, samples, models, and data material.

It gives the right to access information held by a government office. This includes the right to inspect work, documents, records, notes, extracts or certified copies of documents or records.

Although this right is provided in the Constitution, but we need a process through which this right can be exercised. The RTI Act, 2005 lays down the process on how to apply for information, where and to whom to apply, how much fee is to be paid and how, and to whom to file an appeal in case complete or satisfactory information is not given.

For example, one can seek information about house and water tax, ration cards, electricity and water connections, pension payment, medical claims and about all other applications and complaints pending with the public authorities.

Illiteracy: In case a person is illiterate, he can request the Public Information Officer to help him.

Video Conferencing: UP state government has decided to provide a new facility for RTI applicants. Applicants from across the UP State can now pursue their cases from their native place, as the UP State Information Commission will conduct hearings through video conferencing connecting all the 71 districts of the state.

The facility will start in collaboration with the National Information Centre. Required apparatus will be installed in NIT centre in all the districts to connect them to their main centre in Lucknow through Internet. Although the commission does not possess the required infrastructure as present, for the time being the facility will start on an experimental basis using the video conferencing centre set-up at Yojana Bhawan connecting it to NIT centres in the districts.

The initiative, which is already in practice at the Central Information Commission in New Delhi and in some other states, assumes significance as the cases taken up in the UPSIC are from other districts (*HT* dated 16th May 2011).

Bureaucrats' assets in MP under RTI ambit: Madhya Pradesh is the first state in the country to bring asset details of bureaucrats in public domain following a recent order of Central Information Commission in this regard. Acting on an application, the income tax department has started giving details of assets of Madhya Pradesh cadre IAS officers.

In a recent order the Central Information Commission in New Delhi had said, "Disclosure of information such as assets of a Public servant, which is routinely collected by the Public authority and routinely provided by the Public servant, cannot be construed as an invasion on the privacy of an individual. If people who aspire to be public servants must declare their property details, it is only logical that the details of assets of those who are public servants must be considered to be disclosable."

He further said, "Making details of bureaucrats' assets public, it will help ensuring people's trust in the system and add to transparency. Bringing details of babu's assets in public domain will help government in checking corruption."

The recent searches by the Income Tax department in Bhopal and Chhattisgarh have detected wealth to the tune of more than ₹ 500 crore unlawfully amassed among others by IAS couple Arvind Joshi and Tinu Joshi—both principal secretary ranked officers in MP and Chhattisgarh Agriculture Secretary B.L. Agarwal (*HT* dated 10th February 2010).

Inquiry against Babus (Clerks) Covered under RTI Act: The inquiry against corrupt government official cannot be deemed as personal and cannot be kept outside the purview of the RTI Act. Transparency watchdog the Central Information Commission has ruled that such inquiries should be disclosed under RTI Act. It would be safe to hold that investigation or inquiry against a third party employee cannot be brought within the scope of section 8(1)(j) of the RTI Act.

The section exempts personal information from disclosure unless larger public interest is served. The reason is that public authority appoints an employee to discharge public functions and it is the manner of his discharge of the function, which is called into question through inquiries and investigations.

In that sense, the inquiry or investigation against the employee of the public authority ceases to be personal to the employee. It relates to overall governance with the public authority as well as its accountability to the larger public for discharging the functions for which the public authority was created.

Each application would have to be examined within the scope of exemption clauses provided under the RTI Act, which provides for seeking approval of the person about whom the information is being sought. Such information cannot be denied only on the ground that it was personal to an employee and that no public interest warranted its disclosure (*HT* dated 12th April 2010).

Supreme Court can't deny Information under RTI: Overturning its previous orders, the Central Information Commission has held that the Supreme Court cannot deny information under the RTI Act even if an applicant has 'other methods' available under the apex court rules, to get it.

Earlier, in a number of cases, the then Chief Information Commissioner had held that if there were existing laws and rules for furnishing information in an organization, information seeker had to use them and not the Right to Information Act.

Accepting the arguments of the Supreme Court, he said that as per Section 22 of the RTI Act, the transparency law would prevail over the existing laws only when there is 'inconsistency' between the two.

The apex court argued that since it already had a mechanism for furnishing information on judicial proceedings and documents, under the Supreme Court rules, these records cannot be provided under the RTI Act as there was no 'inconsistency' between the two.

The Information Commissioner set aside the above arguments. He said that this commission respectfully disagrees with the decision of the then Chief Information Commissioner that the PIO Supreme Court may choose to deny the information sought under the RTI Act and ask an applicant to apply for information under Order XII of the SC Rules.

He said where there are methods of giving information by any public authority which were in existence before the advent of the RTI Act, the citizen may insist on invoking the provisions of the RTI Act to obtain the information.

He further said, "It is the citizen's prerogative to decide under which mechanism, i.e. under the method prescribed by the public authority or the RTI Act, he would like to obtain the information. An information seeker who has filed application under the RTI Act, cannot be forced to obtain the information as per order XII of the SC Rules" (*HT* dated 16th May 2011).

Assets made public tell only half the story: The government intends to complete putting the property returns of all government officers in the public domain by August or September this year. But the property returns will tell only half the story.

The civil service has decided against putting its bank balance and investments in the public domain. Supreme Court judges and politicians contesting elections have to make a full disclosure of their assets, both movable and immovable. Bureaucrats, however, submit the information under two different rules and formats.

Submission of property returns is an annual affair. Civil servants have to submit the list of their immovable assets to the government every January. However, no such annual declaration has to be made in case of their movable assets.

So far, they had to inform the government about any expenditure above a stipulated limit. In case of All India Service officers, this limit was ₹ 15,000. Last week this limit was linked to their salary and fixed at two months basic pay of the officer concerned.

The new rule makes it mandatory for the officer to inform the government about any transaction beyond this limit. This information, however, will not be covered under the transparency move to put assets in public domain.

The public should know about the movable and immovable assets possessed by officers and changes therein, on an annual basis, so that they can draw their own conclusions about the probity or otherwise of All India Service officers. The format of property return is inadequate to ensure full transparency and accountability of bureaucrats (*HT* dated 16th May 2011).

Why it could not control corruption: The Right to Information Act, 2005, and equivalent acts in the states, that require government officials to furnish information requested by citizens or face punitive action, computerization of services and various central and state government acts that established vigilance commissions should have considerably reduced corruption. Or at least it should have opened up avenues to redress grievances.

But this has remained on paper only. The procedure of getting information is so lengthy, expensive and time consuming that majority of applicants leave it in mid-way. Except in one or two cases, no punishment is being awarded. The information being supplied is incomplete. Had the above measures been effective, there would not have been any more scams. But scams are coming to light almost daily.

The only answer to corruption is the severe penalty and confiscation of the assets.

8

RTI Act, 2005—Delay and Denial of Information—Ministry of Defence

The information asked for under the RTI Act, 2005, is either denied or incomplete information is supplied by the Central Public Information officer.

A medical claim regarding Heart Surgery in the Max Hospital, Saket, New Delhi was submitted to the DG, DE, Delhi Cantt. Several reminders were issued, but no action was taken to dispose of the claim even after 14 months of its submission. Then the help of the RTI Act was taken and an application was filed before the Central Public Information officer about the disposal of the claim.

The said CPIO in his letter dated 20th November 2009 invited the attention to the DG, DE, letter dated 23rd November 2009 which clearly showed that he signed the letter dated 20th November in back date. He, without quoting the section of the Act under which it is exempted, informed that the information is not covered under RTI Act.

However, the RTI Act had its effect to a limited extent. The DG, DE, raised four queries on the medical claim, which were replied. Then on 9th February 2010 the DG, DE, without quoting the name of rules, informed that "the claim has been found to be not admissible under the rules". This is the reward we get by using the RTI Act.

The claim was resubmitted to the DG, DE, on 16th February 2010 for passing a reasoned order and the same is still pending in the office of the DG, DE. Again the RTI Act was used and the CPIO did not give the information on the plea that it is exempted u/s 8(g) of the RTI Act.

Indians normally do not like someone pointing out their defects. They take it as an insult and permanent enmity is created. An appeal was filed against the order of the CPIO. The Appellate Authority (DDG Adm.) in her order dated 21 May 2010 mentioned that the medical claim was found not-admissible under the CGHS Rules as the appellant was staying in a non-CGHS area. Thus the Appellate Authority added the bold words on its own while deciding the appeal, the words which are not there in the original order passed while rejecting the claim. She also directed the CPIO to supply the Rule position regarding medical reimbursement claim of CGHS/Non-CGHS beneficiaries. The name of the Rule, whose copy was to be supplied, was not mentioned in the judgement of the Appeal. Moreover, if there was some Rule position, it should have been mentioned and discussed in the order while rejecting the claim. This is all afterwards to fill up the gap in their previous order.

The CPIO supplied the copy of the government order dated 24th August 1998 regarding the Fixed Medical Allowance of ₹ 100 p.m. in lieu of OPD facilities for non-CGHS areas. It does not apply to indoor treatment for Heart Surgery in a recognized hospital.

In the meantime the Delhi High Court in its judgement dated 12th March 2010 held that all retired government employees are entitled to medical reimbursement under Article 21 of the Constitution. The applicant brought this judgement to the kind notice of the DG, DE in his letter dated 12th April 2010. But no action on this letter was taken.

This is how the people are forced to go to court even when the judgement of the High Court or the Supreme Court is already there. Going to High Court or Supreme Court is time consuming and a costly affair and the people give up their efforts in mid-way.

The applicant then submitted the medical claim to the Secretary, Ministry of Defence (Establishment Section), South

Block, New Delhi-110011 on 16th August 2010 by registered post/AD. But as usual no acknowledgement of the letter was received. The applicant issued four reminders, but no reply has so far been received.

The applicant used the RTI Act and applied to the CPIO of Ministry of Defence on 15th March 2011 to supply the information about the disposal of the claim. But no reply was received. Even the name and designation of the Appellate Authority was not communicated to him by the CPIO.

The applicant went to New Delhi on 18th May 2011. At the reception counter he was informed that the office of the CPIO is in Sena Bhawan opposite to South Block. The receptionist in Sena Bhawan said that the Director (L&C) is the CPIO and he might talk to the officer on telephone. The CPIO said that he did not deal with the medical claims and he might again contact the main ministry in the matter. He refused to divulge the name of his appellate authority.

In case he was not dealing the medical claims, being the CPIO it was his duty to obtain it from the concerned section of the ministry and supply the information to the applicant. Perhaps he had not read through the RTI Act.

The appellant has now filed the appeal to the President of India, through the Defence Secretary, Ministry of Defence, South Block, New Delhi-110011 and handed it over to the receipt clerk in the VIP Dak Counter, South Block, New Delhi and obtained his signatures on the office copy.

It is the summer season. But there is no arrangement for drinking water in the reception offices of the Ministry of Defence. It is understood that the government has reduced the posts of peons in government offices and there is no peon in the reception offices to arrange for drinking water.

Union Public Service Commission

There are complaints that every thing is no longer transparent in UPSC, the recruiting agency for the IAS, IPS and IFS officers, due to rampant corruption in the country. They do not show the marks-sheet of a candidate with the model answer format in spite of orders by the RTI Commissioner and the Delhi High Court. The MP from Hapur, district Ghaziabad, UP, raised the point in Parliament. If the UPSC does not remain transparent and fair the entire system of administration called the steel administration may collapse.

Government Servant Property Returns: Shri Bal Sharan Singh, Director General, Defence Estates, was living in Flat No. 4292 (G.F.), Pocket–5 & 6, Sector–B, Vasant Kunj, New Delhi, which now costs more than a crore of rupees. He built a colourful boundary wall with gate of this flat. R.W.A. Managing Committee of Vasant Kunj prepared a Residents' Directory and the position of Shri Bal Sharan Singh is shown therein as under:

Flat No: 4292

Name: Bal Sharan Singh

Profession: Govt. Service

Residence Telephone No: 26124783

When his CPIO was asked about the property return of Shri Bal Sharan Singh and whether this flat was included in his property return or not, he replied that the information asked for was exempt u/s 8(1)(j) of the RTI Act and hence could not be supplied.

In an order the Central Information Commissioner, New Delhi, said, "Disclosure of information such as assets of a public servant, which is routinely collected by the public authority and routinely provided by the public servant, cannot be construed as an invasion on the privacy of an individual. If people who aspire to be public servants must declare their property details, it is only logical that the details of assets of those who are public servants must be considered to be disclosable" (*HT* dated 10th February 2010).

The Central Information Commission has also ruled that annual confidential reports of government servants cannot be treated as secret. Citizens' right to information has greater primacy with regard to privacy. He further said that privacy is a cultural notion related to social norms and cannot be considered a valid exercise to constrain the citizens' fundamental right to information. Parliament has not codified the right to privacy, so far. Hence, in balancing the right to information of citizens and the individual's right to privacy, the citizen's right to information would be given greater weightage. He also said that information such as property details, conviction or acquittal of a public servant and provided by public servants, cannot be construed as an invasion of privacy (*HT* dated 23rd May 2011).

But the CPIOs do not take cognizance of such rulings of RTI Commissioner. Every applicant is being forced to approach the RTI Commissioner by filing at least two appeals. This is all time consuming and waste of money.

Thus to a common man the RTI Act has not proved useful. In fact he loses the sympathy of the office where his case has been pending for disposal. For the removal of corruption the only remedy is the exemplary punishment to be provided in the anti-corruption laws.

9

The Right to Information Act, 2005 (22 of 2005)

[15 June 2005]

An Act to provide for setting out the practical regime of right to information for citizens to secure access to information under the control of public authorities, in order to promote transparency and accountability in the working of every public authority, the constitution of a Central Information Commission and State Information Commissions and for matters connected therewith or incidental thereto.

Whereas the Constitution of India has established democratic Republic;

And whereas democracy requires an informed citizenry and transparency of information which are vital to its functioning and also to contain corruption and to hold Governments and their instrumentalities accountable to the governed;

And whereas revelation of information in actual practice is likely to conflict with other public interests including efficient operations of the Governments, optimum use of limited fiscal resources and the preservation or confidentiality of sensitive information;

And whereas it is necessary to harmonize these conflicting interests while preserving the paramountcy of the democratic ideal;

Now, therefore, it is expedient to provide for furnishing certain information to citizens who desire to have it.

BE it enacted by Parliament in the Fifty-sixth Year of the Republic of India as follows:

CHAPTER I
PRELIMINARY

1. Short title, extent and commencement. (1) This Act may be called the Right to Information Act, 2005.

(2) It extends to the whole of India except the State of Jammu and Kashmir.

(3) The provisions of sub-section (1) of section 4, sub-sections (1) and (2) of section 5, sections 12, 13, 15, 16, 24, 27, and 28 shall come into force at once, and the remaining provisions of this Act shall come into force on the one hundred and twentieth day (12th October 2005) of its enactment.

2. Definitions. In this Act, unless the context otherwise requires,

(a) "appropriate Government" means in relation to a public authority which is established, constituted, owned, controlled or substantially financed by funds provided directly or indirectly:

  (i) by the Central Government or the Union territory administration, the Central Government;

  (ii) by the State Government, the State Government;

(b) "Central Information Commission" means the Central Information Commission constituted under sub-section (1) of section 12;

(c) "Central Public Information Officer" means the Central Public Information Officer designated under sub-section (1) and includes a Central Assistant Public Information Officer designated as such under sub-section (2) of section 5;

(d) "Chief Information Commissioner" and "Information Commissioner" mean the Chief Information Commissioner and Information Commissioner appointed under sub-section (3) of section 12;

(e) "competent authority" means—

(i) the Speaker in the case of the House of the People or the Legislative Assembly of a State or a Union territory having such Assembly and the Chairman in the case of the Council of States of a Legislative Council of States;

(ii) the Chief Justice of India in the case of the Supreme Court;

(iii) the Chief Justice of the High Court in the case of a High Court;

(iv) the President or the Governor, as the case may be, in the case of other authorities established or constituted by or under the constitution;

(v) the administrator appointed under article 239 of the Constitution;

(f) "information" means any material in any form, including records, documents, memos, e-mails, opinions, advices, press releases, circulars, orders, logbooks, contracts, reports, papers, samples, models, data material held in any electronic form and information relating to any private body which can be accessed by a public authority under any other law for the time being in force;

(g) "prescribed" means prescribed by rules made under this Act by the appropriate Government or the competent authority, as the case may be;

(h) "public authority" means any authority or body or institution of self-government established or constituted,

(a) by or under the Constitution;

(b) by any other law made by Parliament;

(c) by any other law made by State Legislature;

(d) by notification issued or order made by the appropriate Government, and includes any—

(i) body owned, controlled or substantially financed;

(ii) non-Government Organization substantially financed, directly or indirectly by funds provided by the appropriate Government;

(i) "record" includes—

(i) any document, manuscript and file;

(ii) any microfilm, microfiche and facsimile copy of a document;

(iii) any reproduction of image or images embodied in such microfilm (whether enlarged or not); and

(iv) any other material produced by a computer or any other device;

(j) "right to information" means the right to information accessible under this Act which is held by or under the control of any public authority and includes the right to—

(i) inspection of work, documents, records;

(ii) taking notes, extracts, or certified copies of documents or records;

(iii) taking certified samples of material;

(iv) obtaining information in the form of diskettes, floppies, tapes, video cassettes or in any other electronic mode or through printouts where such information is stored in a computer or in any other device;

(k) "State Information Commission" means the State Information Commission constituted under sub-section (1) of section 15;

(l) "State Chief Information Commissioner" and "State Information Commissioner" mean the State Chief Information Commissioner and the State Information Commissioner appointed under sub-section (3) of section 15;

(m) "State Public Information Officer" means the State Public Information Officer designated under sub-section (1) and includes a State Assistant Public Information Officer designated as such under sub-section (2) of section 5;

(n) "third party" means a person other than the citizen making a request for information and includes a public authority.

CHAPTER II
RIGHT TO INFORMATION AND OBLIGATIONS OF PUBLIC AUTHORITIES

3. Right to information. Subject to the provisions of this Act, all citizens shall have the right to information.

4. Obligations of public authorities. (1) Every public authority shall—

(a) maintain all its records duly catalogued and indexed in a manner and the form which facilitates the right to information under this Act and ensure that all records that are appropriate to be computerized are, within a reasonable time and subject to availability of resources, computerized and connected through a network all over the country on different systems so that access to such records is facilitated;

(b) publish within one hundred and twenty days from the enactment of this Act—

(i) the particulars of its organization, functions and duties;

(ii) the powers and duties of its officers and employees;

(iii) the procedure followed in the decision-making process, including channels of supervision and accountability;

(iv) the norms set by it for the discharge of its functions;

(v) the rules, regulations, instructions, manuals and records, held by it or under its control or used by its employees for discharging its functions;

(vi) a statement of the categories of documents that are held by it or under its control;

(vii) the particulars of any arrangement that exists for consultation with, or representation by, the members of the public in relation to the formulation of its policy or implementation thereof;

(viii) a statement of the boards, councils, committees and other bodies consisting of two or more persons constituted as its part or for the purpose of its advice, and as to whether meetings of those boards, councils, committees and other bodies are open to the public, or the minutes of such meetings are accessible for public;

(ix) a directory of its officers and employees;

(x) the monthly remuneration received by each of its officers and employees, including the system of compensation as provided in its regulations;

(xi) the budget allocated to each of its agency, indicating the particulars of all plans, proposed expenditures and reports on disbursements made;

(xii) the manner of execution of subsidy programmes, including the amounts allocated and the details of beneficiaries of such programmes;

(xiii) particulars of recipients of concessions, permits or authorizations granted by it;

(xiv) details in respect of the information, available to or held by it, reduced in an electronic form;

(xv) the particulars of facilities available to citizens for obtaining information, including the working hours of a library or reading room, if maintained for public use;

(xvi) the names, designations and other particulars of the Public Information Officers;

(xvii) such other information as may be prescribed, and thereafter update these publications every year;

(c) publish all relevant facts while formulating important policies or announcing the decisions which affect public;

(d) provide reasons for its administrative or quasi judicial decisions to affected persons.

(2) It shall be a constant endeavour of every public authority to take steps in accordance with the requirements of clause (b) of sub-section (1) to provide as much information suo motu to the public at regular intervals through various means of

communications, including internet, so that the public have minimum resort to the use of this Act to obtain information.

(3) For the purpose of sub-section (1), every information shall be disseminated widely and in such form and manner which is easily accessible to the public.

(4) All materials shall be disseminated taking into consideration the cost effectiveness, local language and the most effective method of communication in that local area and the information should be easily accessible, to the extent possible in electronic format with the Central Public Information Officer or State Public Information Officer, as the case may be, available free or at such cost of the medium or the print cost price as may be prescribed.

Explanation. For the purposes of sub-sections (3) and (4), "disseminated" means making known or communicated the information to the public through notice boards, newspapers, public announcements, media broadcasts, the internet or any other means, including inspection of offices of any public authority.

5. **Designation of Public Information Officers.** (1) Every public authority shall, within one hundred days of the enactment of this Act, designate as many officers as Central Public Information Officers or State Public Information Officers, as the case may be, in all administrative units or offices under it as may be necessary to provide information to persons requesting for the information under this Act.

(2) Without prejudice to the provisions of sub-section (1), every public authority shall designate an officer, within one hundred days of the enactment of this Act, at each sub-divisional level or other sub-district level as a Central Assistant Public Information Officer or a State Assistant Public Information Officer, as the case may be, to receive the applications for information or appeals under this Act for forwarding the same forthwith to the Central Public Information Officer or the State Public Information Officer or senior officer specified under sub-section (1) of section 19 or the Central Information Commission or the State Information Commission, as the case may be:

Provided that where an application for information or appeal is given to a Central Assistant Public Information Officer or a State Assistant Public Information Officer, as the case may be, a period of five days shall be added in computing the period for response specified under sub-section (1) of section 7.

(3) Every Central Public Information Officer or State Public Information Officer, as the case may be, shall deal with requests from persons seeking information and render reasonable assistance to the persons seeking such information.

(4) The Central Public Information Officer or State Public Information Officer, as the case may be, may seek the assistance of any other officer as he or she considers it necessary for the proper discharge of his or her duties.

(5) Any officer, whose assistance has been sought under sub-section (4), shall render all assistance to the Central Public Information Officer or State Public Information Officer, as the case may be, seeking his or her assistance and for the purposes of any contravention of the provisions of this Act, such other officer shall be treated as a Central Public Information Officer or State Public Information Officer, as the case may be.

6. Request for obtaining information. (1) A person, who desires to obtain any information under this Act, shall make a request in writing or through electronic means in English or Hindi in the official language of the area in which the application is being made, accompanying such fee as may be prescribed, to:

(a) the Central Public Information Officer or State Public Information Officer, as the case may be, of the concerned public authority;

(b) the Central Assistant Public Information Officer or State Assistant Public Information Officer, as the case may be, specifying the particulars of the information sought by him or her:

Provided that where such request cannot be made in writing, the Central Public Information Officer or State Public Information Officer, as the case may be, shall render all reasonable assistance to the person making the request orally to reduce the same in writing.

(2) An applicant making request for information shall not be required to give any reason for requesting the information or any other personal details except those that may be necessary for contacting him.

(3) Where an application is made to a public authority requesting for an information,—

(i) which is held by another public authority; or

(ii) the subject matter of which is more closely connected with the functions of another public authority,

the public authority, to which such application is made, shall transfer the application or such part of it as may be appropriate to that other public authority and inform the applicant immediately about such transfer:

Provided that the transfer of an application pursuant to this sub-section shall be made as soon as practicable but in no case later than five days from the date of receipt of the application.

7. Disposal of request. (1) Subject to the proviso to sub-section (2) of section 5 or the proviso to sub-section (3) of section 6, the Central Public Information Officer or State Public Information Officer, as the case may be, on receipt of a request under section 6 shall, as expeditiously as possible, and in any case within thirty days of the receipt of the request, either provide the information on payment of such fee as may be prescribed or reject the request for any of the reasons specified in sections 8 and 9:

Provided that where the information sought for concerns the life or liberty of a person, the same shall be provided within forty-eight hours of the receipt of the request.

(2) If the Central Public Information Officer or State Public Information Officer, as the case may be, fails to give decision on the request for information within the period specified under sub-section (1), Central Public Information Officer or State Public Information Officer, as the case may be, shall be deemed to have refused the request.

(3) Where a decision is taken to provide the information on payment of any further fee representing the cost of providing the

information, the Central Public Information Officer or State Public Information Officer, as the case may be, shall send an intimation to the person making the request, giving—

(a) the details of further fees representing the cost of providing the information as determined by him, together with the calculations made to arrive at the amount in accordance with fee prescribed under sub-section (1), requesting him to deposit that fees, and the period intervening between the dispatch of the said intimation and payment of fees shall be excluded for the purpose of calculating the period of thirty days referred to in that sub-section;

(b) information concerning his or her right with respect to review the decision as to the amount of fees charged or the form of access provided, including the particulars of the appellate authority, time limit, process and any other forms.

(4) Where access to the record or a part thereof is required to be provided under this Act and the person to whom access is to be provided is sensorily disabled, the Central Public Information Officer or State Public Information Officer, as the case may be, shall provide assistance to enable access to the information, including providing such assistance as may be appropriate for the inspection.

(5) Where access to information is to be provided in the printed or in any electronic format, the applicant shall, subject to the provisions of sub-section (6), pay such fee as may be prescribed:

Provided that the fee prescribed under sub-section (1) of section 6 and sub-sections (1) and (5) of section 7 shall be reasonable and no such fee shall be charged from the persons who are of below poverty line as may be determined by the appropriate Government.

(6) Notwithstanding anything contained in sub-section (5), the person making request for the information shall be provided the information free of charge where a public authority fails to comply with the time limits specified in sub-section (1).

(7) Before taking any decision under sub-section (1), the Central Public Information Officer or State Public Information Officer, as the case may be, shall take into consideration the representation made by a third party under section 11.

(8) Where a request has been rejected under sub-section (1), the Central Public Information Officer or State Public Information Officer, as the case may be, shall communicate to the person making the request,—

(i) the reasons for such rejection;

(ii) the period within which an appeal against such rejection may be preferred; and

(iii) the particulars of the appellate authority.

(9) An information shall ordinarily be provided in the form in which it is sought unless it would disproportionately divert the resources of the public authority or would be detrimental to the safety or preservation of the record in question.

8. Exemption from disclosure of information. (1) Notwithstanding anything contained in this Act, there shall be no obligation to give any citizen,—

(a) Information, disclosure of which would prejudicially affect the sovereignty and integrity of India, the security, strategic, scientific or economic interests of the State, relation with foreign State or lead to incitement of an offence;

(b) Information which has been expressly forbidden to be published by any court of law or tribunal or the disclosure of which may constitute contempt of court;

(c) Information, the disclosure of which would cause a breach of privilege of parliament or the state legislature;

(d) Information including commercial confidence, trade secrets or intellectual property, the disclosure of which would harm the competitive position of a third party, unless the competent authority is satisfied that larger public interest warrants the disclosure of such information;

(e) Information available to a person in his fiduciary relationship, unless the competent authority is satisfied that the larger public interest warrants the disclosure of such information;

(f) Information received in confidence from foreign government;

(g) Information, the disclosure of which would endanger the life or physical safety of any person or identify the source of information or assistance given in confidence for law enforcement or security purposes;

(h) Information which would impede the process of investigation or apprehension or prosecution of offenders;

(i) Cabinet papers including records of deliberations of the Council of Ministers, Secretaries and other officers:

Provided that the decisions of Council of Ministers, the reasons thereof, and the material on the basis of which the decisions were taken shall be made public after the decision has been taken, and the matter is complete, or over:

Provided further that those matters which come under the exemptions specified in this section shall not be disclosed;

(j) Information which relates to personal information the disclosure of which has no relationship to any public activity or interest, or which would cause unwarranted invasion of the privacy of the individual unless the Central Public Information Officer or State Public Information Officer or the appellate authority, as the case may be, is satisfied that the larger public interest justifies the disclosure of such information:

Provided that the information, which cannot be denied to the Parliament or a State Legislature shall not be denied to any person.

(2) Notwithstanding anything in the Official Secrets Act, 1923 (19 of 1923) nor any of the exemptions permissible in accordance with sub-section (1), a public authority may allow access to information, if public interest in disclosure outweighs the harm to the protected interests.

(3) Subject to the provisions of clauses (a), (c) and (i) of sub-section (1), any information relating to any occurrence, event or

matter which has taken place, occurred or happened twenty years before the date on which any request is made under section 6 shall be provided to any person making a request under that section:

Provided that where any question arises as to the date from which the said period of twenty years has to be computed, the decision of the Central Government shall be final, subject to the usual appeals provided for in this Act.

9. Grounds for rejection to access in certain cases. Without prejudice to the provisions of section 8, a Central Public Information Officer or State Public Information Officer, as the case may be, may reject a request for information where such a request for providing access would involve an infringement of copyright subsisting in a person other than the state.

10. Severability. (1) Where a request for access to information is rejected on the ground that it is in relation to information which is exempt from disclosure, then, notwithstanding anything contained in this Act, access may be provided to that part of the record which does not contain any information which is exempt from disclosure under this Act and which can reasonably be severed from any part that contains exempt information.

(2) Where access is granted to a part of the record under sub-section (1), the Central Public Information Officer or State Public Information Officer, as the case may be, shall give a notice to the applicant, informing,—

(a) that only part of the record requested, after severance of the record containing information which is exempt from disclosure, is being provided;

(b) the reasons for the decision, including any findings on any material question of fact, referring to the material on which those findings were based;

(c) the name and designation of the person giving the decision;

(d) the details of the fees calculated by him or her and the amount of fee which the applicant is required to deposit; and

(e) his or her rights with respect to review of the decision regarding non-disclosure of part of the information, the amount of fee charged or the form of access provided, including the particulars of the senior officer specified under sub-section (1) of section 19 or the Central Information Commission or the State Information Commission, as the case may be, time limit, process and any other form of access.

11. Third party information. (1) Where a Central Public Information Officer or the State Public Information Officer, as the case may be, intends to disclose any information or record, or part thereof on a request made under this Act, which relates to or has been supplied by a third party and has been treated as confidential by that third party, the Central Public Information Officer or State Public Information Officer, as the case may be, shall, within five days from the receipt of the request, give a written notice to such third party of the request and of the fact that the Central Public Information Officer or State Public Information Officer, as the case may be, intends to disclose the information or record, or part thereof, and invite the third party to make a submission in writing or orally, regarding whether the information should be disclosed, and such submission of the third party shall be kept in view while taking a decision about disclosure of information:

Provided that except in the case of trade or commercial secrets protected by law, disclosure may be allowed if the public interest in disclosure outweighs in importance any possible harm or injury to the interests of such third party.

(2) Where a notice is served by the Central Public Information Officer or State Public Information Officer, as the case may be, under sub-section (1) to a third party in respect of any information or record or part thereof, the third party shall, within ten days from the date of receipt of such notice, be given the opportunity to make representation against the proposed disclosure.

(3) Notwithstanding anything contained in section 7, the Central Public Information Officer or State Public Information Officer, as the case may be, shall, within forty days after receipt

of the request under section 6, if the third party has been given an opportunity to make representation under sub-section (2), make a decision as to whether or not to disclose the information or record or part thereof and give in writing the notice of his decision to the third party.

(4) A notice given under sub-section (3) shall include a statement that the third party to whom the notice is given is entitled to prefer an appeal under section 19 against the decision.

CHAPTER III
THE CENTRAL INFORMATION COMMISSION

12. Constitution of Central Information Commission. (1) The Central Government shall, by notification in the Official Gazette, constitute a body to be known as the Central Information Commission to exercise the powers conferred on, and to perform the functions assigned to it, under this Act.

(2) The Central Information Commissioner shall Consist of—

(a) the Chief Information Commissioner, and

(b) such number of Central Information Commissioners not exceeding ten as may be deemed necessary.

(3) The Chief Information Commissioner and Information Commissioners shall be appointed by the President on the recommendation of a committee consisting of—

(i) the Prime Minister, who shall be the Chairperson of the committee;

(ii) the Leader of Opposition in the Lok Sabha; and

(iii) a Union Cabinet Minister to be nominated by the Prime Minister.

Explanation. For the purposes of removal of doubts it is hereby declared that where the Leader of Opposition in the House of the People has not been recognized as such, the Leader of the single largest group in opposition of the Government in the House of the People shall be deemed to be the Leader of the Opposition.

(4) The general superintendence, direction and management of the affairs of the Central Information Commission shall vest in the Chief Information Commissioner who shall be assisted by the Information Commissioners and may exercise all such powers and do all such acts and things which may be exercised or done by the Central Information Commission autonomously without being subjected to directions by any other authority under this Act.

(5) The Chief Information Commissioner and Information Commissioners shall be persons of eminence in public life with wide knowledge and experience in law, science and technology, social service, management, journalism, mass media or administration and governance.

(6) The Chief Information Commissioner or an Information Commissioner shall not be a Member of Parliament or Member of the Legislature of any State or Union territory, as the case may be, or hold any other office of profit or connected with any political party or carrying on any business or pursuing any profession.

(7) The headquarters of the Central Information Commission shall be at Delhi and the Central Information Commission may, with the previous approval of the Central Government, establish offices at other places in India.

13. Term of office and conditions of service. (1) The Chief Information Commissioner shall hold office for a term of five years from the date on which he enters upon his office and shall not be eligible for reappointment:

Provided that no Chief Information Commissioner shall hold office as such after he has attained the age of sixty-five years.

(2) Every Information Commissioner shall hold office for a term of five years from the date on which he enters upon his office or till he attains the age of sixty-five years, whichever is earlier, and shall not be eligible for reappointment as such Information Commissioner:

Provided that every Information Commissioner shall, on vacating his office under this sub-section be eligible for appointment as the Chief Information Commissioner in the manner specified in sub-section (3) of section 12:

Provided further that where the Information Commissioner is appointed as the Chief Information Commissioner, his term of office shall not be more than five years in aggregate as the Information Commissioner and the Chief Information Commissioner.

(3) The Chief Information Commissioner or an Information Commissioner shall, before he enters upon his office, make and subscribe before the President or some other person appointed by him in that behalf, an oath or affirmation according to the form set out for the purpose in the First Schedule.

(4) The Chief Information Commissioner or an Information Commissioner may, at any time, by writing under his hand addressed to the President, resign from his office:

Provided that the Chief Information Commissioner or an Information Commissioner may be removed in the manner specified under section 14.

(5) The salaries and allowances payable to and other terms and conditions of service of—

(a) the Chief Information Commissioner shall be the same as that of the Chief Election Commissioner;

(b) an Information Commissioner shall be the same as that of an Election Commissioner:

Provided that if the Chief Information Commissioner or an Information Commissioner, at the time of his appointment, is in receipt of a pension (other than a disability or wound pension) in respect of any previous service under the Government of India or under the Government of a State, his salary in respect of the service as the Chief Information Commissioner or an Information Commissioner shall be reduced by the amount of that pension including any portion of pension which was commuted and pension equivalent of other forms of retirement benefits excluding pension equivalent of retirement gratuity:

Provided further that if the Chief Information Commissioner or an Information Commissioner if, at the time of his appointment, is in receipt of retirement benefits in respect of any previous service rendered in a Corporation established by or under any Central Act or State Act or a Government company owned or controlled by the Central Government or the State Government, his salary in respect of the service as the Chief Information Commissioner or an Information Commissioner shall be reduced by the amount of pension equivalent to the retirement benefits:

Provided also that the salaries, allowances and other conditions of service of the Chief Information Commissioner and the Information Commissioner shall not be varied to their disadvantage after their appointment.

(6) The Central Government shall provide the Chief Information Commissioner and the Information Commissioners with such officers and employees as may be necessary for the efficient performance of their functions under this Act, and the salaries and allowances payable to, and the terms and conditions of service of the officers and other employees appointed for the purpose of this Act shall be such as may be prescribed.

14. Removal of Chief Information Commissioner or Information Commissioners. (1) Subject to the provision of sub-section (3), the Chief Information Commissioner or any Information Commissioner shall be removed from his office only by order of the President on the ground of proved misbehaviour or incapacity after the Supreme Court, on a reference made to it by the President, has, on inquiry, reported that the Chief Information Commissioner or any Information Commissioner, as the case may be, ought on such ground be removed.

(2) The President may suspend from office, and if deem necessary prohibit also from attending the office during inquiry, the Chief Information Commissioner or Information Commissioner in respect of whom a reference has been made to the Supreme Court under sub-section (1) until the President has passed orders on receipt of the report of the Supreme Court on such reference.

(3) Notwithstanding anything contained in sub-section (1), the President may by order remove from office the Chief Information Commissioner or any Information Commissioner if the Chief Information Commissioner or a Information Commissioner, as the case may be,—

(a) is adjudged an insolvent; or

(b) has been convicted of an offence which, in the opinion of the President, involves moral turpitude; or

(c) engages during his term of office in any paid employment outside the duties of his office; or

(d) is, in the opinion of the President, unfit to continue in office by reason of infirmity of mind or body; or

(e) has acquired such financial or other interest as is likely to affect prejudicially his functions as the Chief Information Commissioner or a Information Commissioner.

(4) If the Chief Information Commissioner or an Information Commissioner is, in any way, concerned or interested in any contract or agreement made by or on behalf of the Government of India or participates in any way in the profit thereof or in any benefit or emolument arising therefrom otherwise than as a member and in common with the other members of an incorporated company, he shall, for the purposes of sub-section (1), be deemed to be guilty of misbehaviour.

CHAPTER IV
THE STATE INFORMATION COMMISSION

15. Constitution of State Information Commission. (1) Every State Government shall, by notification in the Official Gazette, constitute a body to be known as the...........(name of the State) Information Commission to exercise the powers conferred on, and to perform the functions assigned to it, under this Act.

(2) The State Information Commission shall consist of—

(a) The State Chief Information Commissioner; and

(b) Such number of State Information Commissioners, not exceeding ten, as may be deemed necessary.

(3) The State Chief Information Commissioner and the State Information Commissioners shall be appointed by the Governor on the recommendation of a committee consisting of—

(i) the Chief Minister, who shall be the Chairperson of the committee;

(ii) the Leader of Opposition in the Legislative Assembly; and

(iii) a Cabinet Minister to be nominated by the Chief Minister.

Explanation. For the purposes of removal of doubts, it is hereby declared that where the Leader of Opposition in the Legislative Assembly has not been recognized as such, the Leader of the single largest group in opposition of the Government in the Legislative Assembly shall be deemed to be the Leader of the Opposition.

(4) The general superintendence, direction and management of the affairs of the State Information Commission shall vest in the State Chief Information Commissioner who shall be assisted by the State Information Commissioners and may exercise all such powers and do all such acts and things which may be exercised or done by the State Information Commission autonomously without being subjected to directions by any other authority under this Act.

(5) The State Chief Information Commissioner and the State Information Commissioners shall be persons of eminence in public life with wide knowledge and experience in law, science and technology, social service, management, journalism, mass media or administration and governance.

(6) The State Chief Information Commissioner or a State Information Commissioner shall not be a Member of Parliament or Member of the Legislature of any State or Union territory, as the case may be, or hold any other office of profit or connected with any political party or carrying on any business or pursuing any profession.

(7) The headquarters of the State Information Commission shall be at such place in the State as the State Government may, by notification in the Official Gazette, specify and the State

Information Commission may, with the previous approval of the State Government establish offices at other places in the State.

16. Term of office and conditions of service. (1) The State Chief Information Commissioner shall hold office for a term of five years from the date on which he enters upon his office and shall not be eligible for reappointment:

Provided that no State Chief Information Commissioner shall hold office as such after he has attained the age of sixty-five years.

(2) Every State Information Commissioner shall hold office for a term of five years from the date on which he enters upon his office or till he attains the age of sixty-five years, whichever is earlier, and shall not be eligible for reappointment as such State Information Commissioner:

Provided that every State Information Commissioner shall, on vacating his office under this sub-section, be eligible for appointment as the State Chief Information Commissioner in the manner specified in sub-section (3) of section 15:

Provided further that where the State Information Commissioner is appointed as the State Chief Information Commissioner, his term of office shall not be more than five years in aggregate as the State Information Commissioner and the State Chief Information Commissioner.

(3) The State Chief Information Commissioner or a State Information Commissioner, shall before he enters upon his office make and subscribe before the Governor or some other person appointed by him in that behalf, an oath or affirmation according to the form set out for the purpose in the First Schedule.

(4) The State Chief Information Commissioner or a State Information Commissioner may, at any time by writing under his hand addressed to the Governor, resign from his office:

Provided that the State Chief Information Commissioner or a State Information Commissioner may be removed in the manner specified under section 17.

(5) The salaries and allowances payable to and other terms and conditions of service of—

(a) the State Chief Information Commissioner shall be the same as that of an Election Commissioner;

(b) the State Information Commissioner shall be the same as that of the Chief Secretary to the State Government:

Provided that if the State Chief Information Commissioner or a State Information Commissioner, at the time of his appointment is, in receipt of a pension (other than a disability or wound pension) in respect of any previous service under the Government of India or under the Government of a State, his salary in respect of the service as the State Chief Information Commissioner or a State Information Commissioner shall be reduced by the amount of that pension including any portion of pension which was commuted and pension equivalent of other forms of retirement benefits excluding pension equivalent of retirement gratuity:

Provided further that where the State Chief Information Commissioner or a State Information Commissioner if, at the time of his appointment is, in receipt of retirement benefits in respect of any previous service rendered in a Corporation established by or under any Central Act or State Act or a Government company owned or controlled by the Central Government or the State Government, his salary in respect of the service as the State Chief Information Commissioner or the State Information Commissioner shall be reduced by the amount of pension equivalent to the retirement benefits:

Provided also that the salaries, allowances and other conditions of service of the State Chief Information Commissioner and the State Information Commissioners shall not be varied to their disadvantage after their appointment.

(6) The State Government shall provide the State Chief Information Commissioner and the State Information Commissioners with such officers and employees as may be necessary for the efficient performance of their functions under this Act, and the salaries and allowances payable to and the terms and conditions of service of the officers and other employees appointed for the purpose of this Act shall be such as may be prescribed.

17. Removal of State Chief Information Commissioner or State Information Commissioner. (1) Subject to the provisions of sub-section (3), the State Chief Information Commissioner or any State Information Commissioner shall be removed from his office only by order of the Governor on the ground of proved misbehaviour or incapacity after the Supreme Court, on a reference made to it by the Governor, has on inquiry, reported that the State Chief Information Commissioner or a State Information Commissioner, as the case may be, ought on such ground be removed.

(2) The Governor may suspend from office, and if deem necessary prohibit also from attending the office during inquiry, the State Chief Information Commissioner or a State Information Commissioner in respect of whom a reference has been made to the Supreme Court under sub-section (1) until the Governor has passed orders on receipt of the report of the Supreme Court on such reference.

(3) Notwithstanding anything contained in sub-section (1), the Governor may by order remove from office the State Chief Information Commissioner or a State Information Commissioner if a State Chief Information Commissioner or a State Information Commissioner, as the case may be,—

(a) is adjudged an insolvent; or

(b) has been convicted of an offence which, in the opinion of the Governor, involves moral turpitude; or

(c) engages during his term of office in any paid employment outside the duties of his office; or

(d) is, in the opinion of the Governor, unfit to continue in office by reason of infirmity of mind or body; or

(e) has acquired such financial or other interest as is likely to affect prejudicially his functions as the State Chief Information Commissioner or a State Information Commissioner.

(4) If the State Chief Information Commissioner or any State Information Commissioner is, in any way, concerned or interested in any contract or agreement made by or on behalf of the

Government of the State or participates in any way in the profit thereof or in any benefit or emoluments arising therefrom otherwise than as a member and in common with the other members of an incorporated company, he shall, for the purposes of sub-section (1), be deemed to by guilty of misbehaviour.

CHAPTER V
POWERS AND FUNCTIONS OF THE INFORMATION COMMISSIONS, APPEAL AND PENALTIES

18. Powers and functions of Information Commission. (1) Subject to the provisions of this Act, it shall be the duty of the Central Information Commission or State Information Commission as the case may be to receive and inquire into a complaint from any person,—

(a) who has been unable to submit a request to a Central Public Information Officer, or State Public Information Officer as the case may be, either by reason that no such officer has been appointed under this Act, or because the Central Assistance Public Information Officer or State Assistant Public Information Officer, as the case may be, has refused to accept his or her application for information or appeal under this Act for forwarding the same to the Central Public Information Officer or State Public Information Officer or Senior Officer specified in sub-section (1) of section 19 or the Central Information Commission or the State Information Commission, as the case may be;

(b) who has been refused access to any information requested under this Act;

(c) who has not been given a response to a request for information or access to information within the time limits specified under this Act;

(d) who has been required to pay an amount of fee which he or she considers unreasonable;

(e) who believes that he or she has been given incomplete, misleading or false information under this Act; and

(f) in respect of any other matter relating to requesting or obtaining access to records under this Act.

(2) Where the Central Information Commission or State Information Commission, as the case may be, is satisfied that there are reasonable grounds to inquire into the matter, it may initiate an inquiry in respect thereof.

(3) The Central Information Commission or State Information Commission, as the case may be, shall, while inquiring into any matter under this section, have the same powers as are vested in a civil court while trying a suit under the Code of Civil Procedure, 1908, in respect of the following matter, namely:

(a) summoning and enforcing the attendance of persons and compel them to give oral or written evidence on oath and to produce the document or things;

(b) requiring the discovery and inspection of documents;

(c) receiving evidence on affidavit;

(d) requisitioning any public record or copies thereof from any court or office;

(e) issuing summons for examination of witnesses or documents; and

(f) any other matter which may be prescribed.

(4) Notwithstanding anything inconsistent contained in any other Act of Parliament, or the State Legislature, as the case may be, the Central Information Commission or the State Information Commission, as the case may be, may during the inquiry of any complaint under this Act, examine any record to which this Act applies which is under the control of the public authority, and no such record may be withheld from it on any grounds.

19. Appeal. (1) Any person who, does not receive a decision within the time specified in sub-section (1) or clause (a) of sub-section (3) of section 7, or is aggrieved by a decision of the Central Public Information Officer or the State Public Information Officer, as the case may be, may within thirty days from the expiry of such period or from the receipt of such a decision prefer an appeal to such officer who is senior in rank to the

Central Public Information Officer or the State Public Information Officer, as the case may be, in each public authority:

Provided that such officer may admit the appeal after the expiry of the period of thirty days if he or she is satisfied that the appellant was prevented by sufficient cause from filing the appeal in time.

(2) Where an appeal is preferred against an order made by a Central Public Information Officer or a State Public Information Officer, as the case may be, under section 11 to disclose third party information, the appeal by the concerned third party shall be made within thirty days from the date of the order.

(3) A second appeal against the decision under sub-section (1) shall lie within ninety days from the date on which the decision should have been made or was actually received, with the Central Information Commission or the State Information Commission:

Provided that the Central Information Commission or the State Information Commission, as the case may be, may admit the appeal after the expiry of the period of ninety days if it is satisfied that the appellant was prevented by sufficient cause from filing the appeal in time.

(4) If the decision of the Central Public Information Officer or State Public Information Officer, as the case may be, against which an appeal preferred relates to information of a third party, the Central Information Commission or State Information Commission, as the case may be, shall give a reasonable opportunity of being heard to that third party.

(5) In any appeal proceedings, the onus to prove that a denial of a request was justified shall be on the Central Public Information Officer or State Public Information Officer, as the case may be, who denied the request.

(6) An appeal under sub-section (1) or sub-section (2) shall be disposed of within thirty days of the receipt of the appeal or within such extended period not exceeding a total of forty-five days from the date of filing thereof, as the case may be, for reasons to be recorded in writing.

(7) The decision of the Central Information Commission or State Information Commission, as the case may be, shall be binding.

(8) In its decision, the Central Information Commission or State Information Commission, as the case may be, has the power to,—

(a) require the public authority to take any such steps as may be necessary to secure compliance with the provision of this Act, including—

(i) by providing access to information, if so requested, in a particular form;

(ii) by appointing a Central Public Information Officer or State Public Information Officer, as the case may be;

(iii) by publishing certain information or categories of information;

(iv) by making necessary changes to its practices in relation to the maintenance, management and destruction of records;

(v) by enhancing the provision of training on the right to information for its officials;

(vi) by providing it with an annual report in compliance with clause (b) of sub-section (1) of section 4;

(b) require the public authority to compensate for any loss or other detriment suffered;

(c) impose any of the penalties provided under this Act;

(d) reject the application.

(9) The Central Information Commission or State Information Commission, as the case may be, shall give notice of its decision, including any right of appeal, to the complainant and the public authority.

(10) The Central Information Commission or State Information Commission, as the case may be, shall decide the appeal in accordance with such procedure as may be prescribed.

20. Penalties. (1) Where the Central Information Commission or State Information Commission, as the case may be, at the time of deciding any complaint or appeal is of the opinion that the Central Public Information Officer or the State Public Information Officer, as the case may be, has, without any reasonable cause, refused to receive an application for information or has not furnished information within the time specified under sub-section (1) of section 7 or malafidely denied the request for information or knowingly given incorrect, incomplete or misleading information or destroyed information which was the subject of the request or obstructed in any manner in furnishing the information, it shall impose a penalty of two hundred and fifty rupees each day till application is received or information is furnished, so however, the total amount of such penalty shall not exceed twenty-five thousand rupees:

Provided that the Central Public Information Officer or the State Public Information Officer, as the case may be, shall be given a reasonable opportunity of being heard before any penalty is imposed on him:

Provided further that the burden of proving that he acted reasonably and diligently shall be on the Central Public Information Officer or State Public Information Officer, as the case may be.

(2) Where the Central Information Commission or the State Information Commission, as the case may be, at the time of deciding any complaint or appeal is of the opinion that the Central Public Information Officer or the State Public Information Officer, as the case may be, has, without any reasonable cause and persistently, failed to receive an application for information or has not furnished information within the time specified under sub-section (1) of section 7 or malafidely denied the request for information or knowingly given incorrect, incomplete or misleading information or destroyed information which was the subject of the request or obstructed in any manner in furnishing the information, it shall recommend for disciplinary action against the Central Public Information Officer or the State Public Information Officer, as the case may be, under the service rules applicable to him.

CHAPTER VI
MISCELLANEOUS

21. Protection of action taken in good faith. No suit, prosecution or other legal proceeding shall lie against any person for anything which is in good faith done or intended to be done under this Act or any rule made thereunder.

22. Act to have overriding effect. The provisions of this Act shall have effect notwithstanding anything inconsistent therewith contained in the Official Secrets Act, 1923 (19 of 1923), and any other law for the time being in force or in any instrument having effect by virtue of any law other than this Act.

23. Bar of jurisdiction of courts. No court shall entertain any suit, application or other proceeding in respect of any order made under this Act and no such order shall be called in question otherwise than by way of an appeal under this Act.

24. Act not to apply to certain organizations. (1) Nothing contained in this Act shall apply to the intelligence and security organizations specified in the Second Schedule, being organizations established by the Central Government or any information furnished by such organizations to that Government:

Provided that the information pertaining to the allegations of corruption and human rights violations shall not be excluded under this sub-section:

Provided further that in the case of information sought for is in respect of allegations of violation of human rights, the information shall only be provided after the approval of the Central Information Commission, and notwithstanding anything contained in section 7, such information shall be provided within forty-five days from the date of the receipt of request.

(2) The Central Government may, by notification in the Official Gazette, amend the Schedule by including therein any other intelligence or security organization established by that Government or omitting therefrom any organization already specified therein and on the publication of such notification, such organization shall be deemed to be included in or, as the case may be, omitted from the Schedule.

(3) Every notification issued under sub-section (2) shall be laid before each House of Parliament.

(4) Nothing contained in this Act shall apply to such intelligence and security organizations, being organizations established by the State Government, as that Government may, from time to time, by notification in the Official Gazette, specify:

Provided that the information pertaining to the allegations of corruption and human rights violations shall not be excluded under this sub-section:

Provided further that in the case of information sought for is in respect of allegations of violation of human rights, the information shall only be provided after the approval of the State Information Commission and, notwithstanding anything contained in section 7, such information shall be provided within forty-five days from the date of the receipt of request.

(5) Every notification issued under sub-section (4) shall be laid before the State Legislature.

25. Monitoring and reporting. (1) The Central Information Commission or State Information Commission, as the case may be, shall, as soon as practicable after the end of each year, prepare a report on the implementation of the provisions of this Act during that year and forward a copy thereof to the appropriate Government.

(2) Each Ministry or Department shall, in relation to the public authorities within their jurisdiction, collect and provide such information to the Central Information Commission or State Information Commission, as the case may be, as it required to prepare the report under this section and comply with the records for the purposes of this section.

(3) Each report shall state in respect of the year to which the report relates,—

(a) the number of requests made to each public authority;

(b) the number of decisions where applicants were not entitled to access to the documents pursuant to the requests, the provisions of this Act under which these decisions were made and the number of times such provisions were invoked;

(c) the number of appeals referred to the Central Information Commission or state Information Commission, as the case may be, for review, the nature of the appeals and the outcome of the appeals;

(d) particulars of any disciplinary action taken against any officer in respect of the administration of this Act;

(e) the amount of charges collected by each public authority under this Act;

(f) any facts which indicate an effort by the public authorities to administer and implement the spirit and intention of this Act;

(g) recommendations for reform, including recommendations in respect of the particular public authorities, for the development, improvement, modernization, reform or amendment to this Act or other legislation or common law or any other matter relevant for operationalising the right to access information.

(4) The Central Government or the State Government, as the case may be may, as soon as practicable after the end of each year, cause a copy of the report of the Central Information Commission or the State Information Commission, as the case may be, referred to in sub-section (1) to be laid before each House of Parliament or, as the case may be, before each House of the State Legislature, where there are two Houses, and where there is one House of the State Legislature before that House.

(5) If it appears to the Central Information Commission or State Information Commission, as the case may be, that the practice of a public authority in relation to the exercise of its functions under this Act does not conform with the provision or spirit of this Act, it may give to the authority a recommendation specifying the steps which ought in its opinion to be taken for promoting such conformity.

26. Appropriate Government to prepare programmes. (1) The appropriate Government may, to the extent of availability of financial and other resources,—

(a) develop and organise educational programmes to advance the understanding of the public, in particular of disadvantaged communities as to how to exercise the rights contemplated under this Act;

(b) encourage public authorities to participate in the development and organisation of programmes referred to in clause (a) and to undertake such programmes themselves;

(c) promote timely and effective dissemination of accurate information by public authorities about their activities; and

(d) train Central Public Information Officers or State Public Information Officers, as the case may be, of public authorities and produce relevant training materials for use by the public authorities themselves.

(2) The Appropriate Government shall, within eighteen months from the commencement of this Act, compile in its official language a guide containing such information, in an easily comprehensible form and manner, as may reasonably be required by a person who wishes to exercise any right specified in this Act.

(3) The appropriate Government shall, if necessary, update and publish the guidelines referred to in sub-section (2) at regular intervals which shall, in particular and without prejudice to the generality of sub-section (2), include—

(a) the objects of this Act;

(b) the postal and street address, the phone and fax number and, if available, electronic mail address of the Central Public Information Officer or State Public Information Officer, as the case may be, of every public authority appointed under sub-section (1) of section 5;

(c) the manner and the form in which request for access to an information shall be made to Central Public Information Officer or State Public Information Officer, as the case may be;

(d) the assistance available from and the duties of the Central Public Information Officer or State Public Information Officer, as the case may be, of a public authority under this Act;

(e) the assistance available from the Central Information Commission or State Information Commission, as the case may be;

(f) all remedies in law available regarding an act or failure to act in respect of a right or duty conferred or imposed by this Act including the manner of filing an appeal to the Commission;

(g) the provisions providing for the voluntary disclosure of categories of records in accordance with section 4;

(h) the notices regarding fees to be paid in relation to requests for access to an information; and

(i) any additional regulations or circulars made or issued in relation to obtaining access to an information in accordance with this Act.

(4) The appropriate Government must, if necessary, update and publish the guidelines at regular intervals.

27. Power to make rules by Appropriate Government. (1) The Appropriate Government may, by notification in the Official Gazette, make rules to carry out the provisions of this Act.

(2) In particular, and without prejudice to the generality of the foregoing power, such rules may provide for all or any of the following matters, namely:

(a) the cost of the medium or print cost price of the materials to be disseminated under sub-section (4) of section 4;

(b) the fee payable under sub-section (1) if section 6;

(c) the fee payable under sub-sections (1) and (5) of section 7;

(d) the salaries and allowances payable to and the terms and conditions of service of the officers and other employees under sub-section (6) of section 13 and sub-section (6) of section 16;

(e) the procedure to be adopted by the Central Information Commission or State Information Commission, as the case may be, in deciding the appeals under sub-section (10) of section 19; and

(f) any other matter which is required to be, or may be, prescribed.

28. Power to make rules by competent authority. (1) The competent authority may, by notification in the Official Gazette, make rules to carry out the provisions of this Act.

(2) In particular, and without prejudice to the generality of the foregoing power, such rules may provide for all or any of the following matters, namely:

(i) the cost of the medium or print cost price of the materials to be disseminated under sub-section (4) of section 4;

(ii) the fee payable under sub-section (1) of section 6;

(iii) the fee payable under sub-section (1) of section 7; and

(iv) any other matter which is required to be, or may be, prescribed.

29. Laying of rules. (1) Every rule made by the Central Government under this Act shall be laid, as soon as may be after it is made, before each House of Parliament, while it is in session, for a total period of thirty days which may be comprised in one session or in two or more successive sessions, and if, before the expiry of the session immediately following the session or the successive sessions aforesaid, both Houses agree in making any modification in the rule or both Houses agree that the rule should not be made, the rule shall thereafter have effect only in such modified form or be of no effect, as the case may be; so, however, that any such modification or annulment shall be without prejudice to the validity of anything previously done under that rule.

(2) Every rule made under this Act by a State Government shall be laid, as soon as may be, after it is notified, before the State Legislature.

30. Power to remove difficulties. (1) If any difficulty arises in giving effect to the provisions of this Act, the Central Government may, by order published in the Official Gazette, make such provisions not inconsistent with the provisions of this Act as appear to it to be necessary or expedient for removal of the difficulty:

Provided that no such order shall be made after the expiry of a period of two years from the date of the commencement of this Act.

(2) Every order made this section shall, as soon as may be, after it is made, be laid before each House of parliament.

31. Repeal. The freedom of Information Act, 2002 (5 of 2003) is hereby repealed.

THE FIRST SCHEDULE

(See Sections 13(3) and 16(3))

FORM OF OATH OR AFFIRMATION TO BE MADE BY THE CHIEF INFORMATION COMMISSIONER/THE INFORMATION COMMISSIONER/THE STATE CHIEF INFORMATION COMMISSIONER/THE STATE INFORMATION COMMISSIONER

"I,.................., having been appointed Chief Information Commissioner/Information Commissioner/State Chief Information Commissioner/State Information Commissioner swear in the name of God that I will bear true faith and allegiance to the Constitution of India as by law established, that I will uphold the sovereignty and integrity of India, that I will duly and faithfully and to the best of my ability, knowledge and judgment perform the duties of my office without fear or favour, affection or ill-will and that I will uphold the Constitution and the laws."

THE SECOND SCHEDULE

(See Section 24)

INTELLIGENCE AND SECURITY ORGANISATION ESTABLISHED BY THE CENTRAL GOVERNMENT

1. Intelligence Bureau.
2. Research and Analysis wing of the Cabinet Secretariat.

3. Directorate of Revenue Intelligence.
4. Central Economic Intelligence Bureau.
5. Directorate of Enforcement.
6. Narcotics Control Bureau.
7. Aviation Research Centre.
8. Special Frontier Force.
9. Border Security Force.
10. Central Reserve Police Force.
11. Indo-Tibetan Border Police.
12. Central Industrial Security Force.
13. National Security Guards.
14. Assam Rifles.
15. Sashtra Seema Bal.
16. Special Branch (CID), Andaman and Nicobar.
17. The Crime Branch-C.I.D.-CB, Dadra and Nagar-Haveli.
18. Special Branch, Lakshadweep Police.
19. Special Protection Group.
20. Defence Research and Development Organization.
21. Border Road Development Board.
22. Financial Intelligence Unit, India.

THE RIGHT TO INFORMATION (REGULATION OF FEE AND COST) RULES, 2005

In exercise of the powers conferred by clauses (b) and (c) of sub-section (2) of section 27 of the Right to Information Act, 2005 (22 of 2005), the Central Government hereby makes the following rules, namely:

1. Short title and commencement. (1) These rules may be called the Right to Information (Regulation of Fee and Cost) Rules, 2005.

(2) They shall come into force on the date of their publication in the Official Gazette.

2. Definitions. In the rules, unless the context otherwise requires,

(a) 'Act' means the Right to Information Act, 2005;

(b) 'section' means section of the Act;

(c) All other words and expressions used herein but not defined and defined in the Act shall have the meanings assigned to them in the Act.

3. A request for obtaining information under sub-section (1) of section 6 shall be accompanied by an application fee of rupees ten by way of cash against proper receipt or by demand draft or bankers cheque payable to the Accounts Officer of the public authority.

4. For providing the information under sub-section (1) of section 7, the fee shall be charged by way of cash against proper receipt or by demand draft or bankers cheque payable to the Accounts Officer or the public authority at the following rates:

(a) rupees two for each page (in A4 or A3 size paper) created or copied;

(b) actual charge or cost price of a copy in larger size paper;

(c) actual cost or price for samples or models; and

(d) for inspection of records, no fee for the first hour; and a fee of rupees five for each subsequent hour (or fraction thereof).

5. For providing the information under sub-section (5) of section 7, the fee shall be charged by way of cash against proper receipt or by demand draft or bankers cheque payable to the Accounts Officer of the public authority at the following rates:

(a) for information provided in diskette or floppy rupees fifty per diskette or floppy; and

(b) for information provided in printed form at the price fixed for such publication or rupees two per page of photocopy for extracts from the publication.

---

1. *Vide* G.S.R. 336, dated 16th September, 2005, published in the Gazette of India, Pt. II, sec. 3(i), dated 1st October, 2005.

2. Subs. by G.S.R. 649 (E), dated 27th October, 2005, for clause (d) (w.e.f. 28-10-2005).

THE CENTRAL INFORMATION COMMISSION (APPEAL PROCEDURE) RULES, 2005

In exercise of the powers conferred by clauses (e) and (f) of sub-section (2) of section 27 of the Right to Information Act, 2005 (22 of 2005), the Central Government hereby makes the following rules, namely:

1. Short title and commencement. (1) These rules may be called the Central Information Commission (Appeal Procedure) Rules, 2005.

(2) They shall come into force on the date of their publication in the Official Gazette.

2. Definitions. In these rules, unless the context otherwise requires,

(a) "Act" means the Right to Information Act, 2005;

(b) "section" means section of the Act;

(c) "Commission" means the Central Information Commission;

(d) words and expressions used herein and not defined but defined in the Act, shall have the meanings respectively assigned to them in that Act.

3. Contents of appeal. An appeal to the Commission shall contain the following information, namely:

(i) name and address of the appellant;

(ii) name and address of the Central Public Information Officer against the decision of whom the appeal is preferred;

(iii) particulars of the order including number, if any, against which the appeal is preferred;

(iv) brief facts leading to the appeal;

(v) if the appeal is preferred against deemed refusal, the particulars of the application, including number and date and name and address of the Central Public Information Officer to whom the application was made;

(vi) prayer or relief sought;

(vii) grounds for the prayer or relief;

(viii) verification by the appellant; and

(ix) any other information which the Commission may deem necessary for deciding the appeal.

4. Documents to accompany appeal. Every appeal made to the commission shall be accompanied by the following documents, namely:

(i) self-attested copies of the Orders or documents against which the appeal is being preferred;

(ii) copies of documents relied upon by the appellant and referred to in the appeal; and

(iii) an index of the documents referred to in the appeal.

5. Procedure in deciding appeal. In deciding the appeal the commission may,—

(i) here oral or written evidence on oath or on affidavit from concerned or interested person;

(ii) peruse or inspect documents, public records or copies thereof;

(iii) inquire through authorized officer further details or facts;

(iv) here Central Public Information Officer, Central Assistant Public Information Officer or such Senior Officer who decided the first appeal, or such person against whom the complaint is made as the case may be;

(v) hear third party; and

(vi) receive evidence on affidavits from Central Public Information Officer, Central Assistant Public Information Officer, such Senior Officer who decided the first appeal, such person against whom the complaint lies or the third party.

6. Service of notice by Commission. Notice to be issued by the Commission may be served in any of the following modes, namely:

(i) service by the party itself;

(ii) by hand delivery (dasti) through Process Server;

(iii) by registered post with acknowledgement due; or

(iv) through Head of Office or Department.

7. Personal presence of the appellant or complainant. (1) The appellant or the complainant, as the case may be, shall in every case be informed of the date of hearing at least seven clear days before that date.

(2) The appellant or the complainant, as the case may be, may at his discretion at the time of hearing of the appeal or complaint by the Commission be present in person or through his duly authorized representative or may opt not to be present.

(3) Where the Commission is satisfied that the circumstances exist due to which the appellant or the complainant, as the case may be, is being prevented from attending the hearing of the Commission, then, the Commission may afford the appellant or the complainant, as the case may be, another opportunity of being heard before a final decision is taken or take any other appropriate action as it may deem fit.

(4) The appellant or the complainant, as the case may be, may seek the assistance of any person in the process of the appeal while presenting his points and the person representing him may not be a legal practitioner.

8. Order of the Commission. Order of the Commission shall be pronounced in open proceedings and be in writing duly authenticated by the Registrar or any other officer authorized by the Commission for this purpose.

---

1. *Vide* G.S.R. 650(E), dated 28th October 2005, published in the Gazette of India, Extraordinary, Pt. II, Sec. (i), dated 28th October 2005.

Address and Members of Central Information Commission

CENTRAL INFORMATION COMMMISSION

Block No. 4 (5th Floor), Old Jnu Campus, New Delhi-110067

Chief Information Commissioner
Shri Wajahat Habibullah
Information Commissioners
Shri A.N. Tiwari
Shri O.P. Kejariwal
Shri M.M. Ansari
Smt. Padma Balasubramanian

10

Indian Republic

Paitric Henry, American lawyer, has said that the constitution is not the weapon of the government to control the people, but is the weapon of the people to control the government.

Some years ago, when the Government of India was asked to make a special presentation at the World Economic Forum at Davis, it showcased the country's achievement under the title: "The World's Fastest-Growing Democracy". The words, carefully chosen, were aimed at Western liberals whose attractions to the world's fastest growing economy were tempered by reservations about its political system. This was not an isolated occurrence—for, as manifest most recently in the decision of our Ambassador to Norway to attend the Nobel Peace Prize ceremony, the Indian Establishment is not shy of claiming moral superiority over China on account of our democratic traditions.

This positioning of India as the Asian nice guy can backfire, as when those Western liberals (most famously, President Obama) chastise us for endorsing the military regime in Myanmar. The scolding has been dismissed as hypocritical on the grounds that the United States has historically been very keen on supporting dictators against democrats in Asia (remember Suharto, Zia, Musharraf), in Africa (Mobutu and many others) and in Latin America (Pinochet, Somoza, Sundry Brazilian generals). But as we mark our 62nd Republic day, it is harder to dismiss a criticism made by an increasing number of Indians that there has been sharp erosion of republican values and processes within India itself.

This erosion is evident most strikingly in two spheres—first the Rule of Law and second the freedom of the Press. One of India's most respected lawyers Shanti Bhushan, claims that of the 16 Chief Justices of the Supreme Court he has appeared before, at least half of them were corrupt. Other senior lawyers confirm that the claim is credible. Levels of corruption in the lower courts may be even higher. That judgments can be fixed is widely believed—so much so that a powerful journalist is now known to have advised Nira Radia how to doctor a case in her client's favour.

Apart from cash, violence and intimidation can also pervert the law or stop it from pursuing the true ends of justice. Even where manifestly guilty of looting the public exchequer, politicians do not spend extended time in prison. This is in part because judges and prosecutors worry about their own safety if the party of the accused were to return to power.

The frailties of the legal system are abundantly on display in India's conflict zones—such as Kashmir, Manipur, and the Naxalite affected areas of central and eastern India. Police officers and soldiers who commit human rights violations are rarely charged and never punished. In Dantewada, Chhattisgarh a district whose tragic recent history I have been closely following, tribals who have had their homes burnt or women raped by a vigilant group promoted by the state government, are simply too terrified to register a complaint. Even if they had the necessary legal support, local police stations did not accept FIR's and local courts did not entertain cases. Out of despair, a brave tribal leader named Kartam Joga moved the Supreme Court. His reward was a spate of spurious cases filed by the state government, who then threw him away in jail, in an act of vicious retribution.

The sufferings of the tribals are a product of the barbaric methods adopted both by the Maoists and by State-sponsored persons called vigilants. The Maoists are accountable to nobody. But it is a sign of the abdication of its Constitutional responsibilities that when the Supreme Court chastised the Chhattisgarh government for its failure to rehabilitate displaced tribals, it set up an inquiry committee composed of the same politicians—Raman Singh, Mahendra Karma, etc.—who had energetically promoted the vigilants.

This callousness of a professedly democratic regime towards the human rights of its citizens provides ammunition to extremists who wish to secede from India or convert it into a one-party State. But our democratic claims are also undermined by increasing curbs on the freedom of the press. Sometimes, it is newspaper owners and the managers who are at fault, as when they enter into private treaties with corporate houses to provide favourable coverage, or pass off party propaganda as impartial assessments (what is called 'paid news'). At other times, it is individual journalist who are guilty, as when they act as spokesmen for particular businessmen or industrial houses.

A third threat to the freedom of the Press comes from government interference. Consider the curbs on setting up community radio stations, or the banning of news broadcasts from privately owned radio channels. These are a product of a general fear of free expression. Speaking in more particular terms, state governments often withdraw departmental advertisements (a key source of revenue) from newspapers, which have been critical of its policies. Sometimes, the intimidation is less subtle; as when politicians threaten independent minded journalist, and even (as has happened in Dantewada) have them beaten up by hired goons.

That India, unlike China, has regular elections, and that Indians, unlike the Chinese, can live anywhere they want, are freedoms to cherish and be grateful for. Among other visible (and admirable) strength of Indian democracy are the independence of institutions such as the Election Commission and the Office of the Comptroller and Auditor General and the sturdy apolitical character of our armed forces. Set against these gains are the corruption and corrosion of our political class, the corruption and corrosion of legal system, and the increasingly self-serving nature of our press. Rather than brag about how much more democratic we are than China, we should pay attention to how far Indian democracy has fallen short of the ideals envisaged and the standards laid out by our own

Constitution framed in 1950 (By Rama Chandra Guha, *HT* dated 26th January 2011).

Let us take the Sonawane case. That oil Mafia exists and kerosene adulteration is highly profitable is no secret. An estimated 40 per cent of kerosene is diverted towards adulterating diesel or petrol or for resale. Six years ago when Indian Institute of Management graduate Manjunath Shanmugan was killed by the oil Mafia in Uttar Pradesh, the government promised a 'clean up'. The kerosene 'marker' system that was introduced was discontinued after it was found to be an adulteration check, which was ineffective. The fact is that the muscle of the oil Mafia has less to do with policing and more to do with flawed government policies.

Petrol costs ₹ 60 per litre and subsidized kerosene ₹ 12 per litre. The price difference is a temptation for oil black marketeers. The documentary evidence suggests that a small percentage of the subsidy on kerosene reaches the poor, exploited as it is by the middlemen. Yet governments seem reluctant to review oil policies that result in the killing of honest and brave officers like Manjunath and Sonawane (By Rajdeep Sardesai, *HT* dated 28th January 2011).

But one aspect has not been touched by the author of this article. On 25 January 2011, the additional collector was doused with petrol and burnt to death by a gang of petrol robbers when he raided them in Manmad, Nashik, Maharashtra. Twenty-sixth Januray 2011 was a republic day and a holiday. On twenty-seventh itself the authorities launched a massive crack down across Maharashtra raiding 200 places and arrested 180 persons. This shows that the information about the Mafia and their places of hide were already known to the authorities, otherwise how could they identified 180 persons and their 200 places in a day only. That means the petrol Mafia was guilty of adulteration with the connivance of some government officers. In fact no politician or businessman can indulge in corruption without the connivance of the government servants.

Kunal Shinde, the son of Popat, in his statement to the police said that seeing the oil adulteration in process, Sonawane stopped his car, and after learning that pilferage was taking place at Popat's behest, the additional collector then summoned him and demanded a huge amount of bribe to settle the matter (*HT* dated 31st January 2011).

When the matter was not settled, perhaps then the Mafia gang leader killed the officer without realizing its consequences. The government officers showed to the Mafia that they can do and are doing adulteration with their connivance only. Otherwise they cannot do it and if they do it, this is what would happen to them. After sometime the things would settle down and the Mafia would become active again with their connivance.

Popat Shinde also got 70 per cent burns in this incidence and died on 31 January 2011 in J.J. Hospital. Shinde's family members have alleged that Sonawane was constantly harassing him for a cut in an oil deal. Shinde was under severe mental stress as he was not able to arrange the bribe money for Sonawane. The frustration forced him to take the drastic step (*HT* dated 1st February 2011).

The Central government has also become active. They have shown to the Mafia that they have all the methods to stop the adulteration of petrol if they do not behave, otherwise where they were sleeping all these days. They unveiled steps to reduce the scope for diversion of subsidized kerosene. Nothing actually would happen and the steps would remain in the file or would be found to be impracticable. If we want corruption to be controlled and democracy to continue, first the law to be made is to punish the government servants with severe penalty if they are found to be involved in corruption. Then only they would not allow others to commit such crimes.

The additional collector was killed at the back of a dhaba (local hotel) where food was never cooked or served. It was a dhaba for namesake only. It was just a front for running the adulteration racket. A long wall, high enough to hide tankers behind it, runs along the back of the dhaba. It is behind the wall that the tanker would be parked and the oil they carried pilfered. It is almost a cottage industry in these parts of Maharashtra. Government officials and the police know about its existence and allegedly benefit from it.

Drivers/cleaners of transport trucks steal fuel. This is then mixed as required by operators. Pilferage is in small quantities so that petrol pump owners accept it as loss in transit or evaporated. Apart from those directly involved in the trade and regulating officials, even local farmers benefit as they get cheap fuel for their tractors and water pumps.

A small operator gets ₹ 10-12 lakhs a month. Police, revenue civil supplies, and Oil Company officials get kickbacks of 1.50-2.50 lakhs per month. Regulatory agencies at times resort to arms-twisting to get higher bribes or some work done by them. The raids cost the operators in terms of money and running around government officials, including criminal cases being made out against them (*HT* dated 29th January 2011).

However, the question is who is responsible for the death of Yashwant Sonawane, the additional district collector, Nashik. Is the Oil Mafia alone is responsible for it or the government officials are also responsible for it? The government officers would continue to lose their lives so long their colleagues are a partner in the crime. Otherwise such murders rarely happen while doing government duty.

No one now has any faith in the Police. The wife of the killed officer is unhappy with the probe into the killing of her husband. But it is the women who can help in removing corruption if they keep their spending within the income of their husbands. But the desire in women to have unlimited costly garments and jewellery never ends.

While talking about Indian Republic he remembered an American story. The name of the story is 'The greatest man of the world'.

The hero of this story is a well-built farmer. Somehow, by assembling parts, he is able to make an aeroplane and is able to fly it. With his genius, the whole country gets amazed and feels proud of him. The government makes announcement to honour the farmer publicly by the President. Before the celebrations the assistants of the President teach him for weeks how he should behave and shake hands with the President and what has he to say on the mike.

The big hall arranged for this occasion is full. The celebrations begin. The bodyguards of the President bring the farmer on the stage. He shakes hands with the President and speaks the words taught to him. But then in excitement he starts speaking in colloquial language all sorts of words, which are not suitable for the occasion. All the people in the hall become non-plus. Suddenly the bodyguards of the President take him to the back of the stage and start beating him. Now on the stage the President is praising him for his genius, while in the background he is being thrashed and is crying.

The republic of India enacts the same scene. On one hand the common man is crying due to rise in prices, bribes and scandals worth lakhs of crores of rupees, rampant corruption, steep rise in crime and justice being purchased. On the other hand the whole world is being mesmerized by the show of fighter-bombers, the units of Army, Navy and Air Force. In the scenery no where the suicides of 2 lakh farmers due to poverty is shown and also the number of people killed in fake encounters in addition to those killed in floods and famine.

No profit out of mining leases is being given to the Tribals. It goes into the pockets of the politicians, government officers and the middlemen. Those who protest against the injustice being done in government, are being branded Nexalites or Maoists and are being killed by the armed police. The social workers like Vinayak Sen are being sentenced for life imprisonment and Arundhati Roy is being threatened.

The whole republic is just breathing and crying under the feet of big corporates or under the monopoly of the market and the rulers feel helpless that they can neither control the rise in prices nor the administrative scandals. About 1.75 lakh crores can be a normal budget of a big state. More money than the budget of the whole country is lying in foreign banks and the government is unable to do anything in the absence of legal framework.

The capital of India has been converted into the capital of crime. The government says that they would protect the honour of ladies. Here every day there is a rape or murder. Criminals can shoot anyone anywhere without fear. Even the literate youth do not appear to have any future as the number of jobs goes on reducing. After all how many people can go to foreign lands for employment. To guide them there is neither any philosophy nor any principle. The media is also affected by the culture of corporate sector and is itself passing through the danger of incredibility.

In this era, to give punishment to a big criminal appears to be impossible even if it is Arushi-Hemraj murder case or Nithari girl's rape and murder cases or the work of demon like Rathore. In the country players are being bought and sold openly. The poor and oppressed want to become rich through crimes.

No political party now has any philosophy or principle. The words Socialism, Communism and Democracy have lost their meanings. The youth are busy in protests on small matters. The Property of the state is burnt and destroyed on minor issues.

In this situation to improve things, there appears to be only one solution and that is democratic dictatorship by having Presidential type of government. Then the laws would not take years to be framed to bring back crores and crores of rupees from foreign banks. Criminals can be hanged in the streets by the nearest lamppost. Pt. Jawaharlal Nehru, the first Prime Minister of India, had said before independence that in free India, corrupt and black marketeers will be hanged on the nearest lamppost.

What a great man says happens. It is the question of time. It could not happen during the lifetime of Pt. Jawaharlal Nehru because perhaps the necessity was not felt for it. But it would certainly happen. The life of the common man has become miserable. The corrupt and the black marketeers have broken all limits. A central minister is getting involved in a scandal to the tune of more than a State's normal budget. The rich who are 10 per cent of the population are holding the entire wealth of the nation. They have made the country's economy hollow. So some people may have to be hanged by the nearest lamppost. They would not learn from what happened due to corruption in other countries. They want to experience it themselves. So let us do it and fulfill the words of the Great man [By Rajendra Yadav, *Amar Ujala* (Hindi) dated 26th January 2011].

We may do something concrete by framing draconian laws of excessive punishment and award severe penalty to the corrupt government servants. Only a few may have to be punished in each State instead of hanging many by the nearest lampposts.

We are proud of our Republic. We are the biggest Republic of the world and on this strength we have been facing the biggest challenges successfully. There is a large population and there is the greatest number of youths in the country. Due to one of the biggest financial power we are being counted among the big nations.

But under republic the political arrangements we have now, its dark side has started appearing and is making us fear. On 26 January 1950, we had adopted the republic. Its base was the constitution. We divided the work between legislative bodies and the judiciary. Each of them had to work within its limits.

Today the conditions are that it is the Supreme Court which is having an eye on the 2-G spectrum scam of 1.76 lakhs crores. According to the constitution this job is not of the judiciary, but of the government. Lakhs of cases are pending in the courts for disposal. If any pillar of democracy stops doing its duty, who else would do it? The other can do it only at the cost of its own work. The Supreme Court is doing it at the cost of its own work. If it continues like this the Democracy is going to fail. It is a question of time only.

On one side the government does not stop patting its back at 8 to 9 per cent of increase in the financial economy. On the other side 80 per cent population of the country is living below the poverty line. The position of law and order is such that an additional district collector of Nashik was burnt alive by the oil Mafia on 25 January 2011, a day before the Republic day. On education, health, employment, etc. our performance has never been of high standard. What is the guarantee that on this Republic day if we take an oath of allegiance to the constitution, we would be able to do better in the coming years? [*Amar Ujala* (Hindi) dated 26th January 2011 Editorial].

The Indian republic has become 60 years old. In 60 years some positive things have happened and some negative things have also taken place. The positive thing is that our constitution is still in force. The republic has become stronger. The common man still has faith in the constitution. Our country is the biggest republic in the world. Although in between the efforts have been made to break it, yet we are still one. Separatism may have been born in J&K or in the eastern north, but the boundary of the country has not changed. In 60 years the country had to struggle against many internal and external threats. During this period there were four wars, which we fought united to keep our constitution and republic safe.

On the other hand the list of despairs and failures is quite long. The number of the poor has increased since independence. Same is the position of illiterate persons. By following the liberal economic policy to reduce the difference between the rich and the poor, instead of getting reduced, it has increased. The advantage of economic growth has gone to a few only. Most of the people do not appear to gain from the liberal policy. The result is that there is a fall in the living standard of most of the people.

But what we have seen in the last few months, we had never imagined. The corruption has gone to unlimited heights. There is no sphere left where there is no corruption. The reasons are clear. Although we enforced the constitution, but the three pillars of republic, viz. legislative assemblies, governments and the judiciary did not perform their duties sincerely. No work in the republic is transparent.

It is only one fine morning that we read in the newspapers or hear on the TV that there has been a scam in such and such department of the central government or the state government. Even the amount of the scam is beyond countable numbers like so many lakh crores. Nobody is arrested immediately and no responsibility is fixed on anybody. An inquiry is ordered and after months we hear that the CBI has raided the house or shop or business of so many people at so many places. Sometimes a chargesheet is also filed against some persons. But nothing happens. Nobody has so far been punished and sent to jail or his property confiscated.

Sometimes it appears that they are not competent and do not have the strength to deal with the scams taking place every now and then. What happened in the case of Hasan Ali Khan where the ED failed to submit sufficient proof for his custody in a civil court and he was released on bail?

It is the Supreme Court who helped the Enforcement Directorate and overruled the order of the District Judge. The income of Hasan Ali Khan has multiplied by over 100 times in six years from ₹ 529 crore in 2001-02 to ₹ 54,268 crore in 2006-07, revealed by the CAG report tabled in Parliament on 18 March 2011. Hasan Ali did not file tax returns for the last five years. Now he has filed it after receiving the notice from IT department. Where was the IT Department sleeping all these days? (*HT* dated 19th March 2011).

In the absence of responsibility the normal values have declined. The media has ignored its responsibility and the transparency except occasionally. Everything is being sold in the market. There are governments who have attempted to purchase the MLAs and MPs. The legislative assembly is divided into small groups. They put all types of pressures to get profitable ministry/department. This also has become an open secret. The words 'the law is equal for everybody' have remained in the law books only and for quoting in speeches. The influential man gets discharged after committing the crime. Witnesses are purchased and the documents disappear from the file. Sometime even the file disappears.

Now there are differences between the government and the judiciary. The constitution has laid down the areas of work of both. If both work in their areas, then there is no problem. Up till now any differences that arose, have been sorted out. But now it appears that in some areas the division line between the two bodies is not very clear.

The Supreme Court was hearing petition filed by different gutka, pan masala and chewing tobacco-manufacturing companies. They were seeking modification of its ruling banning use of plastic as packing material for their products, by March 1 this year. The Supreme Court had ordered the government to engage an independent agency to test the contents of these sockets to evaluate the risk they pose to consumers. This job was actually of the government and should have been done by it years before. But perhaps due to pressure from the Pan Masala companies the government did not do the job.

The rules have already been framed in September 2009 and only a formal notification is required to be done to implement the law. But the government is holding on this notification. The Supreme Court, therefore, passed an order in December 2010 in which it directed the central government to come out with the law within eight weeks, which expired on 4 February 2011. But the government is still sitting on the notification and pleaded for more time. The Supreme Court refused to grant further time on the plea that one year and 4 months has already passed. So it is not the judiciary who is confronting with the government. But under pressure of the companies the government is not able to work and the people approach the court for ordering the government to do its duty and the confrontation.

But the faith in the constitution makes the republic strong. So far nothing has happened, which could create a constitutional crisis. Let us not be disappointed towards our republic provided we take a decision to remove the present anomalies, which is a big proviso (By Subhash Kashyap, *HT* dated 20th January 2011).

If we look at the previous record of democracy, it becomes clear that democracy has failed to control corruption. In fact, the biggest loser is India. Being the world's largest democracy it is also one of the most corrupt countries in the world. So democracy itself cannot stamp out corruption. As regards economic equality and stability is concerned, here also the democracy is a failure.

If we compare the economics of all democracies and dictatorships between 1950 and 2000, we find that the countries under dictatorial regimes are economically better than those under democratic regimes. The statistics show that within democracies, there are wide economic inequalities. For example, in South Africa and Brazil, the top 20 per cent own 60 per cent of the wealth and the bottom 20 per cent earn less than 3 per cent of the total income. So, democracy is not a guarantee for economic development. But still democracy is much better than autocracy.

We must remember that democracy is not Harry Potter's magic wand that would end our miseries just by chanting of magic charms. Democracy only creates conditions, which will ensure equality of citizens before the law of the country and enhances the dignity of individuals. But for proper functioning of democracy the citizens have to know their rights and duties and enforce them. After all, in a democracy, people are their own masters (By Binayak Ghosh, *HT* dated 17th February 2011).

In ancient Athens, Plato, while criticizing the republic, had said that the biggest drawback of republic is that it allows a common man to speak in assembly on foreign policy, finance and similar other serious issues. He castes his vote on it and after being elected in the executive, executes the decisions, whereas these are the subjects on which the experts only can think about them in the right way. Therefore, he opined and pressed for including in the executive all those who are philosophers and thinkers.

The second fault of republic was that while selecting leaders those reasons come in front which have nothing to do with the skill of running the administration, like money, dynasty, the background of the family and misguiding speeches of candidates.

The third fault of republic is that it can go in the direction of anarchy. When the Athens government sentenced Philosopher Socrates to death by poisoning, Plato was convinced that the republic gives no protection to the common man.

Today the ancient Athens is not there. But what Plato said 2500 years ago is true even now. But this does not mean that we should reject the republic form of government in India and find some other way to govern us. The experts of political science have found that the republic form of Government is much better than other forms.

So far India is concerned; we have adopted the Republic which was born in England. The minimum education and the prosperity required to run this type of government was lacking in India due to illiteracy and poverty. Due to different castes and creeds the feudal societies developed in India, which England had rejected long ago.

After independence, those leaders who joined politics could have created healthy traditions and customs in politics. But they failed to do that. Pandit Jawaharlal Nehru, the first Prime Minister of India, remained in politics till death. Smt. Indira Gandhi followed his example. Jyoti Basu of West Bengal was even ahead of them. On the other hand we have the example of Nelson Mandela, whose sacrifice was greater than all the others mentioned above. He remained in Jail for 27-28 years. If he wanted he could remain President of South Africa for the whole life. But to found a healthy tradition for the republic he left the job after one term only. Lulu Disilva, the president of Brazil, was very popular. He remained president for two terms only. On third time he refused to stand for election although the whole public wanted him to be the President.

Ram Manohar Lohia and Jayaprakash Narayan had drawn the attention to the defects in the Republic. JP had given his voice for complete revolution to change the Republic. Main attack was on the present election process. Among various defects in republic he found the major defect in election process, which due to costly election gives protection to incompetent and criminal candidates. JP wanted to continue his protest for a long time. But due to emergency the whole movement lagged behind. The only object remained was the removal of Mrs. Indira Gandhi. The result was that though the emergency was over, but there was no change in the election law and the process.

Now again due to rampant corruption and inflation an environment is developing in the country for revolution, although there is no personality like JP to whom the public may follow. Still efforts are in the way to create the atmosphere for mass protests. A procession was taken out in Delhi and other big cities on 30 January 2011 by about 30,000 people against corruption under the leadership of Baba Ramdev and others to make the stringent laws for the Lokpal and Lokayukt to punish the corrupt persons.

The people should learn the lesson from the Revolution of JP. The opposition political parties may take the advantage of it. Though the revolution should be for a change in the election process and for punishing the corrupt, but JP had taken the help of the social scientists. Today also this may be done. The public protest should be converted into a big revolution. But are we ready for it? [By Udai Prakash Arora, *Amar Ujala* (Hindi) dated 16th February 2011].

The Prime Minister Manmohan Singh is already aware of large-scale corruption and inflation in the country. There are many defects in the election laws. A person who is not a voter from the constituency is being allowed to stand from that constituency. If this provision is amended it may solve the problem of dynasty rule because husband and wife, father/ mother and son cannot stand together in the same election from the same constituency. The person getting less than 50 per cent votes is being declared elected. Here also the problem of minority rule would get solved if the existing provision is amended or a new rule is inserted. There are no stringent laws against disturbing an election. If the same are made, the number of candidates of criminal nature getting elected would reduce.

In Asian and African countries people insist on their rights, but seldom perform their duties. Unluckily rights flow from duties. Someone's duty is another man's right. If duties were not performed, no right would be achieved. This is what is lacking in Asian and African countries. They are kind hearted people. They do not punish those who do not perform their duties sincerely, but show mercy to them.

Prime Minister Manmohan Singh admitted on 16th February 2011 before the press at his house that he had to make some compromises to run a coalition government.

The coalition government is the result of political parties being formed without any ideology. Their number can be restricted by general ideologies like Socialist, Communist, Democratic and Republic Parties. If any member resigns from the party or is removed by the party, his membership should become null and void. In his place the concerned party may nominate any other voter of his constituency for the remaining period to avoid by-elections.

Therefore, for smooth running of republic certain rules and laws need to be amended or new ones to be made for our republic to be successful.

11

French, Russian, Chinese and Jasmine Revolutions

(I) THE FRENCH REVOLUTION

The French Revolution (1789-99) was a period of radical social and political upheaval in French and European history. The absolute monarchy that had ruled France for centuries collapsed in three years. French society underwent an epic transformation. The feudal, aristocratic and religious privileges evaporated under the sustained assault by liberal political groups and the masses on the streets. Old ideas about hierarchy and tradition succumbed to new Enlightenment principles of citizenship and inalienable rights.

The French Revolution began with the convocation of the Estates-General in May 1789. The members of the Third Estate proclaimed the Tennis Court Oath in June. The assault on the Bastille took place in July. The passage of the Declaration of the Rights of Man and of the Citizen took place in August and an epic march on Versailles forced the royal court back to Paris in October 1789. The next few years were dominated by tensions between various liberal assemblies and a conservative monarchy intent on thwarting major reforms.

The modern era unfolded in the shadow of the French Revolution. The growth of republics and liberal democracies, the spread of secularism, the development of modern ideologies and the invention of total war, all mark their birth during the Revolution. Subsequent events that can be traced to the

Revolution include the Napoleon Wars, two separate restorations of the monarchy and two additional revolutions as modern France took shape.

Among the causes of the Revolution are the economic factors, which included hunger and malnutrition in the most destitute segments of the population. There was rise in bread prices after several years of poor grain harvests. It was further aggravated by an inadequate transportation system which hindered the shipment of bulk foods from rural areas to large population centres, contributing greatly to the destabilization of French society in the years leading up to the Revolution.

Another cause was France's near bankruptcy as a result of the many wars fought by previous rulers, as well as the financial strain caused by French participation in the American Revolutionary War. The national debt amounted to some 2 billion livres. The social burdens caused by war included the huge war debt, made worse by the loss of France's colonial possessions in North America and the growing commercial dominance of Great Britain. France's inefficient and antiquated financial system was unable to manage the national debt, something which was both partially caused and exacerbated by the burden of an inadequate system of taxation. To obtain new money to head off default on the government's loans, the king called an Assembly of Notables in 1787.

Meanwhile, the royal court at Versailles was perceived by many as being isolated from and indifferent to the hardships of the lower classes. While in theory King Louis XVI was an absolute Monarch, but in practice he was often indecisive and known to back down when faced with strong opposition. While he did reduce government expenditures, opponents in the parliaments successfully thwarted his attempts at enacting much needed reforms. Those who were opposed to Louis' policies further undermined royal authority by distributing pamphlets that criticized the government and its officials, stirring up public opinion against the monarchy.

Louis XVI ascended to the throne amidst a financial crisis. The nation was nearing bankruptcy and outlays outpaced income.

This was because of France's financial obligations stemming from involvement in the Seven Years War and its participation in the American Revolutionary War. In May 1776, finance minister Turgot was dismissed after he failed to enact much needed reforms.

The next year, Jacques Necker, a foreigner, was appointed Comptroller-General of Finance. He could not be made an official minister because he was a Protestant. Necker realized that the country's tax system, which was perceived as quite regressive, subjected the lower classes to a heavy burden. On the other hand numerous exemptions existed for the nobility and clergy. He argued that the country could not be taxed further and the tax exemptions for the nobility and clergy must be reduced. He proposed that borrowing more money would solve the county's fiscal shortages.

By this time, Necker had earned the enmity of many members of the French court for his overt manipulation of public opinion. They urged the King to dismiss Necker as financial advisor. On 11 July 1789 the King fired him and completely restructured the finance ministry at the same time.

Many Parisians presumed Louis's actions to be aimed against the Assembly and began open rebellion when they heard the news the next day. They were also afraid that soldiers, who were mostly foreign mercenaries, had been summoned to shut down the National Constituent Assembly. The Assembly, meeting at Versailles, went into nonstop session to prevent another eviction from their meeting place. The riots, chaos, and widespread looting began in Paris. The mobs soon had the support of some of the French Guards, who were armed and trained soldiers.

On 14 July, the insurgents set their eyes on the large weapons and ammunition stored inside the Bastille fortress, which was also perceived to be a symbol of royal power. After several hours of combat, the prison fell that afternoon. Despite ordering a cease-fire, which prevented a mutual massacre, the governor was beaten, stabbed and decapitated. His head was placed on a pike and paraded about the city. Although the fortress had held only seven prisoners, the Bastille served as a potent symbol of hating everything of the old Régime. Returning to the city hall, the mob accused the mayor of treachery and butchered him.

By late July, the spirit of popular sovereignty had spread throughout France. In rural areas, many commoners began to form militias and armed themselves against a foreign invasion. Some attacked the nobility due to fear. In addition, wild rumours and paranoia caused widespread unrest and civil disturbances that contributed to the collapse of law and order.

On 4 August 1789, the National Constituent Assembly abolished feudalism, in what is known as the August Decrees. In the course of a few hours, nobles, clergy, towns, provinces, companies and cities lost their special privileges. On 26 August 1789, the Assembly published the Declaration of the Rights of Man and of the Citizen. The National Constituent Assembly functioned not only as a legislature, but also as a body to draft a new constitution.

On 5 October 1789 crowds of women began to assemble at Parisian markets. The women first demanded that city officials address their concerns. The women were shouting that they were facing harsh economic situations especially bread shortages. They also demanded an end to royal efforts to block the National Assembly, and for the King and his administration to move to Paris as a sign of good faith in addressing the widespread poverty.

Getting unsatisfactory responses from city officials, as many as 7,000 women joined the march to Versailles, bringing with them cannons and a variety of smaller weapons. Twenty thousand National Guardsmen under the command of La Fayette responded to keep order, and members of the mob stormed the palace, killing several guards. La Fayette ultimately convinced the king to accede to the demand of the crowd that the monarchy relocates to Paris.

On 6 October 1789, the King and the royal family moved from Versailles to Paris under the "protection" of the National Guards, thus legitimizing the National Assembly. A republic was proclaimed in September 1792 and King Louis XVI was executed the next year.

(II) RUSSIAN REVOLUTION (1917)

The Russian Revolution of 1905 was said to be a major factor to the February Revolutions of 1917. The events of Bloody Sunday triggered a line of protests. A council of workers called the St. Petersburg Soviet was created and there was a beginning of a communist political protest.

World War I prompted a Russian outcry directed at Tsar Nicholas II. After the entry of Turkey on the side of the Central Powers in October 1914, Russia was deprived of a major trade route through Turkey, which followed with a minor economic crisis, in which Russia became incapable of providing munitions to their army in the years leading to 1917. However, the problems were merely administrative and not industrial as Germany was producing great amounts of munitions whilst constantly fighting on two major battlefronts.

The war also developed weariness in the city, owing to a lack of food in response to the disruption of agriculture. The indirect reason was that the government, in order to finance the war, had been printing off millions of ruble notes, and by 1917 inflation had sent prices to four times what they had been in 1914.

The peasantry were consequently faced with the higher cost of purchases, but made no corresponding gain in the sale of their own produce. As a result they tended to hoard their grain and to revert to subsistence farming. Thus the cities were constantly short of food. At the same time rising prices led to demands for higher wages in the factories, and in January and February 1916 revolutionary propaganda lead to widespread strikes. Due to heavy losses during the war the people thought that Tsar Nicholas II was unfit to rule.

In July 1915 a Central War Industries Committee under the chairmanship of Octobrist Guchkov included ten workers' representatives. In September 1915 a combination of Octobrists and Kadets in the Duma demanded the forming of a responsible government. The Tsar rejected these proposals. He had now taken over the position of commander-in-chief of the armed forces. During his absence at his headquarters at Mogilev, he left most of the day-to-day government in the hands of the Empress. She was intensely unpopular, owing to her German origin and the influence that Rasputin, an unsavoury monk, was thought to exercise over her.

An elementary theory of property, believed by many peasants, was that land should belong to those who work at it. They migrated to and from industrial and urban environments. There was overcrowded housing with often deplorable sanitary conditions and long hours at work. On the eve of the war there was a 10-hour workday. By 1916 many were working 11-12 hours a day. There was a constant risk of injury and death from very poor safety and sanitary conditions. There was harsh discipline and inadequate wages.

The rapid industrialization of Russia also resulted in urban overcrowding and poor conditions for urban industrial workers. Between 1890 and 1910, the population of the capital, Saint Petersburg, swelled from 1,033,600 to 1,905,600, with Moscow experiencing similar growth. There was also no running water, and piles of human waste were a threat to the health of the workers. The poor conditions only aggravated the situation, with the number of strikes and incidents of public disorder rapidly increasing in the years shortly before World War I.

Dissatisfaction with Russian autocracy culminated in the huge national upheaval that followed the Bloody Sunday massacre of January 1905, in which hundreds of unarmed protesters were shot by the Tsar's troops. Workers responded to the massacre with a crippling general strike, forcing Nicholas to put forth the October Manifesto, which established a democratically elected parliament. The Tsar undermined this promise of reform.

Russia's first major battle of the war was a disaster. In the 1914 in the battle of Tannenberg, over 30,000 Russian troops were killed or wounded and 90,000 captured, while Germany suffered just 20,000 casualties. However, Austro-Hungarian forces allied to Germany were driven back deep into the Galicia region by the end of the year. In the autumn of 1915, Nicholas had taken direct command of the army, personally overseeing Russia's main theatre of war and leaving his ambitious but incapable wife Alexandra in charge of the government. Reports of corruption and incompetence in the Imperial government began to emerge, and the growing influence of Grigori Rasputin in the Imperial family was widely resented. In December 1916 a small group of nobles assassinated Rasputin.

In 1915, things took a critical turn for the worse when Germany shifted its focus of attack to the Eastern front. The superior German army, which was better led, better trained and better supplied, was terrifyingly effective against the ill-equipped Russian forces, driving the Russians out of Galicia, as well as Russian Poland, during the Gorlice-Tarnow offensive campaign.

By the end of October 1916, Russia had lost between 1,600,000 and 1,800,000 soldiers, with an additional 2,000,000 prisoners of war and 1,000,000 missing, all making up a total of nearly 5,000,000 men. Soldiers went without food and lacked shoes, munitions, and even weapons. Rampant discontent lowered morale, which was further undermined by a series of military defeats.

Already, by the end of 1914, only five months into the war, around 390,000 Russian men had lost their lives and nearly 1,000,000 were injured. Far sooner than expected, scarcely trained recruits had to be called up for active duty.

The army quickly ran short of rifles and ammunition as well as uniforms and food, and, by mid-1915, men were being sent to the front bearing no arms. It was hoped that they could equip themselves with the arms that they recovered from fallen soldiers, of both sides, on the battlefields. With patently good reason, the soldiers did not feel that they were being treated as human beings, or even as valuable soldiers, but rather as raw materials to be squandered for the purposes of the rich and powerful.

By the spring of 1915, the army was in steady retreat. By 1916, however, the situation had improved in many respects. Russian troops stopped retreating, and there were even some modest successes in the offensives that were staged that year at great loss of life. Also, the problem of shortages was largely solved by a major effort to increase domestic production.

By the end of 1915, there were manifold signs that the economy was breaking down under the heightened strain of wartime demand. The main problems were food shortages and rising prices. Not surprisingly, strikes increased steadily from the middle of 1915, and so did crime; but, for the most part, people suffered and endured, scouring the city for food.

Working-class women in St. Petersburg reportedly spent about forty hours a week in food lines, begging, turning to prostitution or crime, tearing down wooden fences to keep stoves heated for warmth, grumbling about the rich, and wondering when and how this would all come to an end.

To quell the riots, the Tsar looked to the army. At least 180,000 troops were available in the capital, but most were either untrained or injured. Around 12,000 could be regarded as reliable. But even these proved reluctant to move in on the crowd, since it included so many women. It was for this reason that when, on March 11 the Tsar ordered the army to suppress the rioting by force, troops began to mutiny. Although few actively joined the rioting, many officers were either shot or went into hiding.

The ability of the garrison to hold back the protestors was all but nullified. Symbols of the Tsarist were rapidly torn down around the city, and governmental authority in the capital collapsed. Meanwhile, the socialist parties established the Petrograd Soviet to represent workers and soldiers. The remaining loyal units switched allegiance the next day.

The Tsar took a train back towards Petrograd, which was stopped on March 14, having been instructed to divert by a group of disloyal troops. When the Tsar finally reached his destination, the Army Chiefs and his remaining ministers suggested in unison that he abdicate the throne. He did so on March 15, on behalf of himself, and then, having taken advice, on behalf of his son, the Tsarevich. Nicholas nominated his brother, the Grand Duke Michael Alexandrovich, to succeed him.

But the Grand Duke realized that he would have little support as ruler, so he declined the crown on March 16 stating that he would take it only if that was the consensus of democratic action. Six days later, Nicholas was reunited with his family at the Alexander Palace at Tsarskoe Selo. On 16 March, a provisional government was announced. The Provisional Government placed him under house arrest with his family.

The centre-left was well represented, and a liberal aristocrat, Prince Georgy Yevgenyevich Lvov, a member of the Constitutional Democratic Party, initially chaired the government. The socialists had formed their rival body four days earlier, the Petrograd Soviet (or workers' council). The Petrograd Soviet and the Provisional Government competed for power over Russia.

The model for the soviet was of workers' councils that had been established in scores of Russian cities during the 1905 revolution. In February 1917, striking workers elected deputies to represent them and socialist activists began organizing a citywide council to unite these deputies with representatives of the socialist parties.

The Petrograd Soviet met in the Tauride Palace, the same building where the new government was taking shape. With Lenin's arrival, the popularity of the Bolsheviks increased steadily. Over the course of the spring, public dissatisfaction with the Provisional Government and the war, in particular among workers, soldiers and peasants, pushed these groups to radical parties.

In early March, the Provisional Government placed Nicholas and his family under house arrest in the Alexander Palace at Tsarskoe Selo, 24 km south of Petrograd. In August 1917 the Kerensky government evacuated the Romanovs to Tobolsk in the Urals, allegedly to protect them from the rising tide of revolution during the Red Terror.

In early September, the Petrograd Soviet freed all jailed Bolsheviks and Trotsky became chairman of the Petrograd Soviet. In the October Revolution, the Bolshevik party, led by Vladimir Lenin, and the workers' Soviets, overthrew the Provisional Government in St Petersburg. The Bolsheviks appointed themselves as leaders of various government ministries and seized control of the countryside, establishing the Cheka to quash dissent.

Civil war erupted between the "Red" (Bolshevik), and "White" (anti-Bolshevik) factions, which was to continue for several years, with the Bolsheviks ultimately becoming victorious. In this way the Revolution paved the way for the Union of Soviet Socialist Republics (USSR).

After the Bolsheviks came to power in October 1917, the conditions of their imprisonment grew stricter and talk of putting Nicholas on trial increased. As the counter-revolutionary White movement gathered force, leading to full-scale civil war by the summer, the Romanovs were moved during April and May 1918 to Yekaterinburg, a militant Bolshevik stronghold.

During the early morning of 16 July, at approximately 0130 AM, Nicholas, Alexandra, their children, their physician, and several servants were taken into the basement and killed. The order came directly from Vladimir Lenin in Moscow as is being alleged.

(III) CHINESE REVOLUTION (1949)

With the breakdown of peace talks between the Chinese Nationalist Party, and the Communist Party of China, an all-out war between these two forces resumed. The Soviet Union provided limited aid to the communists, and the United States assisted the Nationalists with hundreds of millions of dollars worth of military supplies and equipment. The airlifting of many Nationalists troops from central China to Manchuria was also done. It was an area Chiang Kai-Shek saw as strategically vital to defend Nationalist-controlled areas against a communist advance.

The communists were well established in the north and northeast. The Nationalists, who had an advantage in both numbers of men and weapons, controlled a much larger territory and population than their adversaries and enjoyed considerable world support including direct support from the United States. Nevertheless they suffered from a lack of morale and rampant corruption that greatly reduced their ability to fight, as well as their domestic civilian support.

Crucially, during World War II, while Nationalists and Communists were in an alliance against fascist forces (chiefly Japanese troops and their Chinese supporters), the best of the Nationalists troops had already been wounded or killed while the communists had suffered minimal losses. By the time the Chinese Civil War was drawing to a close, Nationalists forces were surviving almost entirely by the grace of their international capitalist sympathizers.

Belatedly, the Nationalists government also sought to enlist popular support through internal reforms. The effort was in vain because of both rampant corruption in government and the accompanying political and economic chaos, including massive hyperinflation. By late 1948 the Nationalists position was extremely bleak. The demoralized and undisciplined Nationalists troops proved no match for the much better formed communist People's Liberation Army.

The latter had managed to not only maintain much of their formations' basic structure and leadership all the way through World War II, but also through all of the Civil War period, as well. In fact, in all, the Communist Party had actively been working towards their moment of victory from even before the World War II.

After numerous operational setbacks in Manchuria, especially in attempting to take the major cities, the communists were finally able to seize the region and capture large Nationalists formations. This provided them with the tanks, heavy artillery, and other combined-arms assets needed to prosecute offensive operations south of the Great Wall. In January 1949 the communists without a fight took Beijing, and its name was changed back to Beijing.

Between April and November, major cities passed from Nationalists to Communist control with minimal resistance. In most cases the surrounding countryside and small towns had come under Communist influence long before the cities. This was part of the strategy of people's war outlined by Mao. One of the decisive battles was the Huai Hai Campaign.

Ultimately, the People's Liberation Army was victorious. On October 1, 1949 Mao Zedong proclaimed the establishment of the People's Republic of China. Chiang Kai-shek, 600,000 Nationalists troops, and about two million Nationalists-sympathizer refugees, predominantly from the former government and business communities of the mainland, retreated to the island of Taiwan and proclaimed the Republic of China. After that, there remained only isolated pockets of resistance to the Communists on the mainland, such as in the far south. A PRC attempt to take the ROC-controlled Island of Kinmen was thwarted in the Battle of Kuningtou, halting a PLA advance towards Taiwan.

In December 1949 Chiang proclaimed Taipei, Taiwan the temporary capital of the Republic, and continued to assert his government as the sole legitimate authority of all China, while the PRC government did likewise. The last fighting between Nationalists and Communist forces ended with the communist capture of Hainan Island in May 1950.

(IV) JASMINE REVOLUTION

If we look into above revolutions we find that preparations had already been made for what was to be done after the revolution. But in the later revolutions it happened that the people took part in the protests against some autocrat, but did not know whom they would like to sit in his chair.

The history of the world is full of revolutions and protests against the autocrats. But in this context we would like to talk about the revolutions in 21st century only. The last year of 20th century gave the gift of two revolutions in 21st century. In January 2000 the public protests forced President Jamil of Ecuador to leave the chair. In the same year in October Slobodan Milosevic of Yugoslavia had to leave his chair. However, in both the countries there was no change in the status of the public.

The new 21st century began with a change in power. In January 2001 President Josef Estrada of Philippine had to resign due to the protests by the army and the public. In December 2001 President Fernando De la of Argentina had to run away after leaving the palace due to protests by the people. In October

2003 President Gonfalon Sanchez De Lozada of Bolivia became the target of change and after struggle had to leave by helicopter. In 5 years they did another revolution in June 2005 and removed Carlos Mesa from the chair who had occupied it after Gonfalon Sanchez De Lozada.

In November 2003 there was a pink revolution in Georgia and in the storm for change President Edward Shevardnadze had to leave the chair. After Georgia the revolution moved to Kyrgyzstan and in March 2005 President Asker Okayed had to run away from the country and Kurmanbek Okayed occupied his chair. In 2010 there was again a public protest and President Kurmanbek Okayed, who had occupied the chair after Asker Okayed, had to run away from the country.

In 2006 in Nepal King Gajanand had to leave his throne due Maoists revolution. But from that time there is political unrest in Nepal. After Kyrgyzstan was the turn of Tunisia. Zined Abidine Ben Ali was the ruler. In Tunisia a principal officer did the injustice with a vegetable seller by beating him and breaking his wooden shop. When the vegetable seller did not get justice the public took to streets. The ruler had to run away from Tunisia.

After Tunisia there was revolution in Egypt. Here in February 2011 due to public protests President Hosni Mubarak had to leave the chair. But now the power in Egypt is in the hands of Army under Mohammad Husain Tanti.

The first round of the great Arab democratic revolt toppled the governments in Tunisia and Egypt. Egypt and Tunisia were more mature States, imbued with a deeper sense of nationhood. There the military declined to clear the streets with gunfire.

Bahrein's Sunni Khalifa ruling family overran the Shia populated island two centuries ago and is still acting as foreign conquerors. They deliberately discriminate between the two religious groups of Sunni and Shia. The Sunni government tried to crush the revolution. So the protestors have decided that they would not agree less than the resignation of the government. Bahrein's Sunni rulers have violently turned on pro-democracy protestors, backed by troops provided by fellow Persian Gulf monarchies. Bahrein's king said that a foreign plot against his island state had been foiled. The numerous arrests and trials of opposition figures is running in military courts. Some leading opposition figures are on trial.

Colonel Muammar Gaddafi took power in a military coup but did little to forge a nation. He is the President of Libya and is ruling for the last 40 years. Libya politics is still tribal politics with Colonel Gaddafi making sure that all the aces lay with his clansmen. The struggle for his removal is continuing. The regime of Colonel Gaddafi has already killed so many protestors that there is no path of political compromise in Libya. As the world dithers on intervention, Libya's dictator Colonel Gaddafi is rapidly rolling up the rebellion that a week ago had seemed on the verge of toppling him. Nato planes pounded Libyan government weapons depots southeast of the town of Zintan on 9 May 2011, in a sign of widening conflict in the Western Mountains region as rebels battle to unseat Muammar Gaddafi.

Iran is playing an increasingly active role in helping the Syrian regime in its crackdown on pro-democracy protestors. A similar story of protests being slowly but surely ground to silence is being repeated in many of the other Arab countries, ranging from Yemen to Algeria, where there had been an expectation of regime change. In Yemen the protestors are agitating for resignation of the government. In Yemen, Oman, Kuwait, Algeria, and Djibouti the people took to the streets demanding political and economic change. The head of the Gulf Cooperative Council said that interference by Iran in the Gulf States would not be tolerated.

In Morocco 5 people have died where King Mohammed VI is the ruler. Perhaps it is Morocco only where the power may not change due to large number of democratic institutions.

If we look towards the result of these protests and revolutions we find that their causes and aims are very limited. In Ecuador the public protest was against financial policies. In Yugoslavia the protest was against cheating and frauds in election. In Philippine the agitation was against corruption by the President Josef Estrada. In Bolivia the allegations against Gonfalon Sanchez De Lozada was the connivance with the oil companies. In

Kyrgyzstan the allegation against Asker Okayed was of cheating and fraud in elections.

Except these allegations all other aims of protest were limited. So their results were not farfetched. In fact these revolutions removed the false hopes that they would bring any changes in the country. After the revolution in 2003 in Bolivia and in 2005 in Kyrgyzstan those who came in power, they could not fulfill the aims of revolution and had to leave the chair due to public protests. In Tunisia a principal officer did the injustice with a vegetable seller. When the vegetable seller did not get justice the people took to streets [By Amartya Prakash, *Amar Ujala* (Hindi) dated 20/02/2001].

Tunisia was the last place where anyone would have expected a revolution to start with. Egypt was the last regime anyone expected to crumble without a fight. Political risk analysts rated Bahrein as among the least likely Arab country to face unrest. Most of the Arab countries remain tribes with flags, their leaders ruling with the help of small crony circles and tightly knit clans. The factors that fossilized Arab Politics are superpower super backing, oil revenues and simple repression, which factors are crumbling. New forces like food inflation and social net working sites are defeating them.

As the weakest Arab despots succumb, the next question is how will the smarter and wealthier Arab States respond? They may survive this wave of protests but it is hoped they realize that the political reform is then the only guarantee of stability (*HT* dated 22nd February 2011).

But what type of political form would suit them is still a mystery. Would democracy with rampant corruption like India, Pakistan, Afghanistan and Iraq suit them or not is a million-dollar question.

The Jasmine revolution in the Arab world is over. It began as a romance and is now ending in tragedy. To a large extent this is not unexpected. The set of circumstances that led to the overthrow of the regimes in Tunisia and Egypt were not to be found in most of the other Arab countries. The country's first exercise in democracy in decades was hailed as a success, but the result of a key referendum raised fears that Islamists will hijack looming elections.

The Persian Gulf nations have sufficient oil and gas-funded resources to pacify their populations. But most important is that most of the Arab nations are still tribal. This has made it difficult to convert protests into mass movement. As has happened in Libya, the ruling leadership has been able to count on tribal backing to ensure that an uprising is converted into a civil war.

In addition, tribal structures have meant that the government can count on the support of some military elements. Combined with greater firepower, the result has been a jasmine withering. The Tunisian and Egyptian militaries crucially declined to violently suppress their own people. The only hope the remnants of the Jasmine revolution have today is international intervention. This in military terms means the United States.

But after the invasions of Iraq and Afghanistan, Washington has no stomach for such action unless there is overwhelming international sanction. This has not been forthcoming unsurprisingly, from countries like China and Russia. But even the democracies have been divided with France pushing the hardest for intervention and more conservative voices like Germany hiding behind a position of non-intervention. India has taken the latter fine, continuing a long tradition of preferring passively when it comes to value-driven foreign policy.

However, the jasmine revolution has left a powerful legacy. The most important of these is the creation of a new political culture in Egypt. Egypt is the largest Arab nation and historically the intellectual leader of that part of the world. Where its revolution takes it will be a key determinant in whether democracy can find a place in the Arab world. Other Arab governments will find it necessary to bend to liberal wind in the decades to come, if that wind blows from Cairo. The revolutions are over, but their formation may have just begun (*HT* dated 17th March 2011).

From these examples it is clear that no revolution can succeed merely by removing the autocrat from the chair till what is to be done is clear and preparations are made for it. Otherwise serpents would leave and the cobras would occupy the chairs.

12

Anna Hazare

Anna Hazare

Baburao Hazare was born on 15 January 1940, in the village of Ralegan Siddhi, district Ahmednagar, Maharashtra. He is popularly known as Anna Hazare. He is an Indian social activist who is especially recognized for his contribution to the development of his village Ralegan Siddhi, and for his efforts to establish it as a model village. For this he was awarded the Padam Bhushan, the third highest civilian award, by the government of India in 1992.

Despite frequent criticism from those in authority and the Press, corruption got sanctified and virtually became a part of life. Such was undoubtedly the case before a certain fragile looking 72-year-old man Anna Hazare came into the picture. This unassuming and modest gentleman is one who had the wisdom and goodness inside him to stand against the widespread corruption in almost every aspect of Indian life.

Hazare's father, Baburao Hazare, worked as an unskilled labourer in Ayurveda Ashram Pharmacy. His grandfather was in the army, posted at Bhingar, when Anna was born. He died in 1945, but Hazare's father continued to stay at Bhingar. In 1952, Hazare's father resigned from his job and returned to his own village, Ralegan Siddhi. Hazare had six younger siblings and the family faced significant hardships. Hazare's childless aunt offered to look after him and his education, and took Anna to Bombay (now Mumbai).

Hazare studied up to the 7th standard in Bombay and then sought employment, due to the economic situation in his household. He started selling flowers at Dadar to support his family. He soon started his own shop and brought two of his brothers to Bombay. Gradually Hazare's income increased to around ₹ 800 per month, a decent income in those times.

Anna Hazare started his career in the Indian Army as a driver in 1963. He spent his spare time reading the works of Vivekananda, Gandhi, and Vinoba Bhave. They inspired him to become a social worker and activist. During the Indo-Pakistan War of 1965, he was the only survivor in an exchange of border fire while driving a truck in Khem Karan sector. During the mid-1970s he survived a road accident while driving.

Anna Hazare has said that the dream of India as a strong nation cannot be realized without self-reliant and self-sufficient villages. This can be achieved only through social commitment and involvement of the common man.

After voluntary retirement from the army, Hazare went to Ralegan Siddhi village in 1975. Initially he organized the youth of the village into an organization named the *Tarun Mandal* (Youth Association). He helped to form the *Pani Puravatha Mandals* (Water Supply Associations) to ensure proper distribution of water.

Hazare and the youth group next decided to take up the issue of alcoholism. At a meeting conducted in the temple, the villagers resolved to close down liquor dens and ban alcohol in the village. Since these resolutions were made in the temple, they became in a sense religious commitment. Over thirty liquor brewing units the owners closed voluntarily. Those who did not succumb to social pressure were forced to close down their businesses when the youth group smashed up their liquor dens. The owners could not complain, as their businesses were illegal.

Some villagers continued to drink in Ralegan Siddhi, as they obtained their liquor from neighbouring villages. The villagers decided that those men would be given three warnings, after which they would be physically punished. Twelve men who were found in a drunken state after warnings were tied to a pole with the help of the youth group and were flogged. Hazare said, "Doesn't a mother administer bitter medicines to a sick child when she knows that the medicine can cure her child? The child may not like the medicine, but the mother does it only because she cares for the child. The alcoholics were punished so that their families would not be destroyed."

Hazare appealed to the government of Maharashtra to bring in a law whereby prohibition would come into force in a village if 25 per cent of the women in the village demanded it. In July 2009 the state government issued a government resolution amending the Bombay Prohibition Act, 1949. As per the amendments, if at least 25 per cent of women voters demand liquor prohibition through a written application to the state excise department, voting should be conducted through a secret ballot. If 50 per cent of the voters vote against the sale of liquor, prohibition should be imposed in the village and the sale of liquor should be stopped. Similar action can be taken at the ward level in municipal areas.

Another circular was issued making it mandatory to get the sanction of the Gram Sabha (the local self-government) for issuing new permits for the sale of liquor. In some instances, when women agitated against the sale of liquor, cases were filed against them. Hazare took up the issue again. In August 2009 the government issued another circular that sought withdrawal of cases against women who sought prohibition of liquor in their villages.

It was decided to ban the sale of tobacco, cigarettes, and beedies in the village. In order to implement this resolution, the youth group performed a unique "Holi" ceremony twenty-two years ago. The festival of Holi is celebrated as a symbolic burning of evil. The youth group brought all the tobacco, cigarettes, and beedies from the shops in the village and burnt them in a 'Holi' fire. Tobacco, cigarettes, or beedies are no longer sold at any shop at Ralegan Siddhi.

Ralegan is located at the foothills, so Hazare persuaded villagers to construct a watershed embankment to stop water and allow it to percolate and increase the groundwater level and improve irrigation in the area. The residents of the village used *shramdan* (voluntary labour) to build canals, small-scale check dams, and percolation tanks in the nearby hills for watershed development. These efforts solved the problem of scarcity of water in the village and made irrigation possible. The first embankment that was built with volunteer efforts developed a leak and had to be reconstructed, this time with government funding.

In order to conserve soil and water by checking runoff, contour trenches and gully plugs were constructed along the hill slopes. Grass, shrubs and 3 lakh (300,000) trees were planted along the hillside and the village. This process was supplemented by afforestation, *nullah bund*s, underground check dams, and cemented *bandhara*s (small diversion weirs) at strategic locations. Ralegan also experimented with drip and bi-valve irrigation. Papaya, lemon, and chillies were planted on a plot of 80 acres (32 ha) entirely irrigated by the drip irrigation system.

Cultivation of water-intensive crops like sugarcane was banned. Crops such as pulses, oilseeds, and certain cash crops with low water requirements were grown. The farmers started growing high-yield varieties of crops and the cropping pattern of the village was changed. Since 1975 Hazare helped farmers of more than 70 villages in drought-prone regions in the state of

Maharashtra. The Government of India plans to start a training centre in Ralegan Siddhi to understand and implement Hazare's watershed development model in other villages in the country.

As a secondary occupation, milk production was promoted in Ralegan Siddhi. Purchase of new cattle and improvement of the existing breed with the help of artificial insemination and timely guidance and assistance by a veterinarian resulted in an improvement in the cattle stock. Milk production has increased. crossbred cows replaced local ones, which gave a lower milk yield.

The number of milk cattle also grew, which resulted in growth from 100 litres (before 1975) to around 2,500 litres per day. The milk was sent to a co-operative dairy (Malganga Dairy) in Ahmednagar. Some milk was given to *Balwadi* (kindergarten) children and neighbouring villages under the child nutrition programme sponsored by the Zilla Parishad.

From the surplus funds generated, the milk society bought a mini-truck and a thresher. The mini-truck was used to transport milk to Ahmednagar and to take vegetables and other produce directly to the market, thus eliminating intermediate agents. The thresher was rented out to farmers during the harvesting season.

In 1932 Ralegan Siddhi got its first formal school, a single classroom primary school. In 1962 the villagers added more classrooms through community volunteer efforts. By 1971, out of an estimated population of 1,209, only 30.43 per cent were literate (72 women and 290 men). Boys moved to the nearby towns of Shirur and Parner to pursue higher education, but due to socio-economic conditions, girls could not do the same and were limited to primary education.

Hazare, along with the youth of Ralegan Siddhi, worked to increase literacy rates and education levels. In 1976 they started a pre-school and a high school in 1979. The villagers formed a charitable trust, the *Sant Yadavbaba Shikshan Prasarak Mandal*, which was registered in 1979.

The trust obtained a government grant of ₹ 4 lakhs (400,000) for the school building using the National Rural Education Programme. This money funded a new school building that was built over the next two months using volunteer labour. A new hostel was constructed to house 200 students from poorer sections of society.

After the opening of the school, a girl from Ralegan Siddhi became the first female in the village to complete her Secondary School Certificate in 1982. Since then the school has been instrumental in bringing in many changes in the village. Traditional farming practices are taught in this school in addition to the government curriculum.

Ralegan Siddhi villagers have largely eliminated the social barriers and discrimination that existed due to the caste system in India. People of all castes come together to celebrate social events. The Dalits have been integrated into the social and economic life of the village. The villagers have built houses for the Dalits, and have helped them to repay their loans to free themselves from their indebtedness.

Most rural poor get into a debt trap as they incur heavy expenses at the time of marriage of their son or daughters. It is an undesirable practice but has almost become a social obligation in India. Ralegan's people have started celebrating marriages collectively. Joint feasts are held, where the expenses are further reduced by the *Tarun Mandal* taking responsibility for cooking and serving the food. The Tarun Mandal members belonging to the oppressed castes bought the vessels, the loudspeaker system, the mandap, and the decorations. From 1976 to 1986, 424 marriages were held under this system.

The Gandhian philosophy on rural development considers the Gram Sabha as an important democratic institution for collective decision-making in the villages of India. Hazare campaigned between 1998 and 2006 for amending the Gram Sabha Act, so that the villagers have a say in the development works in their village. The state government initially refused, but eventually gave in due to public pressure. As per the amendments, it is mandatory to seek the sanction of the Gram Sabha (an assembly of all village adults, and not just the few elected representatives in the gram panchayat) for expenditures on development works in the village.

In case of expenditure without the sanction of the Gram Sabha, 20 per cent of Gram Sabha members can lodge a complaint to the chief executive officer of the zila parishad (the district-level governing body) with their signatures. The chief executive officer is required to visit the village and conduct an inquiry within 30 days and submit a report to the divisional commissioner, who has the power to remove the sarpanch or deputy sarpanch and dismiss the gram sevak involved. Hazare was not satisfied, as the amended Act did not include the right to recall a sarpanch. He insisted that this should be included and the state government relented.

In Ralegan Siddhi, Gram Sabha meetings are held periodically to discuss issues relating to the welfare of the village. Projects like watershed development activities are undertaken only after they are discussed in the Gram Sabha. All decisions like *Nashabandi* (bans on alcohol), *Kurhadbandi* (bans on tree felling), *Charai bandi* (bans on grazing), and *Shramdan* were taken in the Gram Sabha. Decisions are taken in a simple majority consensus. The decision of the Gram Sabha is accepted as final.

In addition to the panchayat, there are several registered societies that take care of various projects and activities of the village. Each society presents an annual report and statement of accounts in the Gram Sabha. The *Sant Yadavbaba Shikshan Prasarak Mandal* monitors the educational activities. The *Vividh Karyakari Society* gives assistance and provides guidance to farmers regarding fertilizers, seeds, organic farming, and financial assistance. The *Sri Sant Yadavbaba Doodh Utpadhak Sahakari Sanstha* gives guidance regarding the dairy business. Seven co-operative irrigation societies provide water to the farmers from cooperative wells. The *Mahila Sarvage Utkarsh Mandal* attends the welfare needs of women.

In 1991, Hazare launched the *Bhrashtachar Virodhi Jan Aandolan* (BVJA) (People's Movement against Corruption), a popular movement to fight against corruption in Ralegan Siddhi. In the same year he protested against the collusion between 40 forest officials and timber merchants. This protest resulted in the transfer and suspension of these officials.

In May 1997, Hazare protested against alleged malpractice in the purchase of powerlooms by the *Vasantrao Naik Bhathya Vimukt Jamati Vikas Manch* and the *Mahatma Phule Magasvargiya Vikas Mandal*. These institutions were directly under the charge of the then Maharashtra Social Welfare Minister Babanrao Gholap of the Shiv Sena. Their managing committees were dissolved after the Shiv Sena-Bhartiya Janata Party government came to power in the state in 1995.

Hazare also raised the issue of an alleged massive land purchase by Gholap's wife Shashikala in Nashik between April and September 1996. He forwarded the available documentary evidence to the then Maharashtra Governor P.C. Alexander. On 4 November 1997, Gholap filed a defamation suit against Hazare for accusing him of corruption. He was arrested in April 1998 and was released on a personal bond of ₹ 5,000.

On 9 September 1998, Hazare was imprisoned in the Yerawada Jail to serve a three months sentence mandated by the Mumbai Metropolitan Court. The sentencing came as a huge shock at that time to all social activists. Leaders of all political parties except the BJP and the Shiv Sena came in support of him. Later, due to public protests, the Government of Maharashtra ordered his release from the jail. After release, Hazare wrote a letter to then chief minister Manohar Joshi demanding Gholap's removal for his role in alleged malpractice in the Awami Merchant Bank. Gholap resigned from the cabinet on 27 April 1999.

In 2003, Hazare raised corruption charges against four NCP ministers of the Congress-NCP government. He started his 'fast unto death' on 9 August 2003. He ended his fast on 17 August 2003 after the then chief minister Sushil Kumar Shinde formed a one-man commission headed by the retired justice P.B. Sawant to probe his charges. The P.B. Sawant commission report, submitted on 23rd February 2005, indicted Sureshdada Jain, Nawab Malik, and Padmasinh Patil.

The report exonerated Vijaykumar Gavit. The report also indicted Hazare for corruption for the use of ₹ 2.20 lakh of funds from the *Hind Swaraj Trust*, which he heads, for his birthday celebrations, in spite of a subsequent donation of

₹ 2.48 lakh by industrialist Abhay Firodia to the trust for that purpose. Suresh Jain and Nawab Malik resigned from the cabinet in March 2005.

In the early 2000s Hazare led a movement in Maharashtra State which forced the state government to pass a stronger Maharashtra Right to Information Act. This Act was later considered as the base document for the Right to Information Act 2005 (RTI), enacted by the Union Government. It also ensured that the President of India assented to this new Act. Law professor Alasdair Scott Roberts said: The state of Maharashtra —home to one of the world's largest cities, Mumbai, adopted a Right to Information Act in 2003, prodded by the hunger strike of prominent activist, Anna Hazare ("All corruption can end only if there is freedom of information", said Hazare, who resumed his strike in February 2004 to push for better enforcement of the Act).

On 20 July 2006 the Union Cabinet amended the Right to Information Act, 2005 to exclude the file noting by the government officials from its purview. Hazare began his 'fast unto death' on 9 August 2006 in Alandi against the proposed amendment. He ended his fast on 19 August 2006, after the government agreed to change its earlier decision.

Awards given to Anna Hazare

2011 – Rabindranath Tagore International Peace Prize, awarded by the Indian Institute of Planning and Management.

2008 – On 15 April 2008 Hazare received the World Bank's 2008 Jit Gill Memorial Award for Outstanding Public Service: "Hazare created a thriving model village in Ralegan Siddhi, in the impoverished Ahmednagar region of Maharashtra State, and championed the right to information and the fight against corruption."

1992 – Padma Bhushan award, by the Government of India.

1990 – Padma Shri award, by the Government of India.

1989 – Krishi Bhushana award by the Government of Maharashtra.

1986 – Indira Priyadarshini Vrikshamitra award by the Government of India on 19 November 1986 from the hands of Prime Minister of India Rajiv Gandhi.

Ahmednagar Municipal Corporation felicitated Anna Hazare on 15 January 1987 and by the Pune Municipal Corporation.

Anna Hazare's hunger strike at Jantar Mantar in Delhi

On 5 April 2011, Hazare initiated a movement for passing a stronger anti-corruption Lokpal (Ombudsman) bill. He began a fast unto death from 5 April 2011 at Jantar Mantar in Delhi to exert pressure on the government. His fast, his strength, his will, and above all the flawless logic behind his actions, were the qualities that were responsible for Anna Hazare's popularity, so much so that a pamphlet highlighting his mission gave him the title of Mahatma.

Along with members of the India Against Corruption movement, former justice of the Supreme Court of India and Lokayukta of Karnataka N. Santosh Hegde and Prashant Bhushan, a senior lawyer in the Supreme Court, had drafted an alternate bill called the Jan Lokpal Bill 2010 (People's Ombudsman Bill). This bill provides more stringent provisions and wider powers to the Lokpal (Ombudsman). The fast led to nationwide protests in support of Hazare.

The Prime Minister of India Manmohan Singh rejected his demand. Anna Hazare stated, "I will fast until Jan Lokpal Bill is passed." He pressed for the demand to form a joint committee of the representatives of the Government and the civil society to draft a new bill with stronger penal actions and more independence to the *Lokpal* and *Lokayukta*s (Ombudsmen in the States).

The movement attracted attention in the media, and thousands of supporters. Almost 150 people reportedly joined Hazare in his fast. He said that he would not allow any politician to sit with him in this movement. Politicians like Uma Bharti and Om Prakash Chautala were driven away by protesters when they came to visit the site where the protest was taking place. Social activists, including Medha Patkar, Arvind Kejriwal, former IPS officer Kiran Bedi, and Jayaprakash Narayan lent their support to Hazare's hunger strike and anti-corruption campaign.

People have shown support in Internet social media such as Twitter and Facebook. In addition to spiritual leaders Sri Sri Ravi Shankar, Swami Ramdev, Swami Agnivesh and former Indian cricketer Kapil Dev, many celebrities showed their public support through Twitter.

The movement gathered significant support from India's youth, visible through the local support and on social networking sites like Facebook and Twitter. There have also been protests in Bangalore, Mumbai, Chennai, Ahmedabad, Guwahati, Shillong, and Aizawl, among other cities of India.

Anna Hazare doesn't look like the tough he talks about. He is short stature, moves slowly and talks softly. Dressed in a white dhoti-kurta, a Gandhi cap on his head, Hazare sits cross-legged on the stage. Resting on a pile of white cushions, he surveys the crowd that has gathered at the site of his fast at Jantar Mantar in the national capital. Sometimes he claps his hands, joining the drumbeat of supporters singing revolutionary songs. Sometimes, he takes quick gulps of water from a steel glass offered by an attendant. Then as the sun climbs higher, he lies down, trying to sleep even as crowds swarm the stage from where he is challenging the government.

Due to Anna Hazare's movement against corruption, Agriculture minister Sharad Pawar had to resign on 6 April 2011 from the sub-committee of ministers preparing the draft of Lokpal Bill. So he became an eyesore for his party. In the past also the party of Sharad Pawar suffered the maximum loss due to Hazare. The three Cabinet Ministers Sureshdada Jain, Nawab Malik and Dr. Vijay Kumar Gavit of his party had to resign from the ministry. Such has been the character of Hazare. He had been constantly fighting against injustice and corruption [*Dainik Jagran* (Hindi) dated 9th April 2011].

Anna Hazare is a Gandhian with a difference. He is more like a street fighter. He is not scared of taking on anyone because he believes his cause is just. And he is a man of many causes. At Jantar Mantar, groups of farmers from Maharashtra talk of him as a hero. For them he is a living legend. All his actions—the fight against the liquor Mafia; the battle against corruption in government offices; the crusade for a Right to Information Act in Maharashtra; the campaign against the Mumbai underworld —have become the stuff of legend. And now he has many new converts in his fight against corruption. "I read somewhere that corruption is a middle class fad. That's wrong. The worst victims of corruption in India are the poor. My fight is for the people living in the countryside who have to pay bribes to get what is legally due to them" says Hazare. "I will continue to fight for the people".

"Look at this man. From which angle does he look like a fascist? He is 71 and on hunger strike to fight corruption and the politicians are calling him a fascist and a blackmailer. When politicians, cutting across party line, speak the same language, we have to be careful", says Ramesh Sharma, a social activist. He has been camping at Jantar Mantar since April 5, when Hazare began his fast unto death to force the government to accept civil society's recommendations on the Lokpal bill.

Indeed politicians have been talking much the same language. Congress spokesman Manish Tiwari said that Hazare had no locus standi on the issue. Mohan Singh of the Samajwadi Party accused him of employing "fascist tactics" and the Rashtriya Janta Dal's Raghuvansh Prasad Singh poured vitriol on him for "dictating" terms to the government.

Janata Party president Subramanian Swamy extends his "active support" to Hazare. Ravnish Singh, a jobless schoolteacher from Haryana, sees "hope for the country" in him. Student Shruti Khanna gets "inspiration from him to do something for the country". Housewife Malti Rana from Faridabad feels as if "Gandhiji has come back to give us independence from the corrupt politicians".

Today he is anna or elder brother for much of India. Every time a politician opens his mouth against Hazare, he gets a few hundred new followers, thousands of Facebook pages get updated and millions show their support for the man who has become a symbol of the fight against corruption. Bollywood actor Anupam Kher calls him a "selfless man who is risking his life for the sake of the nation".

"There is a lot of anger among the people and they don't know how to express it. Suddenly they see an old man fasting to death not for any personal gain and they rally around him", says an IAS officer who walked by Jantar Mantar to soak in the atmosphere. The officer, who doesn't want to be named for obvious reasons, adds, "the government miscalculated the impact of his fast. In this country a selfless act of sacrifice can pull a lot of people".

Simplicity is Anna Hazare's greatest attraction. Integrity is another major factor that distinguishes him from other public figures. "They call him names now but Raghuvansh Prasad and Mohan Singh have done nothing to fight corruption. Being honest personally is not enough, they are members of parties which are synonymous with corruption", says Ramesh Sharma, the social activist. "Lobbyists, arms dealers and political fixers can influence the government policy but there is no place for an old Gandhian in this system."

Hazare has been an activist for 40 years, but has never touched hearts and minds in the way he did during his hunger strike for the Jan Lokpal Bill. In a matter of five days, Anna Hazare has become a much larger figure than when he arrived in Delhi on April 2. Now, with the Lokpal Bill issue settled for the moment, the fighter in Anna Hazare must surely be looking for his next big cause (*The Times of India* dated 10th April 2011).

When asked, if his fast didn't amount to blackmailing the government, he said, "Yes, so? As long as I'm alive and as long as it benefits the people, I'll keep blackmailing the government. What's the problem? In 63 years, so many have been elected to Parliament, but they haven't understood one basic thing, the people are the masters and the representatives are their servants".

When asked if he thought an empowered Lokpal will end corruption, he said, "No, but it will certainly put the brakes on corruption to a great extent. Decentralization is going to be my big area of focus. We focused on the Lok Sabha and the Vidhan Sabha but completely omitted the Gram Sabha. In fact, that's where the real power should lie" (*The Times of India* dated 18th April 2011).

Anna Hazare has found support from an unlikely quarter, the Maoists. The CPI (Maoist) central committee has issued a statement dated 13th April 2011 in support of Hazare's recent movement against corruption, calling for "intensifying mass struggle to put an end to institutionalized corruption" (*The Times of India* dated 18th April 2011).

It was an experience not to be missed. Like any other ordinary citizen, concerned over the rampant corruption in Indian political and social system, I too could not resist the magnetic pull of Gandhian Anna Hazare. I went to see and hear him on the Jan Lokpal issue over which he had staged fast-unto-death.

It was an experience one could have had only during the freedom struggle or during the JP movement. Since I did not have the privilege to be a party to either of the two, I e-mailed to some of my friends: "If you have missed the Anna Hazare crusade, you have missed a chance to understand what a movement is!"

Thousands of people, so dedicated to the cause of rooting out corruption from the fabric of Indian society endured the heat and dust of Delhi near the historic Jantar Mantar. There were groups within groups, spearheading the movement; and were very clear that *"Dil kya cheez hai, jaan bhi denge hum desh ke liye*. They had full conviction in Hazare and were ready to sacrifice their lives. The sweet smell of success was in the air."

An old lady, 97, had come all the way from Haridwar, and she was excited at being a part of the movement. A frail, old man, in his 90s, a former freedom fighter, said that it was his "second fight for freedom from the cancer of corruption". One can't understand their feelings and their zeal for a cause until one is face-to-face with him. Their cause was so great that they felt that even if they had to sacrifice their lives, it would be "too small and insignificant".

But they were convinced that their sacrifice will "keep the candle of emotion, conviction and truth burning" to lead the future generations. Just as they followed the Gandhian ways of Puran Swaraj movement, they were convinced that the young would follow them tomorrow to guide the country on the right path.

All this made one realize the power and the significance of the saying that faith moves mountains and that nothing is impossible if one is bent upon doing it (By P.P. Wangchuk, *HT* dated 14th April 2011).

On 8 April 2011 the Government of India accepted all demands of the movement. The government issued a gazette notification on the formation of a joint committee (of government and civil society representatives) to draft an effective Lokpal Bill. The fast ended on 9 April 2011. Hazare first offered lemon juice to some of his supporters who were fasting with him. Hazare then broke his fast by taking some lemon juice. He addressed the people and set a deadline of 15 August 2011 to pass the Lokpal Bill in the Indian Parliament.

Today Anna Hazare is a symbol of the fight against corruption, of which virtually every citizen in this country is a victim. Anna has touched the nerve of the people.

13

India Fights Corruption

War on Corruption
(*HT* dated 9th April 2011)

India has provided institutions like Central Information Commission, Central Vigilance Commission, and Central Bureau of Investigation and Ombudsman at state level for redress of public grievances. But these institutions do not have powers to make independent inquiries against politicians and bureaucrats and punish them. So these institutions are without a force (toothless) and have not proved effective.

To make them effective powers must be given to these institutions to hold independent inquiries after they are satisfied that *prima facie* there is a case of corruption against the person both in public and private sectors, irrespective of his position.

Powers must be given to them for confiscation of property and other punishment.

Observing that the "growing corruption" at the national level is rattling the common man at present, the Bihar unit of BJP on April 3rd said that it would launch a statewide agitation on the issue from April 6 next (*HT* dated 4th April 2011).

The Lokayuktas (anti-corruption ombudsmen) of 17 states have opposed the already embattled government's draft Lokpal Bill, 2010, saying that the proposed multimember body will have an adverse effect on the functioning of the institution. The committee of Lokayuktas has pointed out that the proposal in the draft bill to have a three-member Lokpal, which is likely to be followed in the states, "would substantially" alter the character of the institution, leading to reduction in the effectiveness to tackle corruption (*HT* dated 8th April 2011).

Veteran social activist Anna Hazare announced that he would sit on dharna in Delhi against corruption and the people gave their full support to this whistle blower against corruption. He began a fast unto death at Jantar Mantar, New Delhi on 5th April 2011 demanding enactment of a comprehensive Lokpal (Ombudsman) Bill to give wider powers to Ombudsman to check corruption. But the government was not in a mood to give powers to Ombudsman to inquire and punish the guilty independently. Shri Anna Hazare requested the Prime Minister to convene a joint committee to frame the proposed law, which request the PM rejected (*HT* dated 6th April 2011).

A group of entrepreneurs sitting in their office went through a brain storming discussion in their bid to formulate strategy to extend their support to this cause. "We have decided to invite people to light candles at Baccha Park, Meerut, UP to burn the demon of corruption", said Vivek Garg of Tanya Automobile, who has been spearheading 'light a candle campaign' along with his colleagues Pankaj Gupta, Sanjeev and Arun Hazela, all associated with Indian Industries Association. "We have invited people from different walks of society, including media persons, to join hands in the fight against corruption", said Sanjeev as his other colleagues summed up their endeavour with a slogan "India Fights Corruption".

The IIMT group has also been working relentlessly to register its anger against corruption in the form of a signature campaign. "Around 10,000 students, their faculties and other staff of IIMT family signed the charter against corruption, which they would hand over to the district magistrate on April 5", said Yogesh Mohan, chairman of the IIMT Group of Industries. Following his directions, Directors of the group propagated the message to the faculties of different courses who briefed students. Supporting the campaign of Hazare, the charter reads, "IIMT Group of Colleges, starts a signature campaign, a small effort from them all to be a part and parcel of the 'hunger strike' by Hazare. We the students and staff of IIMT family altogether stand upright against the 'corruption bug' that is prevalent in every nook and corner of Indian society." Some people are even planning to extend their support to Hazare in Delhi.

There is only one issue sticking in people's minds and it is corruption. From the time of 2010 Commonwealth Games scam to the 2-G telecom scam, the public faith in government institutions is now at an all-time low level. The sub-committee formed by government to draft the Lokpal Bill is headed by Defence Minister A.K. Antony, also has Agriculture Minister Sharad Pawar and Law Minister M. Veerappa Moily as members. Moily said that the government did not say no to the demand for a joint committee to draft the Bill after the sub-committee held discussions with representatives of Hazare and other members of civil society.

Arvind Kejriwal activist has questioned the credibility of the members. "The government says that its committee will draft the bill—who are in the committee? Sharad Pawar who has been involved in land scams in Maharashtra; Moily, who drafted this weak legislation; or Kapil Sibal, who does not see any corruption in the 2-G scam." The Jan Lokpal Bill calls for the setting up of Ombudsman—a Lokpal at the Centre and Lokayuktas in states—independent of government control to look into cases of corruption in public life (*HT* dated 7th April 2011).

Civil society activists and youth leaders representing various voluntary organizations staged a protest at Shaheed Samarak

Park, Agra, on 6 April 2011 in support of Anna Hazare, who was on a fast-unto-death in Delhi to press for a tougher anti-corruption law, viz. Lokpal Bill. They came from all quarters and from all sections of the society. The issue of corruption raised by Hazare touched one and all. They all were of the opinion that a severe punishment should be provided in the Bill to create a fear in the public about corruption.

On the day of the fast, thousands came forward in support of his crusade. "This is democracy and they want people's participation in drafting the Bill, i.e. 50 per cent from civil society and 50 per cent from the government", Anna Hazare said (*HT* dated 7th April 2011). The Union government began negotiations with the representatives of social activist Anna Hazare, and even agreed to some of their demands.

Prime Minister Manmohan Singh deputed Union Minister Kapil Sibal for talks with the social activists. After the first round of talks, both parties stuck to their proposals and demands but later ironed out some of the differences. While the government said that it would set up an informal joint committee for drafting the Lokpal Bill, Shri Hazare was demanding that it be officially notified to ensure its legal validity. Similarly, there was also no consensus on who will head the committee.

While the government wanted Finance Minister Pranab Mukherjee to lead the committee, the activists wanted Shri Hazare to head it. However, the two negotiators later said that a retired Supreme Court Judge should head the committee. After the meeting Shri Sibal said that they could evolve a procedure with which they can move ahead. He also said that the government was ready to form a joint committee immediately, comprising five members from the government and the civil society each, and also introduce the Lokpal Bill in the monsoon session of Parliament (*Hindu* dated 8th April 2011).

As support to the agitation by veteran social activist Anna Hazare in favour of Jan Lokpal Bill gathered momentum, Mrs. Sonia Gandhi, the UPA chairperson and Congress President, appealed to Shri Hazare to give up his fast and assured him that his views would receive the government's full attention. Without getting into the nitty-gritty of the demands of the followers of Shri Hazare on setting up a Lokpal institution, she also said that there could be no two opinions on the urgent necessity of combating graft and corruption. I believe that the laws in these matters must be effective and must deliver the desired results as we move forward to fight this menace.

The nature of support extended by the Opposition parties to Mr. Hazare's agitation was also generic. They are neither endorsing the version of the Bill proposed by Mr. Hazare nor getting into the specific demand for a government/civic society joint committee to work on the draft Bill.

In response to questions of a news conference here on whether his party backed the Lokpal Bill put forth by Mr. Hazare, BJP spokesman said that they agree with the sentiments and cause. Asked about reported statement of Mr. Hazare that he and his supporters had lost faith in political parties, the spokesman contended that the BJP did not agree with all the views of the veteran activist. In fact the BJP Party itself wanted to start an agitation on this issue. But due to the agitation of Shri Hazare it had to abandon or pend its programme.

The Communist Party of India (Marxist) on April 7 backed the move for an effective Lokpal Bill suggesting that the government set up a mechanism to consult all parties, social activists and concerned citizens groups to finalize a new draft legislation. In a statement, the party Polit Bureau said that the need for an effective Lokpal legislation assumed importance in the backdrop of the spate of corruption scandals and Mr. Hazare's fast highlighting this need.

The party was advocating the setting up of a strong Lokpal authority to look into complaints of corruption against public servants and government officials. The efforts to bring about such legislation did not make headway in the past. The draft proposed by the government of India is inadequate and will not serve the purpose (*Hindu* dated 8th April 2011).

Anna's fight became a mass crusade. A large number of students turned up on April 8 to support Anna Hazare's campaign against corruption in Agra. They took to the streets, staged plays and resolved to fight against corruption. Besides, lawyers also took out a 'Prabhat Pheri' to extend their support to the cause. Large groups of people, especially youngsters, were seen heading towards Shaheed Smarak, which saw only a handful of people supporting the cause two days back. However, the night on April 7 witnessed the strength of people as they collected to participate in the candle march to support Anna Hazare. Freedom fighter Rani Saroj Gaurihar led the candle march and hundreds followed.

The mood was similar on April 8 as students raised slogans and held banners against corruption. Besides, Lalit Kala Sansthan staged street plays all over city to raise awareness about corruption. A large turnout of people was also seen in front of Sri Gandhi Khadi Ashram at Sanjay Place where veteran Gandhian Krishna Chandra Sahai came despite his illness. He also participated in the day long fast and supported the cause. Mahant Yogesh Puri from Man Kameshwar Temple and Qazi Sayyad Mohd Sabir also joined the mass movement against corruption. "We have organized a daylong fast and are committed to fight against corruption", said Harish Chimti, conducting the meet.

During namaz on April 8 at Jama Masjid, people offered prayers for Anna Hazare's long life and extended full support to the cause raised by him. The Shahi Imam led the prayer and hundreds offered prayers at the historical mosque of Agra. Meanwhile, in Aligarh also a number of people came forward to support the cause. While some groups organized candle marches, others observed fasts.

Activists of various organizations staged demonstrations and observed a fast at the district magistrate's office on April 8. Doctors, teachers, members of the Manav Upkar Vyapar Mandal, Bharat Vikas Parishad, and Bar Association observed day long fast to express their solidarity. Besides, the Association of Private Doctors also started a signature campaign to gather more support for Hazare. A silent dharna was also staged in Jama Masjid at Upper Kot under the auspices of NGO Lata Gramudyog. Hundreds of students gathered at Ganesh Shanker Vidyarthi Statute on April 8 morning and marched up to the clock tower with candles.

Like a chain reaction Anna Hazare's campaign is engulfing the entire nation and people have taken to the streets to express their solidarity for the veteran social activist. Similar demonstrations were held in other cities like Dehradun, Hapur, Ghaziabad, Shillong, etc. In Dehradun Bahuguna staged a dharna in support of Anna Hazare's campaign. In Shillong teachers and students of the premier North Eastern Hill University held a demonstration in favour of a strong Lokpal Bill. Himachal Pradesh government promised to bring an Anti-graft Bill in the next assembly session providing for confiscation of wealth amassed through corrupt means. Bihar State government has already passed such legislation.

It may be mentioned that officials of AMUSU reached Jantar Mantar in Delhi and extended their support to the campaign on April 7 (*HT* dated 9th April 2011). Lending his full support to Anna Hazare campaign, Bihar CM Nitish Kumar said, "I have full support to Anna Hazare for his campaign against corruption —it is the manifestation of people's pledge against corruption. There is widespread resentment, indignation and discontent brewing in the people's mind against corruption." Battling against the allegations of corruption, Karnataka Chief Minister B.S. Yeddyurappa extended support to Anna Hazare, saying, "Time has come for enactment of such a legislation to eradicate corruption in the country." Yeddyurappa, facing charges in a land scam, demanded that the Centre take immediate steps to bring in the Anti-corruption law (*The Times of India* dated 9th April 2011).

A demo of democracy is on. It is exciting to even imagine how, after a long download, the full version will look and feel like. After 26/11, we had seen protests and candlelight vigils by citizens. But the anger was directed mainly at faceless enemies, and the demand was for an action that fell in the shadowy zone between war and tough diplomacy. This time around, the enemy is clear, corrupt politicians. The immediate goal can be held between fingers: revised pages of the Lokpal Bill.

From the gathering avalanche of tweets, Facebook posts, online signatures and even ground support for Anna Hazare, it is evident that the government will concede a lot of ground on the Bill, and soon. Even the un-embarrassable politicians, who make money from even the smallest of drain or road contracts in the country, seem embarrassed this time.

The real concern, however, lies in the afterlife of the Bill. Will this spontaneous movement, helped by Twitter, Facebook, news channels and other children of information technology, get washed away when work, kitchen, child's school fees rush in? Is the inert-to-intrepid Middle India prepared for the long haul of revolution?

The Bill will not magically erase corruption. Rivers of rot run deep in this country. If this is to be the watershed moment of our democracy, we need a long organized and determined citizens' movement that looks beyond the shrill thrill of protest and its likely success. The process has to begin with the T, and go on to three 'Ts': involvement, information and implementation.

Frankly, it is comfortable to be cynical and say all this will fizzle out, Utopia does not exist. But if we aim for Utopia, we might end up at least a few miles closer to it. The time has come to make up our minds on how we can contribute beyond our tiny, selfish worlds.

There is a tough job ahead. If we take it up, homemakers, writers, businessmen, policemen, soldiers, marketing professionals, accountants, technicians, road makers, and artists—all will be needed (By Abhijit Majumder, *HT* dated 9th April 2011).

Could India go the way of Tunisia and Egypt? The very thought was dismissed during the Jasmine Revolution because India is different. It is a working democracy whose citizens own the nation and can let off steam through protest. And yet, here is our Tunisia moment. India was actually a boiler fit to burst, and Anna Hazare just had to touch the valve to set it off. We share two crucial features with the citizens of the North African nations. The first is disgust at the careless greed of oligarchies, which rule our lives and the second is the impatience at being held hostage by a culture of corruption that democracy has failed to address.

In fact, illicit funding of elections is one of its sources. So now, 'blackmail' is going to solve a problem that four decades of protest, media activism and legal action could not. As his detractors have said, Hazare's fast amounts to blackmail. But in desperate times, when all other options have been exhausted, moral coercion becomes a valid political act. Now, even if the government keeps stonewalling, the movement has gathered the critical mass to keep going and force a change.

But the quality of this change remains to be decided by us. The Jan Lokpal Bill proposed by Hazare and his associates is far better than the government's Lokpal Bill, which is so much toothless that you would like to hand over some dentures to it. But it remains a work in progress and the concerned citizens' duty is to read it (at www.annahazare.org) (chapters 14 & 15) and suggest improvements. This will be a landmark legislation, the first to be publicly debated and drafted by the people and by their elected representatives. When it is tabled in Parliament, it must set a benchmark in perfection (By Pratik Kanjilal, *HT* dated 9th April 2011).

There is a strong likelihood of agreement between government and Anna Hazare on a set of demands related to Lokpal Bill. There are indications that of the two outstanding issues, government is likely to agree to issue a notification about the setting up of a joint committee. The government is still reluctant on agreeing to the other demand that Hazare should head the joint committee. Hazare himself said that at the most, he could be an advisor or member of the committee. Sonia Gandhi having backed the public outcry over Lokpal Bill, there is a strong possibility that April 8 could see a solution.

On April 7, two rounds of negotiations between HRD Minister Kapil Sibal and Swami Agnivesh and Arvind Kejriwal resulted in government agreeing to the demand for a joint committee with 50:50 representatives of civil society and the government. The government is also veering around to accepting activists' demand for a fixed timeline to finalize the Lokpal Bill.

After the first round of negotiations, government offered to set up an informal joint committee. But Hazare's representatives rejected it. Hazare said that it was not acceptable and he would continue his fast unto death. The activists cited the case of Maharashtra to argue that the government could notify even committees consisting of civil society members. Both sides struck a conciliatory note. Sibal said, "We had two rounds of discussions. We have agreed on almost all issues but there is no agreement on two issues, that is issuing an official notification to form the committee and making Hazare chairman of the committee" (*The Times of India* dated 9th April 2011).

The stalemate over the campaign for an effective Lokpal Bill deepened on April 8 with the government rejecting Anna Hazare's two crucial demands on the joint committee while the Gandhian announced "jail bharo" protest from April 13 across the country. Earlier in the day, Hazare and supporters made it clear that they were not jockeying for posts and would want former chief justice of India J.S. Verma or retired Supreme Court Judge Santosh Hegde to be the chairman of the draft committee. Congress president Sonia Gandhi, who had on April 7 appealed to Hazare to end the fast, met Prime Minister Manmohan Singh on April 8 and discussed the stalemate between the two sides. Senior ministers Pranab Mukherjee, Sibal and Gandhi's political secretary Ahmed Patel were also present. After the meeting, sources said the government was ready to negotiate. Mukherjee appealed to Hazare to end his fast and join the committee for drafting the Bill.

With talks between the government and Anna Hazare still stuck on the issue of the latter being named the chief and formal notification of the consultation committee, the prime minister stepped up efforts by meeting President Pratibha Patil and Congress chief Sonia Gandhi on the issue.

Prime Minister Manmohan Singh, who held discussions with Sonia, her political secretary Ahmed Patel, HRD minister Kapil Sibal and finance minister Pranab Mukherjee earlier in the day held a second round of deliberations with senior ministers. Minority affairs minister Salman Khurshid, Sibal, Mukherjee and law minister Veerappa Moily met the Prime Minister at his official residence. So far Sibal had been holding discussions with Hazare's emissaries—Swami Agnivesh and Arvind Khejriwal.

In the evening, Hazare said that he had suggested co-chairpersons for the joint committee on drafting the Bill and said that he would be part of the committee to keep up the pressure on government. Swami Agnivesh, Kiran Bedi and Arvind Kejriwal, who have been part of the campaign, were at Sibal's house for a third round of discussions (*The Times of India* dated 9th April 2011).

As Hazare, 71, ended his hunger strike on 9th April 2011, so did hundreds of other crusaders who had also undertaken the fast unto-death for a Lokpal (Ombudsman) bill with more teeth to battle corruption in public life. It was 10.52 a.m., a historical moment they said, that would go down in posterity as the end of the most spontaneous and powerful people's mobilization since independence, one that had nothing to do with politicians or politics.

The diminutive, bespectacled man sipped from a glass of juice and cheers resonated across the vast expanse that is India. Anna Hazare had broken his 97-hour fast, marking the culmination of an unparalleled people's movement against corruption that saw the government promise a more powerful anti-graft bill in the next session of parliament.

Hazare, who began his fast on the morning of April 5, congratulated the people for the success of the movement that saw Prime Minister Manmohan Singh issue a statement promising that the Lokpal Bill would be introduced this July. Terming the movement a second freedom struggle, he said the system had to be changed. "We have got a lot of strength from the people", said the former soldier. "I have broken the fast today because the government has agreed to our demand by issuing this order", he said, triumphantly flashing the gazette notifying the formation of a 10-member panel that would draft a stringent Lokpal Bill to combat corruption in high places.

"The fact that civil society and government have joined hands to evolve a consensus to move this historic legislation augurs well for our democracy. I am pleased that Anna Hazare has agreed to give up his fast", the Prime Minister said in a statement. "This is a scourge that confronts all of us." According to the notification—a point the government was reluctant to agree to but gave in as the civil society leaders insisted on it—the drafting committee of the Lokpal bill would comprise five ministers and five nominees of Hazare, including himself. It is expected to complete its task by June 30.

The five ministers are Pranab Mukherjee, P. Chidambaram, M. Veerappa Moily, Kapil Sibal and Salman Khursheed. The civil society members are Anna Hazare, N. Santosh Hegde former Supreme Court Judge, Shanti Bhushan advocate, Prashant Bhushan advocate, and activist Arvind Kejriwal. The representative of the committee of Lokayuktas should also be made a member of this committee to tell them their experiences and the difficulties being faced by them.

The chairperson of the committee is finance minister Mukherjee, co-chair Shanti Bhushan and the convenor, law minister Moily. Shanti Bhushan, former law minister, said he expected the proposed Lokpal Bill to be passed unanimously by both the houses of parliament. He added that all strata of society were worried about graft, "whether it is small or big like the 2-G spectrum scam". While experts sorted out the legalities, there was exultation in India. It was an emotive moment for the many thousands of unlikely activists who said they had been pulled into the movement because of the ideal of a clean India.

There was the public anger and the political risk ahead of polls. The government just could not afford to be seen on the wrong side of this debate. The mood could be sliced with a knife as images of swelling crowds at Jantar Mantar and copycat demonstrations in other cities flashed on TVs in ministerial offices.

Cries of "*bhrashtachar nahi chalega* (Corruption will not be tolerated)" pushed up anxiety levels and senior figures in the government mulled the damaging fallout of being seen as unresponsive to popular rage. The Lokpal Bill symbolized a rising anger about graft.

"It is not the specifics of the bill, but frustration about the political class being corrupt and governance maladies from broken roads to price rise that is spilling out", conceded a political source. Anna Hazare's fast provided the spark that set off a fire.

This is hardly what Congress wants in a poll session despite some harsh words, with which the party spokespersons used to attack civil society activists. But the contempt for Hazare's group soon gave way to circumspection and even deference as the anti-graft mood came to a boil.

The government's response, felt many in the party, was too wooden and mired on legal technicalities like a professed fear of setting a precedent by issuing a notification or government order on a joint committee of activists and ministers to draft the Lokpal Bill. This was despite several notifications regularly issued for panels that include non-officials.

The need of the hour was for a political response. The meeting of the Cabinet on April 6 provided a reckoner for the government with ministers pointing out that the stir ought not to be allowed to linger. There was also the danger of it being hijacked by elements not interested in a resolution. The discussions ended with a stringent gag order not to divulge the debate in the Cabinet.

Congress chief Sonia Gandhi's intervention a day later intended to prod the government to get moving. It delivered a political touch that the government's stiff response is lacking. Surprisingly, the government needed more time to negotiate the demand that an activist should head the panel but the political impetus began to work.

A meeting at Prime Minister Manmohan Singh's residence on April 8 morning attended by Finance Minister Pranab Mukherjee, Defence Minister A.K. Antony and of course Sonia set the ball rolling. Crisis management moved beyond Telecom Minister Kapil Sibal with Health Minister Ghulam Nabi Azad, Minority affairs minister Salman Khurshid and Parliamentary affairs minister P.K. Bansal being roped in. The government then virtually capitulated before Hazare's demands (*The Times of India* dated 10th April 2011).

If banners at the site of the fast are anything to go by, the personal probity for the PM was no comfort. Anna Hazare may have mentioned several times that he was not aware of any instance of personal corruption on the part of PM Manmohan Singh. But his image as an honest man, who just happens to head a corrupt government, does not seem to be cutting much ice with the common man any more.

SMSs asking why youth icon Rahul Gandhi was missing in action when the young are thronging Jantar Mantar to make protests, the answer is that he has been taking the rounds since April 8 morning (By Abantika Ghosh, *The Times of India* dated 10th April 2011).

After the formation of the joint panel, Prime Minister Manmohan Singh said that his government intended to introduce the historic legislation in the monsoon session of Parliament. What if the ministers and society representatives on the panel don't reach a consensus? Let's keep our fingers crossed. But if it happens, it would be yet another milestone for Indian democracy (*HT* dated 10th April 2011).

Democracy is a government of the people and for the people. The people are both the rulers and the ruled. The people of India have now realized that the executive has become a part of those who are indulging in corruption and are looting the public exchequer. They also have found that there is no mechanism to punish the corrupt both fast and severely to eradicate or control corruption. The executive was not taking any interest in framing any such law.

The law 'The Lokpal Bill 2010' framed by them excluded the Bureaucrats without whose connivance no corruption can take place in India. To punish the politicians, sanction of the speaker of Lok Sabha or of the chairperson of Rajya Sabha is compulsory. In such a situation the people used their right of peaceful agitation. They demanded that the government should redraft the law 'The Lokpal Bill 2010'. They also provided to the government a draft of the said bill framed by their experts and demanded that their five members be co-opted in the panel for drafting.

The agitation spread to the whole of India like wild fire under the leadership of Anna Hazare. Within five days the government accepted all their demands. The government is fully competent to seek the help of any expert in drafting a bill. The bill has to be passed by both houses of parliament. If the bill is not passed by the parliament the political parties fully know that they may suffer in the next election.

The first meeting of the joint committee to redraft the Lokpal Bill took place on 16th April 2011 in the room of the Finance Minister Pranab Mukerjee, the chairman of the committee. It was attended by Union ministers P. Chidambaram, Kapil Sibal, M. Veerappa Moily, and Salman Khurshid and Anna Hazare, Arvind Kejriwal, Santosh Hegde, Shanti Bhushan and Prashant Bhushan from the civil society. The government agreed to audio-record all the meetings and hold public consultations before a final draft of the anti-graft law is prepared.

Joint Committee Meeting

The Chief Justice of India S.H. Kapadia at the fifth M.C. Setalvad memorial lecture said that there was a need for "clean men in black robes" and asked the political class not to protect corrupt judges.

Acknowledging that the people will not tolerate the prevailing state of affairs, Prime Minister Manmohan Singh on 21 April 2011 pledged swift and exemplary action to deal with corruption. To do this, he took a number of steps.

He had told IAS, IPS, IFS and other senior bureaucrats that there is a growing feeling in the people that our laws, systems and procedures are not effective in dealing with corruption. We must recognize that there is little public tolerance now for the prevailing state of affairs. Mr. Singh also said that the government hopes to introduce the Lokpal Bill during the monsoon session of Parliament (*HT* dated 22nd April 2011).

It is far easier to punish the corrupt than to wipe out corruption. The former provides a strong, unwavering disincentive to be dishonest, while the latter is a noble wish and nothing else. A more unbiased party has nudged the UPA government hard into action: the Indian public.

A batch of Public Interest Litigation were filed in the Supreme Court challenging constitutional validity of the notification on the composition of the committee to draft the Jan Lokpal Bill. On 29 April 2011 the Supreme Court refused to go into it saying that the petitions were premature and can't be taken for hearing as the Lokpal Bill was yet to be passed. It is still not the law and some of the views in the petition are untenable in law (*HT* dated 30th April 2011).

In a gathering at St Francis College, Lucknow social activist Arvind Kejriwal has said on 1 May 2011 that if the Lokpal Bill is not passed by Parliament a similar agitation like that of April 5 would be started. He also said that the issue of bringing all the anti-corruption bodies, including the state vigilance commissions and central vigilance commissions under the ambit of Lokpal would also be taken up in the meetings to follow (*HT* dated 3rd May 2011).

The meeting of the drafting committee was held on 23 May 2011. It was agreed that assets obtained through corrupt means would be confiscated to make good the loss to the exchequer. In case of a complaint of corruption, the Lokpal can order an "interdiction", that is an order preventing the public servant from transferring any asset. At the conclusion of the investigation, if the person is convicted for corruption, the court will have to decide what is the loss caused to the government and allocate that loss to the guilty party.

Civil society sources said that the government in principle agreed to this proposal, but said that the modalities needed to be worked out and there were still certain reservations on the timing of this "confiscation" of property. The committee agreed that any assets owned by a public servant that have not been declared but found later, will be considered obtained through corrupt means. The onus will be then on the individual to prove otherwise.

The committee also agreed that the Lokpal would have the power to verify assets declared by elected political representatives with his declared sources of income in his tax returns (*The Times of India* dated 25th May 2011).

Hazare's team and the Centre agreed in principle on a provision to attach the properties of corrupt government officials after completion of investigation of charges against them. They also agreed on recovering the losses caused by the corrupt officials by auctioning the properties acquired by using ill-gotten wealth.

Sharp differences emerged at a meeting of the Lokpal Bill drafting committee on 29 May 2011 with the government opposing proposals for keeping the Prime Minister, higher judiciary, and acts of MP's inside Parliament under the purview of the anti-corruption watchdog (*HT* dated 31st May 2011).

Civil society members are expected to make a strong pitch for graver punishment for high ranking officials in cases of corruption, in the next meeting of the joint committee to draft the Lokpal Bill. They would also demand that a corrupt government official is to serve a minimum of one-year rigorous imprisonment and a maximum punishment of life imprisonment. "Punishment shall be higher if the status or rank of the accused is higher," reads a recommendation of the civil society members led by Anna Hazare (*HT* dated 30th May 2011).

The government has asked for the opinion of the chief ministers of states and the political parties on sticky issues. They have also asked whether there should be a Lokpal and Lokayukt and whether the entity should be a single or multi-member body. The civil society members in the panel on 1st June 2011 invited government nominees for a public debate on contentious issues that could be telecast live (*HT* dated 2nd June 2011).

On 1 June 2011 the Prime Minister Manmohan Singh sent four of his top ministers to meet Ramdev at the Delhi airport where he had flown from Ujjain in Madhya Pradesh. Addressing reporters in Gurgaon, he said that more than 70 lakh people die of hunger every year in the country according to the global hunger index. What should be the punishment for those indirectly responsible for their death? No one sees 70 lakh people dying, but if a corrupt is being hanged, they say 'save him'. Seeking the gallows for those who committed corruption to the tune of ₹ 1,05,01,000 crore or ₹ 1 lakh crore, he asked which demand he raised was unreasonable?

Pressing ahead with his plans for a fast-unto death against corruption, Yoga Guru Baba Ramdev on 2 June 2011 hinted at maximum punishment for the corrupt. The government was busy to persuade Ramdev not to go ahead with it, but the yoga guru did not agree. He met his close aides to finalize the strategy for his hunger strike in demand of government action against corruption and on the black money issue.

Anna Hazare on 2 June 2011 associated himself with yoga guru Ramdev's proposed hunger strike, but warned him not to be swayed by the government's overtures because it plays fraud by first agreeing to demands and then backing out. Hazare said that he would join Ramdev at his fast-unto-death on 4 June 2011 and emphasized that there was no divide in civil society on the issue of corruption (*HT* dated 3rd June 2011).

The nearly six-hour long meeting between government representatives and Baba Ramdev ended inconclusively on 3 June 2011 with the yoga guru saying that he was going ahead with his fast-unto-death against corruption from 4 June 2011.

Shri Sibal said that they had constructive dialogue on several issues and the government had addressed all the issues Baba had raised in writing. Most of these issues are of national concern and the government is already seized of many of them. However, the minister said that these were issues that could not be resolved in a day as they have long-term implications (*HT* dated 4th June 2011).

But the minister did not tell when the issue of corruption and black money would be resolved. Shri Anna Hazare wants the issue of corruption to be resolved by a fixed programme whereas Baba Ramdev wants immediate action on recovery of black money. Government is perhaps hesitating because many of its officers and ministers may be involved in corruption and black money. But the government may not be able to delay it for long. Time has come to act on both these issues. Further delay may be harmful for the government and the country as a whole.

I have given a solution for both in this book so that the snake is killed while the stick is not broken.

14

The (Government) Lokpal Bill, 2010

A
BILL

to provide for the establishment of the institution of lokpal to inquire into allegations of corruption against public functionaries and for matters connected therewith.

Be it enacted by parliament in the Sixty-first Year of the Republic of India as follows:

CHAPTER – I
PRELIMINARY

1. Short title and commencement: (1) This Act may be called the Lokpal Act, 2010.

(2) It shall come into force on such date as the Central Government may, by notification in the Official Gazette, appoint.

2. Definitions: In this Act, unless the context otherwise requires,

(a) "Chairperson" means the Chairperson of the Lokpal;

(b) "competent authority", in relation to—

(i) the Prime Minister, means the House of the People;

(ii) a member of the Council of Ministers, other than the Prime Minister, means the Prime Minister; and

(iii) a member of Parliament, other than a Minister means the Council of States in the case of a member of that Council and the House of the People in the case of a member of that House;

(c) "memorandum of complaints" means a memorandum of complaints alleging that a public functionary has committed any offence punishable under the Prevention of Corruption Act; 1988, (49 of 1988);

(d) "inquiry" means every inquiry conducted under this Act by the Lokpal;

(e) "Lokpal" means the institution established under section 3;

(f) "Member" means a Member of the Lokpal;

(g) "prescribed" means prescribed by rules made under this Act;

(h) "public functionary" means a person who—

(i) holds or has held the office of the Prime Minister, Minister, Minister of State or Deputy Minister of the Union; or

(ii) is or has been a member of either House of Parliament.

CHAPTER – II
MACHINERY FOR INQUIRIES

3. Establishment of Lokpal: (1) As from the commencement of this Act, there shall be established, for the purpose of making inquiries in respect of memorandum of complaints under this Act an institution to be called the "Lokpal".

(2) The Lokpal shall consist of—

(a) a Chairperson who is or has been a Chief Justice or a Judge of the Supreme Court; and

(b) two Members who are or have been the judges of the Supreme Court or the Chief Justices of the High Courts.

(3) The Chairperson and every other Member shall, before entering upon his office, make and subscribe before the President, or a person appointed in that behalf by the President, an oath or affirmation in the form set out in the Schedule.

4. Appointment of Chairperson and Members: (1) The Chairperson and Members shall be appointed by the President by warrant under his hand and seal.

(2) Every appointment under sub-section (1) shall be made after obtaining the recommendations of a Committee consisting of:

(a)	the Vice-President of India	Chairman;
(b)	the Prime Minister	Member;
(c)	the Speaker of the House of the People	Member;
(d)	the Minister in-charge of the Ministry of Home Affairs in the Government of India	Member;
(e)	the Minister in-charge of the Ministry of Law and Justice in the Government of India	Member;
(f)	the Leader of the House other than the House in which the Prime Minister is a member of Parliament	Member;
(g)	the Leader of the Opposition in the House of the People	Member;
(h)	the Leader of the Opposition in the Council of States	Member:

Provided that in case, there is no Leader of Opposition in the House of the People or the Council of States, the leader of the single largest group or party in opposition to the Government, as the case may be, in such House or Council shall be deemed to be a member of the Committee specified in clause (g) or clause (h), as the case may be:

Provided further that no sitting judge of the Supreme Court or sitting Chief Justice of a High Court shall be appointed except after consultation with the Chief Justice of India.

(3) No appointment of a Chairperson or a Member shall be invalid merely by reason of any vacancy in the Committee.

5. **Chairperson and Members to be ineligible to hold other office:** The Chairperson or a Member shall not be a member of Parliament or a member of the Legislature of any State or Union territory and shall not hold any office of trust or profit (other than his office as the Chairperson or a Member) or be connected with any political party or carry on any business or practise any profession and accordingly, before he enters upon his office, a

person appointed as the Chairperson or a Member, as the case may be, shall, if—

(a) he is a member of Parliament or of the Legislature of any State or Union territory, resign such membership; or

(b) he holds any office of trust or profit, resign from such office; or

(c) he is connected with any political party, sever his connection with it; or

(d) he is carrying on any business, sever his connection (short of divesting himself of ownership) with the conduct and management of such business; or

(e) he is practicing any profession, cease to practise such profession.

6. Term of office and other conditions of service of Chairperson and Members: (1) The Chairperson and every other Member shall hold office as such for a term of three years from the date on which he enters upon his office or until he attains the age of seventy years, whichever is earlier:

Provided that he may—

(a) by writing under his hand addressed to the President, resign his office, or

(b) be removed from his office in the manner provided in section 7.

(2) On ceasing to hold office, the Chairperson and every other Member shall be ineligible for—

(i) reappointment in the Lokpal;

(ii) any diplomatic assignment appointment as administrator of a Union territory and such other assignment or appointment which is required by law to be made by the President by warrant under his hand and seal; and

(iii) further employment to any other office of profit under the Government of India or the Government of a State.

(3) The salary, allowances and other conditions of service of—

(i) the Chairperson shall be the same as those of the Chief Justice of India.

(ii) other Members shall be the same as those of a Judge of the Supreme Court:

Provided that if the Chairperson or a Member is, at the time of his appointment, in receipt of a pension (other than a disability or wound pension) in respect of any previous service under the Government of India or under the Government of a State, his salary in respect of service as the Chairperson or, as the case may be, as a Member, be reduced—

(a) by the amount of that pension; and

(b) if he has, before such appointment, received, in lieu of a portion of the pension due to him in respect of such previous service, the commuted value thereof, by the amount of that portion of the pension:

Provided further that the salary, allowances and pension payable to, and other conditions of service of, the Chairperson or a Member shall not be varied to his disadvantage after his appointment.

7. Removal of Chairperson or Member: The Chairperson or a Member shall not be removed from his office except by an order made by the President on the ground of proved misbehaviour or incapacity after an inquiry made by a Committee consisting of the Chief Justice of India and two other Judges of the Supreme Court next to the Chief Justice in seniority, in which the Chairperson or the Member had been informed of the charges against him and given a reasonable opportunity of being heard in respect of those charges.

8. Member to act as Chairperson or to discharge his function in certain circumstances: (1) In the event of the occurrence of any vacancy in the office of the Chairperson by reason of his death, resignation or otherwise, the President may, by notification, authorise the senior-most Member to act as the Chairperson until the appointment of a new Chairperson to fill such vacancy.

(2) When the Chairperson is unable to discharge his functions owing to absence on leave or otherwise, the senior-most Member

available, as the President may, by notification, authorise in this behalf, shall discharge the functions of the Chairperson until the date on which the Chairperson resumes his duties.

9. Staff of Lokpal: (1) The Lokpal shall, for the purpose of assisting it in the discharge of its function (including verification and inquiries in respect of memorandum of complaints) under this Act, appoint a Secretary and such other offices and employees as the President may determine, from time to time, in consultation with the Lokpal.

(2) Without prejudice to the provisions of sub-section (1), the Lokpal may, for the purpose of dealing with any memorandum of complaints or any class of memorandum of complaints, secure—

(i) the services of any officer or employee or investigating agency of the Central Government or a State Government with the concurrence of that Government, or

(ii) the services of any other person or agency.

(3) The terms and conditions of service of the officers and employees referred to in sub-section (1) and of the officers, employees, agencies and persons referred to in sub-section (2) (including such special conditions as may be considered necessary for enabling them to act without fear or favour in the discharge of their functions) shall be such as the President may determine, from time to time, in consultation with the Lokpal.

(4) In the discharge of their functions under this Act, the officers and employees referred to in sub-section (1) and the officers, employees, agencies and persons referred to in sub-section (2) shall be subject to the exclusive administrative control and direction of the Lokpal.

CHAPTER – III
JURISDICTION AND PROCEDURE IN RESPECT OF INQUIRIES

10. Jurisdiction of Lokpal: (1) Subject to the other provisions of this Act, the Lokpal shall inquire into any matter involved in, or arising from, or connected with, any allegation of corruption made in a memorandum of complaints:

Provided that the Lokpal shall not inquire into any matter involved in, or arising from, or connected with, any such allegation of corruption against the Prime Minister in so far as it relates to national security, maintenance of public order, national defence and foreign relations:

Provided that Lokpal shall not inquire into any matter involved in, or arising from or connected with, any such allegation of corruption against any Member of either House of Parliament unless the recommendation of the Speaker of House of People or the Chairman of Council of States, as the case may be, is received by it.

(2) The Lokpal may inquire into any act of conduct of any person other that a public functionary in so far as it considers it necessary so to do for the purpose of its inquiry into any such allegation of corruption:

Provided that the Lokpal shall give such person a reasonable opportunity of being heard and to produce evidence in his defence.

(3) No matter in respect of which a memorandum of complaints may be made under this Act, shall be referred for inquiry under the Commissions of Inquiry Act, 1952 (60 of 1952).

11. Matters not subject to jurisdiction of Lokpal: (1) The Lokpal shall not inquire into any matter concerning any person if the Chairperson or any Member has any bias in respect of such matter or person and if any dispute arises in this behalf, the President shall, on an application made by the party aggrieved, obtain, in such manner as may be prescribed, the opinion of the Chief Justice of India and decide the dispute in conformity with such opinion.

(2) The Lokpal shall not inquire into any memorandum of complaints if the memorandum of complaints is made after the expiry of five years from the date on which the offence mentioned in such memorandum of complaints is alleged to have been committed.

12. Memorandum of complaints: (1) Any person other than a public servant may make a memorandum of complaints under this Act to the Lokpal:

Provided that memorandum of complaints in case of Prime Minister shall be made to the Speaker of the House of People and the Lokpal shall consider only such memorandum of complaints as are referred to it by the Speaker of the House of People:

Provided further that memorandum of complaints in case of Minister, Minister of State, or Deputy Minister of the union and Member of either House of Parliament shall be made to the Speaker of House of People or the Chairman of Council of States, as the case may be, and Lokpal shall consider only such memorandum of complaints as are referred to it by the Speaker of the House or People or the Chairman of Council of States as the case may be:

Explanation: For the purposes of this sub-section, "public servant" means—

(a) any person who is a member of a defence service or of a civil service of the Union or a State or of an all India service or holds any post connected with defence or any civil post under the Union or a State;

(b) any person in the service or pay of a local authority, a corporation established by or under a Central, Provincial or State Act or a Government company, as defined in section 617 of the Companies Act, 1956 (1 of 1956);

(c) any person in the service of any other institution, concern or undertaking which is established by or under a Central, Provincial or State Act or which is controlled, or financed wholly or substantially by funds provided, directly by the Central Government or a State Government.

(2) The memorandum of complaints shall be in the prescribed form and shall set forth particulars of the offence alleged and shall be accompanied by such fees as may be prescribed, if any, an affidavit in support of such particulars and a certificate of deposit furnished under sub-section (3) or, if the complainant is unable to make the deposit, an application for exemption from the requirement as to such deposit.

(3) The complainant shall deposit such sum of money in such manner and with such authority or agency as may be

prescribed and the certificate for such deposit shall be furnished in the prescribed form.

(4) Notwithstanding anything contained in the foregoing sub-sections, any letter written to the Lokpal by a person in any jail or other place of custody or in any asylum or other place for insane persons may, if the Lokpal is satisfied that it is necessary so to do, be treated as a memorandum of complaints made in accordance with the provisions of this section.

(5) Notwithstanding anything contained in any other enactment, it shall be the duty of a police officer or other person in-charge of any jail or other place of custody or of any asylum or other place for insane persons to forward, without opening, any letter addressed to the Lokpal by a person imprisoned or detained in such jail, place of custody, asylum or other place, to the Lokpal without delay.

13. Preliminary scrutiny of memorandum of complaints by Lokpal: (1) if the Lokpal is satisfied, after considering a memorandum of complaints and after making such verification as it deems appropriate that—

(a) the memorandum of complaints is not made within a period of five years as specified in sub-section (2) of section 11; or

(b) the memorandum of complaints is manifestly false and vexatious; the Lokpal shall dismiss the memorandum of complaints after recording its reasons therefor and communicate the same to the complainant and to the competent authority.

(2) The procedure for verification in respect of a memorandum of complaints under sub-section (1) shall be such as the Lokpal deems appropriate in the circumstances of the case and in particular, the Lokpal may, if it deems it necessary so to do, call for the comments of the public functionary concerned.

14. Procedure in respect of inquiries: (1) If, after the consideration and verification under section 13 in respect of a memorandum of complaints, the Lokpal proposes to conduct any inquiry, it—

(a) shall forthwith forward a copy of the memorandum of complaints to the competent authority;

(b) may make such orders as to the safe custody of documents relevant to the inquiry as it deems fit; and

(c) shall, at such time as it considers appropriate, forward a copy of the memorandum of complaints to the public functionary concerned and afford him an opportunity to represent his case.

(2) Every inquiry shall be conducted by the chairperson and the Members sitting jointly and the place in which such inquiry is conducted shall be deemed to be an open court to which the public generally may have access so far as the same can conveniently contain them:

Provided that in exceptional circumstances and for reasons to be recorded in writing, such inquiry may be conducted in camera.

(3) The Lokpal shall hold every such inquiry as expeditiously as possible and in any case complete the inquiry within a period of six months from the date of receipt of the memorandum of complaints:

Provided that the Lokpal may, for reasons to be recorded in writing, complete the inquiry within a further period of six months.

(4) Save as aforesaid, the procedure for conducting any such inquiry shall be such as the Lokpal considers appropriate in the circumstances of the case.

15. Evidence: (1) Subject to the provisions of this section, for the purpose of any inquiry (including the verification under section 13), the Lokpal—

(a) may require any public servant or any other person who, in its opinion, is able to furnish information or produce relevant to such inquiry, to furnish any such information or produce any such document; and

(b) shall have all the powers of a civil court, under the Code of Civil Procedure, 1908 (5 of 1908), while trying a suit in respect of the following matters, namely:

(i) summoning and enforcing the attendance of any person and examining him on oath;

(ii) requiring the discovery and production of any document;

(iii) receiving evidence in affidavits;

(iv) requisitioning any public record or copy thereof from any court or office;

(v) issuing commissions for the examination of witnesses of documents:

Provided that such commission, in case of a witness, shall be issued only where the witness, in the opinion of the Lokpal, is not in a position to attend the proceeding before the Lokpal; and

(vi) such other matters as may be prescribed.

(2) Any proceeding before the Lokpal shall be deemed to be a judicial proceeding within the meaning of section 193 of the Indian Penal Code (45 of 1860).

(3) No obligation to maintain secrecy or other restriction upon the disclosure of information obtained by or furnished to Government or any public servant, whether imposed by any enactment or by any provision of law whatever, shall apply to the disclosure of information for the purposes of any inquiry (including the verification under section 13 under this Act).

(4) The Government or any public servant shall not be entitled, in relation to any such inquiry or verification under section 13 to any such privilege in respect of the production of documents or the giving of evidence as is allowed by any enactment or by any provision of law whatever in legal proceedings.

Explanation: For the purposes of this section, "public servant" shall have the same meaning as is in section 21 of the Indian Penal Code (45 of 1860).

16. Search and seizure: (1) If the Lokpal has reason to believe that any document which, in its opinion, shall be useful for, or relevant to, any inquiry under this Act, are secreted in any place, it may authorise any officer subordinate to it, or any officer of an investigating agency referred to in sub-section (2) of section 9, to search for and to seize such documents.

(2) If the Lokpal is satisfied that any document seized under sub-section (1) would be evidence for the purpose of any inquiry under this Act and that it would be necessary to retain the document in its custody, it may so retain the said document till the completion of such inquiry:

Provided that where any document is required to be returned, the Lokpal shall return the same after retaining copies of such document duly authenticated thereof.

(3) The provision of the Code of Criminal Procedure, 1973 (2 of 1974) relating to searches shall, so far as may be, apply to searches under this section subject to the modification that sub-section (5) of section 165 of the said code shall have effect as if for the word "Magistrate", wherever it occurs therein, the words "Lokpal or any officer authorised by it" were substituted.

17. Reports: (1) After the conclusion of inquiry, the Lokpal shall determine whether all or any of the offences alleged in the memorandum of complaints have or has been proved to its satisfaction and by report in writing shall communicate its findings to the complainant, the public functionary and the competent authority.

(2) The Speaker, in the case of the Prime Minister or a Member of the House of the People, and the Chairman of the Council of States, in the case of a Member of that Council shall, as soon as may be, after the receipt of report under sub-section (1), cause the same to be laid before the House of the People or the Council of States, as the case may be, while it is in session, and if the House of the People or the Council of States, as the case may be, is not in session, within a period of one week from the reassembly of the said House or the Council, as the case may be.

(3) The competent authority shall examine the report forwarded to it under sub-section (1) and communicate to the Lokpal, within a period of ninety days from the date of receipt of the report, the action taken or proposed to be taken on the basis of the report.

(4) The Lokpal shall present annually to the President a consolidated report on the administration of this Act and the President shall, as soon as may be after and in any case not later than ninety days from the receipt of such report, cause the same, together with an explanatory memorandum, to be laid before each House of Parliament.

Explanation: In computing the period of ninety days referred to in this sub-section any, period during which Parliament or, as the case may be, either House of Parliament, is not in session, shall be excluded.

CHAPTER – IV
MISCELLANEOUS

18. Expenditure on Chairperson and members to be charged on the consolidated fund of India: The salaries, allowances and pensions payable to, or in respect of, the Chairperson and Members of the Lokpal, shall be expenditure charged on the Consolidated Fund of India.

19. Intentions, insult or interruptions to Lokpal: (1) Whoever intentionally offers any insult, or causes any interruption, to the Lokpal while the Lokpal or any of its Members is making any verfication or conducting any inquiry under this Act, shall be punished with simple imprisonment for a term which may extend to six months, or with fine or with both.

(2) The provisions of sub-section (2) of section 199 of the Code of Criminal Procedure, 1973 (2 of 1974) shall apply in relation to an offence referred to in sub-section (2) of the said section, subject to the modification that no memorandum of complaints in respect of such offence shall be made by the Public Prosecutor except with the previous sanction of the Lokpal.

20. Power of Lokpal to try certain offences: (1) When any such offence as is described in sub-section (1) of section 19 is committed in the view or presence of the Lokpal, the Lokpal may cause the offender to be detained in custody and at any time on the same day, take cognizance of the offence and, after giving the offender a reasonable opportunity of showing cause why he should not be punished under this section, try such offender summarily, so far as may be, in accordance with the procedure specified for summary trial under the Code of Criminal Procedure, 1973 (2 of 1974) and sentence him to simple imprisonment for a term which may extend to one month, or with fine which may extend to five hundred rupees, or with both.

(2) In every case tried under this section, the Lokpal shall record the facts constituting the offence with the statement, if any, made by the offender as well as the fine and the sentence.

(3) Any person convicted on a trial held under this section may appeal to the Supreme Court.

(4) The provisions of this section shall have effect notwithstanding anything contained in the Code of Criminal Procedure, 1973 (2 of 1974).

21. Disposal of deposit under section 12 etc. and penalty for malafide memorandum of complaints: (1) The sum deposited by a complainant in pursuance of the provisions of section 12 shall—

(a) in a case where the memorandum of complaints is dismissed under sub-section (1) of section 13 shall stand forfeited to the Central Governments.

(b) if the Lokpal, for reasons to be recorded in writing so directs, be utilized for compensating the public functionary complained against; and

(c) in any other case, be refunded to the complainant.

(2) If the Lokpal is satisfied that—

(a) all or any of the allegations made in a memorandum of complaints have or has been substantiated either wholly or partly; and

(b) having regard to the expenses incurred by the complainant in relation to the proceedings in respect of such memorandum of complaints and all other relevant circumstances of the case the complainant deserves to be compensated or rewarded, the Lokpal shall determine the amount which shall be paid to the complainant by way of such compensation or reward and the Lokpal shall determine the person by whom the said compensation or reward shall be paid after giving that person a reasonable opportunity of being heard.

(3) Every person who makes any memorandum of complaints, which is held by the Lokpal to be false and filed with malafide intention to harass the public functionary against whom such memorandum of complaints is filed, shall be punishable as provided in sub-section (4).

(4) When any offence under sub-section (3) is committed, the Lokpal may take cognizance of the offence and after giving the offender a reasonable opportunity of showing cause why he should not be punished for such offence try such offender summarily, so far may be, in accordance with the procedure specified for summary trials under the Code of Criminal Procedure, 1973 (2 of 1974), and if such offender is found guilty of committing the offence, sentence him to imprisonment for a term which shall not be less than one year but which may extend to three years and also to fine which may extend to fifty thousand rupees and may also award where fine is imposed, out of the amount of the fine, to the public functionary against whom such false memorandum of complaints has been made, such amount of compensation as the Lokpal thinks fit.

22. Application of Act 2 of 1974: Notwithstanding anything contained in the Code of Criminal Procedure, 1973 and subject to the other provisions of this Act, any case pending before the Lokpal under sub-section (4) of section 21 shall only be transferred to another criminal court in accordance with the procedure contained in section 406 of that Code and for the purposes of that section the Lokpal shall be deemed to be a Court of Session.

23. Conferment of additional functions on Lokpal: (1) The President may, by order in writing and subject to such conditions or limitations as may be specified in the order, require the Lokpal to inquire into any allegation (being an allegation in respect of which a memorandum of complaints may be made) specified in the order in respect of a public functionary and subject to the provisions of section 13, the Lokpal shall comply with such order.

(2) When the Lokpal is to make any inquiry under sub-section (1), the Lokpal shall exercise the same powers and discharge the same functions as it would in the case of any inquiry made on a memorandum of complaints under this Act and the provisions of this Act (except section 21) shall apply accordingly.

24. Persons likely to be prejudicially affected to be heard: If, at any stage of the inquiry, the Lokpal—

(a) considers it necessary to inquire into the conduct of any person; or

(b) is of opinion that the reputation of any person is likely to be prejudicially affected by the inquiry, the Lokpal shall give to that person a reasonable opportunity of being heard in the inquiry and to produce evidence in his defence:

Provided that nothing in this section shall apply where the credit of a witness is being impeached.

25. Protection of action taken in good faith: (1) No suit, prosecution or other legal proceedings shall lie against the Lokpal or against any officer, employee, agency or person referred to in section 9, in respect of anything which is in good faith done or intended to be done under this Act.

(2) Save as otherwise provided in this Act, no proceedings or decision of the Lokpal shall be called in question in any Court.

26. Power to delegate: The Lokpal may, by general or special order in writing, and subject to such conditions and limitations as may be specified therein, direct that any power conferred or duties imposed on it by or under this Act [except the power under sub-section (1) of section 12 the power to dismiss a memorandum of complaints under sub-section (1) of section 13, and the powers under section 21] may also be exercised or discharged by the officers, employees and agencies referred to in section 9, as may specified in the order.

27. Power to make rules: (1) The President may, by notification in the Official Gazette, make rules for the purpose of carrying out the provisions of this Act.

(2) In particular, and without prejudice to the generality of the foregoing power, such rules may provide for—

(a) the manner in which the President shall obtain the opinion of the Chief Justice of India under sub-section (1) of section 11;

(b) the form of memorandum of complaints under sub-section (2) of section 12 and the fees, if any, to be accompanied therewith;

(c) the manner in which and the authorities or agencies with whom deposit shall be made under sub-section (3) of section 12 and the form in which certificate shall be furnished in respect of such deposits;

(d) the matters referred to in sub-clause (vi) of clause (b) of sub-section (1) of section 15; and

(e) any other matter which is to be or may be prescribed.

(3) Every rule made under this Act shall be laid, as soon as may be after it is made, before each House of Parliament, while it is in session, for a total period of thirty days which may be comprised in one session or in two or more successive sessions, and if, before the expiry of the session immediately following the session or the successive sessions aforesaid, both Houses agree in making any modification in the rule, or both Houses agree that the rule should not be made, the rule shall thereafter have effected only in such modified form or be of no effect, as the case may be; so, however, that any such modification or annulment shall be without prejudice to the validity of anything previously done under that rule.

28. Removal of doubts: For the removal of doubts, it is hereby declared that nothing in this Act shall operate to confer or enable the conferring of any jurisdiction on the Lokpal to make any inquiry—

(a) into any allegation of corruption against or any act or conduct of—

(i) the President, the Vice-President, the Speaker of the House of the People, the Deputy Speaker of the

House of the People, Deputy Chairman of the Council of States;

(ii) the Chief Justice or any other Judge of the High Court or the Supreme Court;

(iii) the Comptroller and Auditor-General of India, the Attorney General of India, Chairman and other members of National Commission for Scheduled Castes and Scheduled Tribes, the Chief Election Commissioner, other Election Commissioners, the Chairman and other Members of the Union Public Service Commission or any other authority appointed under the Constitution of India; and

(b) upon its own knowledge or information.

29. Saving: Nothing contained in this Act shall be construed as affecting the constitution of, or the continuance of, functioning or exercise of powers by any Commission of Inquiry appointed under the Commissions of Inquiry Act, 1952 (60 of 1952) before the commencement of this Act and no memorandum of complaints shall be made under this Act in respect of any matter referred for inquiry to such Commission before such commencement.

30. Amendment of Act 60 of 1952: In section 3 of the Commissions of Inquiry Act, 1952, in sub-section (1), for the words "The appropriate Governments may", the words, brackets and figures "Subject to the provisions of sub-section (3) of section 10 of the Lokpal Act, 2007, the appropriate Government may" shall be substituted.

THE SCHEDULE
[See section 3(3)]

1. A.B. ....having been appointed Chairperson (or a Member) of the Lokpal so swear in the name of God/solemnly affirm that I will bear true faith and allegiance to the Constitution of India as by law established, that I will duly and faithfully and to the best of my ability, knowledge and judgement perform the duties of my office without fear or favour, affection or ill-will.

15

Jan Lokpal Bill, 2010

An act to create effective anti-corruption and grievance redressal systems at centre so that effective deterrent is created against corruption and to provide effective protection to whistleblowers.

1. Short title and commencement: (1) This Act may be called the Anti-Corruption, Grievance Redressal and Whistleblower Protection Act, 2010.

(2) It shall come into force on the one hundred and twentieth day of its enactment.

2. Definitions: In this Act, unless the context otherwise requires,

(1) "Action" means any action taken by a public servant in the discharge of his functions as such public servant and includes decision, recommendation or finding or in any other manner and includes willful failure or omission to act and all other expressions relating to such action shall be construed accordingly;

(2) "Allegation" in relation to a public servant includes any affirmation that such public servant—

(a) has indulged in misconduct, if he is a government servant;

(b) has indulged in corruption;

(3) "complaint" includes any grievance or allegation or a request by whistleblower for protection and appropriate action;

(4) "corruption" includes anything made punishable under Chapter IX of the Indian Penal Code or under the Prevention of Corruption Act, 1988:

Provided that if any person obtains any benefit from the government by violating any laws or rules, that person along with the public servants who directly or indirectly helped that person obtain those benefits, shall be deemed to have indulged in corruption.

(5) "Government" or "Central Government" means Government of India;

(6) "Government Servant" means any person who is or was any time appointed to a civil service or post in connection with the affairs of the Central Government or High Courts or Supreme Court either on deputation or permanent or temporary or on contractual employment but would not include the judges;

(7) "grievance" means a claim by a person that he sustained injustice or undue hardship in consequence of mal-administration;

(8) "Lokpal" means—

(a) Benches constituted under this Act and performing their functions as laid down under various provisions of this Act; or

(b) Any officer or employee, exercising its powers and carrying out its functions and responsibilities, in the manner and to the extent, assigned to it under this Act, or under various rules, regulations or orders made under various provisions of this Act;

(c) For all other purposes, the Chairperson and members acting collectively as a body;

(9) "Mal-administration" means action taken or purporting to have been taken in the exercise of administrative function in any case where,—

(a) such action or the administrative procedure or practice governing such action is unreasonable, unjust, oppressive or improperly discriminatory; or

(b) there has been willful negligence or undue delay in taking such action or the administrative procedure or practice governing such action involves undue delay;

(10) "Misconduct" means misconduct as defined in CCS Conduct Rules and which has vigilance angle;

(11) "Public authority" means any authority or body or institution of self-government established or constituted—

(a) by or under the Constitution;

(b) by any other law made by Parliament;

(c) by notification issued or order made by the Government, and includes any body owned, controlled or substantially financed by the Government;

(12) "Public servant" means a person who is or was at any time,—

(a) the Prime Minister;

(b) a Minister;

(c) a Member of Parliament;

(d) Judges of High Courts and Supreme Court;

(e) a Government servant;

(f) the Chairman or Vice-Chairman (by whatever name called) or a member of a local authority in the control of the Central Government or a statutory body or corporation established by or under any law of the Parliament of India, including a co-operative society, or a Government Company within the meaning of section 617 of the Companies Act, 1956 and members of any Committee or Board, statutory or non-statutory, constituted by the Government;

(g) such other authorities as the Central Government may, by notification, from time to time, specify;

(13) "Vigilance angle" includes—

(a) All acts of corruption;

(b) Gross or willful negligence; recklessness in decision-making; blatant violations of systems and procedures; exercise of discretion in excess, where no ostensible/ public interest is evident; failure to keep the controlling authority/superiors informed in time;

(c) Failure/delay in taking action, if under law the government servant ought to do so, against subordinates on complaints of corruption or dereliction of duties or abuse of office by the subordinates;

(d) Indulging in discrimination through one's conduct, directly or indirectly;

(e) Victimizing Whistleblowers;

(f) Any undue/unjustified delay in the disposal of a case, perceived after considering all relevant factors, would reinforce a conclusion as to the presence of vigilance angle in a case;

(g) Make unfair investigation or inquiry to either unduly help culprits or fabricate the innocent;

(h) Any other matter as notified from time to time by Lokpal;

(14) "Whistleblower" is any person who faces threat of—

(a) professional harm, including but not limited to illegitimate transfers, denial of promotions, denial of appropriate perks, departmental proceedings, discrimination or

(b) physical harm or

(c) is actually subjected to such harm; because of either making a complaint to Lokpal under this Act or for filing an application under Right to Information Act.

3. Establishment of the institution of Lokpal and appointment of Lokpal: (1) There shall be an institution known as Lokpal, which shall consist of one Chairperson and ten members along with its officers and employees. The Lokpal shall be headed by its Chairperson.

(2) The Chairperson and members of Lokpal shall be selected in such manner as laid down in this Act.

(3) A person appointed as Chairperson or member of Lokpal shall, before entering upon his office, make and subscribe before the President, an oath or affirmation in the form as prescribed.

(4) The Government shall appoint the Chairperson and members of the first Lokpal and set up the institution with all its logistics and assets within six months of enactment of this Act.

(5) The Government shall fill up a vacancy of the Chairperson or a member caused due to—

- (a) Retirement, 3 months before the member or the Chairperson retires.
- (b) Any other unforeseen reason, within a month of such vacancy.

CHAIRPERSON AND MEMBERS OF LOKPAL

4. The Chairperson and members of Lokpal not to have held certain offices: The Chairperson and members of Lokpal shall not be serving or former member of either the Parliament or the Legislature of any State and shall not hold any office or trust of profit (other than the office as Chairperson or member) or would have ever been connected with any political party or carry on any business or practice any profession and accordingly, before he enters upon his office, a person appointed as the Chairperson or member of Lokpal shall—

- (i) if he holds any office of trust or profit, resign from such office; or
- (ii) if he is carrying on any business, sever his connection with the conduct and management of such business; or
- (iii) if he is practicing any profession, suspend practice of such profession;
- (iv) if he is associated directly or indirectly with any other activity, which is likely to cause conflict of interest in the performance of his duties in Lokpal, he should suspend his association with that activity:

Provided that if even after the suspension, the earlier association of that person with such activity is likely to adversely affect his performance at Lokpal, that person shall not be appointed as a member or Chairperson of Lokpal.

5. Term of office and other conditions of service of Lokpal: (1) A person appointed as the Chairperson or member of Lokpal shall hold office for a term of five years from the date on which he enters upon his office:

Provided further that:

(a) the Chairperson or member of Lokpal may, by writing under his hand addressed to the President, resign his office;

(b) the Chairperson or member may be removed from office in the manner provided in this Act.

(2) There shall be paid to the Chairperson and each member every month a salary equal to that of the Chief Justice of India and that of the judge of the Supreme Court respectively.

(3) The allowances and pension payable to and other conditions of service of the Chairperson or a member shall be such as may be prescribed:

Provided that the allowances and pension payable to and other conditions of service of the Chairperson or members shall not be varied to his disadvantage after his appointment.

(4) The administrative expenses of the office of the Lokpal including all salaries, allowances and pensions payable to or in respect of persons serving in that office, shall be charged on the Consolidated Fund of India.

(5) There shall be a separate fund by the name of "Lokpal fund" in which penalties/fines imposed by the Lokpal shall be deposited and in which 10 per cent of the loss of Public Money detected/prevented on account of investigations by Lokpal shall also be deposited by the Government. Disposal of such fund shall be completely at the discretion of the Lokpal and such fund shall be used only for enhancement/upgradation/extension of the infrastructure of Lokpal.

(6) The Chairperson or members shall not be eligible for appointment on any position in Government of India or Government of any state or for fighting elections, if he has ever held the position of the Chairperson or a member for any period:

Provided however that a member or Chairperson may be reappointed for one more term or a member may be appointed as the Chairperson, however, that any person shall not serve for more than a total of two terms.

6. Appointment of the Chairperson and members: (1) The Chairperson and members shall be appointed by the President on the recommendation of a selection committee.

(2) Following persons shall not be eligible to become Chairman or Member in Lokpal:

(a) Any person who was ever chargesheeted for any offence under IPC or PC Act or was ever penalized under CCS Conduct Rules.

(b) Any person who is less than 40 years in age.

(3) At least four members of Lokpal shall have legal background.

(4) The members and Chairperson should have unimpeachable integrity and should have demonstrated their resolve and efforts to fight against corruption in the past.

(5) A selection committee consisting of the following shall be set up:

(a) The Chairpersons of both Houses of Parliament

(b) Two senior most judges of Supreme Court

(c) Two senior most Chief Justices of High Courts

(d) All Nobel Laureates of Indian Origin

(e) Chairperson of National Human Rights Commission

(f) Last two Magsaysay Award winners of Indian origin

(g) Comptroller and Auditor General of India

(h) Chief Election Commissioner

(i) Bharat Ratna Award winners

(j) After the first set of selection process, the outgoing members and Chairperson of Lokpal.

(6) The senior most judge of Supreme Court shall act as the Chairperson of the selection committee.

(7) The following selection process shall be followed:

(a) Recommendations shall be invited through open advertisements in prescribed format.

(b) Each person recommending shall be expected to justify the selection of his candidate giving examples from the past achievements of the candidate.

(c) The list of candidates along with their recommendations received in the format mentioned above shall be displayed on a website.

(d) Each member of the selection committee, on the basis of the above material, shall recommend such number of names as there are vacancies.

(e) A priority list shall be prepared with the candidate receiving recommendations from maximum number of members of selection committee at the top. The candidates recommended by same number of members shall be treated at par.

(f) This priority list shall be displayed on the website.

(g) Around three times the names as there are vacancies, shall be shortlisted from the top.

(h) Public feedback shall be invited on the shortlisted names by putting these names on the website.

(i) The selection committee may decide to use any means to collect more information about the background and past achievements of the shortlisted candidates.

(j) Selection committee shall invite shortlisted candidates for discussions, video recordings of which shall be made public.

(k) All the material obtained so far about the candidates shall be made available to each member of the selection committee in advance. The members shall make their own assessment of each candidate.

(l) The selection committee shall meet and discuss the material so received about each candidate. The final selections for the Chairperson and members shall be made preferably through consensus:

Provided that if three or more members, for reasons to be recorded in writing, object to the selection of any member, he shall not be selected.

(m) All meetings of selection committee shall be video recorded and shall be made public.

(8) The Prime Minister shall recommend the names finalized by the selection committee to the President immediately, who shall order such appointments within a month of receipt of the same.

(9) If any of the members of the selection committee retires while a selection process is going on, that member will continue on the selection committee till the end of that process.

7. Removal of Chairperson or members: (1) The Chairperson or any member shall not be removed from his office except by an order of the President.

(2) They can be removed on one or more of the following grounds:

(a) Proved misbehaviour;

(b) Professional or physical incapacity;

(c) If he is adjudged to be insolvent;

(d) Has been charged of an offence which involves moral turpitude;

(e) If he engages during his term of office in any paid employment outside the duties of his office;

(f) Has acquired such financial interests or other interests, which are likely to affect prejudicially his functions as member or Chairperson;

(g) If he is guided by considerations extraneous to the merits of the case either to favour someone or to implicate someone through any act of omission or commission;

(h) If any member or Chairperson tries to or actually unduly influences any government functionary;

(i) If he commits any act of omission or commission which is punishable under Prevention of Corruption Act or is a misconduct;

(j) If a member or the Chairperson in any way, concerned or interested in any contract or agreement made by or on behalf of the Government of India or participates in any way in the profit thereof or in any benefit or emolument arising therefrom otherwise than as a member and in common with the other members of an incorporated company, he shall be deemed to be guilty of misbehaviour.

(3) The following process shall be followed for the removal of any member or Chairperson:

(a) Any person may move an application/petition before the Supreme Court seeking removal of one or more of the members of Chairperson of Lokpal alleging one or more of the grounds for removal and providing evidence for the same.

(b) Supreme Court will hear the matter by a bench of three or more Judges on receipt of such petition and may take one or more of the following steps:

(i) order an investigation to be done by a Special Investigation Team appointed by the Supreme Court if a *prima facie* case is made out and if the matter cannot be judged based on affidavits of the parties. The Special Investigation Team shall submit its report within three months.

(ii) pending investigations under sub-clause (i) by Special Investigation Team, the Supreme Court may decide to order withdrawal of part or complete work from that member.

(iii) dismiss the petition if no case is made out.

(iv) if the grounds are proved, recommend to the President for removal of the said member or Chairperson.

(v) direct registration and investigation of cases with appropriate agencies if there is *prima facie* case of commission of an offence punishable under Prevention of Corruption Act.

(c) The three judge bench shall be constituted by a panel of five senior most judges of the Supreme Court:

Provided that if there are any proceedings going on against any judge in Lokpal, he shall not be a part of either the panel or the bench.

(d) The Supreme Court shall not dismiss such petitions in liminae.

(e) If the Supreme Court concludes that the petition has been made with mischievous or malafide motives, the Court may order imposition of fine or imprisonment up to one year against the complainant.

(f) On receipt of a recommendation from the Supreme Court under this section, the Prime Minister shall recommend it to the President immediately and the President shall order removal of said members within a month of receipt of the same.

POWERS AND FUNCTIONS OF LOKPAL

8. Functions of Lokpal: (1) Lokpal shall be responsible for receiving:

(a) Complaints where there are allegations of such acts of omission or commission which are punishable under Prevention of Corruption Act;

(b) Complaints where there are allegations of misconduct by a government servant;

(c) Grievances;

(d) Complaints from whistleblowers;

(2) Lokpal, after getting such inquiries and investigations done as it deems fit, may take one or more of the following actions:

(a) Close the case if *prima facie*, the complaint is not made out; or

(b) Initiate prosecution against public servants as well as those private entities which are party to the act;

(c) Order imposition of appropriate penalties under CCS Conduct Rules:

Provided that if an officer is finally convicted under Prevention of Corruption Act, major penalty of dismissal shall be imposed on such government servant.

(d) Order cancellation or modification of a license or lease or permission or contract or agreement, which was the subject matter of investigation.

(e) Blacklist the concerned firm or company or contractor or any other entity involved in that act of corruption.

(f) Issue appropriate directions to appropriate authorities for redressal of grievance in such time and in such manner as is specified in the order.

(g) Invoke its powers under this Act if its orders are not duly complied with and ensure due compliance of its orders.

(h) Take necessary action to provide protection to a whistleblower as per various provisions of this Act.

(3) *Suo moto* initiate appropriate action under this Act if any case, of the nature mentioned in clauses (1), (2), (3) or (4), comes to the knowledge of the Lokpal from any source.

(4) Issue such directions, as are necessary, from time to time, to appropriate authorities so as to make such changes in their work practices, administration or other systems so as to reduce the scope and possibility for corruption, misconduct and public grievances.

(5) Lokpal shall be deemed to be "Disciplinary authority" or "appointing authority" for the purpose of imposing penalties under CCS Conduct Rules.

(6) Section 19 of Prevention of Corruption Act shall be deleted.

(7) Section 197 of CrPC shall not apply to any proceedings under this Act. All permissions, which need to be sought for initiating investigations or for initiating prosecutions under any

Act shall be deemed to have been granted once Lokpal grants such permissions.

9. Issue of Search Warrant, etc.: (1) Where, in consequence of information in his possession, the Lokpal:

(a) has reason to believe that any person—

(i) to whom a summon or notice under this Act, has, been or might be issued, will not or would not produce or cause to be produced any property, document or thing which will be necessary or useful for or relevant to any inquiry or other proceeding to be conducted by him;

(ii) is in possession of any money, bullion, jewellery or other valuable article or thing and such money, bullion, jewellery or other valuable article or thing represents either wholly or partly income or property which has not been disclosed to the authorities for the purpose of any law or rule in force which requires such disclosure to be made; or

(b) considers that the purposes of any inquiry or other proceeding to be conducted by him will be served by a general search or inspection, he may by a search warrant authorize any Police officer not below the rank of an Inspector of Police to conduct a search or carry out an inspection in accordance therewith and in particular to,

(i) enter and search any building or place where he has reason to suspect that such property, document, money, bullion, jewellery or other valuable article or thing is kept;

(ii) search any person who is reasonably suspected of concealing about his person any article for which search should be made;

(iii) break open the lock of any door, box, locker safe, almirah or other receptacle for exercising the powers conferred by sub-clause (i) where the keys thereof are not available.

Seize any such property, document, money, bullion, jewellery or other valuable article or thing found as a result of such search;

(iv) place marks of identification on any property or document or make or cause to be made; extracts or copies therefrom; or

(v) make a note or an inventory of any such property, document, money, bullion, jewellery or other valuable article or thing.

(2) The provisions of the Code of Criminal Procedure, 1973, relating to search and seizure shall apply, so far as may be, to searches and seizures under sub-section (1).

(3) A warrant issued under sub-section (1) shall for all purposes, be deemed to be a warrant issued by a court under section 93 of the Code of Criminal Procedure, 1973.

10. Evidence: (1) Subject to the provisions of this section, for the purpose of any investigation (including the preliminary inquiry, if any, before such investigation) under this Act, the Lokpal may require any public servant or any other person who, in his opinion is able to furnish information or produce documents relevant to the investigation, to furnish any such information or produce any such document.

(2) For the purpose of any such investigation (including the preliminary inquiry) the Lokpal shall have all the powers of a civil court while trying a suit under the Code of Civil Procedure, 1908, in respect of the following matters, namely:

(a) Summoning and enforcing the attendance of any person and examining him on oath;

(b) Requiring the discovery and production of any document;

(c) Receiving evidence on affidavits;

(d) Requisitioning any public record or copy thereof from any court or office;

(e) Issuing commissions for the examination of witnesses or documents;

(f) ordering payment of compensatory cost in respect of a false or vexatious claim or defence;

(g) ordering cost for causing delay;

(h) Such other matters as may be prescribed.

(3) Any proceeding before the Lokpal shall be deemed to be a judicial proceeding within the meaning of section 193 of the Indian Penal Code.

11. Reports of Lokpal, etc.: (1) The Chairperson of Lokpal shall present annually a consolidated report in prescribed format on its performance to the President.

(2) On receipt of the annual report, the President shall cause a copy thereof together with an explanatory memorandum to be laid before each House of the Parliament.

(3) The Lokpal shall publish every month on its website the list of cases disposed with brief details of each such case, outcome and action taken or proposed to be taken in that case. It shall also publish lists of all cases received by the Lokpal during the previous month, cases disposed and cases which are pending.

12. Lokpal to be a deemed police officer: (1) For the purposes of section 36 of Criminal Procedure Code, the Chairperson, members of Lokpal and the officers in investigation wing of Lokpal shall be deemed to be police officers.

(2) While investigating any offence under Prevention of Corruption Act, 1988, they shall be competent to investigate any offence under any other law in the same case.

13. Powers in case of non-compliance of orders: (1) Each order of Lokpal shall clearly specify the names of the officials who are required to execute that order, the manner in which it should be executed and the time period within which that order should be complied with.

(2) If the order is not complied with within the time or in the manner directed, Lokpal may decide to impose a fine on the officials responsible for the non-compliance of its orders.

(3) The Drawing and Disbursing Officer of that Department shall be directed to deduct such amount of fine as is clearly specified by the Lokpal in its order made in sub-section (2) from the salaries of the officers specified in the order:

Provided that no penalty shall be imposed without giving a reasonable opportunity of being heard:

Provided that if the Drawing and Disbursing Officer fails to deduct the salary as specified in the said order, he shall make himself liable for a similar penalty.

(4) In order to get its orders complied with, the Lokpal shall have, and exercise the same jurisdiction powers and authority in respect of contempt of itself as a High Court has and may exercise, and, for this purpose, the provisions of the Contempt of Courts Act, 1971 (Central Act 70 of 1971) shall have the effect subject to the modification that the references therein to the High Court shall be construed as including a reference to the Lokpal.

13A. Special Judges under section 4 of Prevention of Corruption Act: On an annual basis, Lokpal shall make an assessment of the number of Special Judges required under section 4 of Prevention of Corruption Act, 1988 in each area and the Government shall appoint such number of Judges within three months of receipt of such recommendation:

Provided that Lokpal shall recommend such number of Special Judges so that trial in each case under this Act is completed within a year.

13B. Issue of Letter Rogatory: A bench of Lokpal shall have powers to issue Letters Rogatory in any case pending with Lokpal.

FUNCTIONING OF LOKPAL

14. Functioning of Lokpal: (1) The Chairperson shall be responsible for overall administration and supervision of the institution of Lokpal.

(2) All policy level decisions including formulation of regulations, developing internal systems for the functioning of Lokpal, assigning functions to various officials in Lokpal, delegation of powers to various functionaries in Lokpal, etc. shall be taken by the Chairperson and the members collectively as a body.

(3) The Chairperson shall have an annual meeting with the Prime Minister to assess the needs of Lokpal for finances and manpower. Lokpal shall be provided resources by the Government on the basis of outcome of this meeting.

(4) Lokpal shall function in benches of three or more members. Benches shall be constituted randomly and cases shall be assigned to them randomly by computer. Each bench shall consist of at least one member with legal background.

(5) Such benches shall be responsible for—

(i) granting permission to close any case after a preliminary enquiry.

(ii) granting permission to either close a case after investigations or issuing orders imposing penalties under CCS Conduct Rules and/or for initiating prosecution in that case.

(iii) Issuing orders under section 28 and section 13B.

(6) Lokpal may decide to initiate investigations into any case suo moto also.

(7) The decision to initiate investigation or prosecution against any member of the Cabinet or any judge of High Court or Supreme Court shall be taken in a meeting of all the existing members and the Chairperson. Minutes and records of such meetings shall be made public.

15. Making a complaint to the Lokpal: (1) Subject to the provisions of this Act, any person may make a complaint under this Act to the Lokpal:

Provided that in case of a grievance, if the person aggrieved is dead or for any reason, unable to act for himself, the complaint may be made or if it is already made may be continued by his legal representatives or by any other person who is authorized by him in writing in this behalf.

(2) A complaint could be on a plain paper but should contain all such details as prescribed by Lokpal.

(3) On receipt of a complaint, the Lokpal shall decide whether it is an allegation or a grievance or a request for whistleblower protection or a mixture of two or more of these.

(4) Every complaint shall have to be compulsorily disposed off by the Lokpal:

Provided that no complaint, other than those which are anonymous or pseudonymous, shall be closed without hearing the complainant.

16. Matters which may be investigated by the Lokpal: Subject to the provisions of this Act, the Lokpal may investigate any action which is taken by or with the general or specific approval of a public servant where a complaint involving a grievance or an allegation is made in respect of such action:

Provided that the Lokpal may also investigate such action *suo moto* or if it is referred to it by the government, if such action can be or could have been in his recorded opinion, subject of a grievance or an allegation.

17. Matters not subject to investigation: (1) The Lokpal shall not conduct any investigation under this Act in case of a grievance in respect of any action—

(i) if the complainant has or had, any remedy by way of appeal, revision, review or any other remedy before any other authority provided in any other law and he has not availed of the same.

(ii) taken by a judicial or quasi-judicial body, unless the complainant alleges malafides.

(iii) if the substance of the entire grievance is pending before any court or quasi-judicial body of competent jurisdiction.

(iv) any grievance where there is inordinate and inexplicable delay.

(2) Nothing in this Act shall be construed as authorising the Lokpal to investigate any action which is taken by or with the approval of the Presiding Officer of either House of Parliament.

(3) The provisions of this Act shall be in addition to the provisions of any other enactment or any rule or law under which any remedy by way of appeal, revision, review or in any other manner is available to a person making a complaint under this Act in respect of any action and nothing in this Act shall limit or affect the right of such person to avail of such remedy.

(4) Nothing in this section shall bar Lokpal from entertaining a complaint making an allegation of misconduct or corruption or a complaint from a whistleblower seeking protection.

18. Provisions relating to complaints and investigations: (1) (a) The Lokpal, on receipt of a complaint in the nature of an allegation or a grievance or a combination of the two, or in a case initiated on his own motion, may on perusing the documents, either decide to proceed to enquire or investigate into that complaint or decide, to make such preliminary inquiry before proceeding to enquire or investigate into such complaint or direct any other person to make such preliminary inquiry as it deems fit for ascertaining whether there exists reasonable ground for conducting the investigation. The outcome of such preliminary enquiry, and if the complaint is being closed along with reasons for the same and all material collected during preliminary enquiry, shall be communicated to the complainant:

Provided that if any case is closed, all documents related thereto shall thereafter be treated as public. Every month, a list of all such cases shall be put on the website with reasons for closing a case. All material connected with such closed cases will be provided to anyone seeking it under Right to Information Act:

Provided further that if the complaint contains verifiable and specific information about misconduct or corruption, then that case shall not be rejected even if the complaint is anonymous:

Provided further that no complaint of allegation shall be rejected by questioning the motives or intention of the complainant:

Provided further that all hearings before Lokpal shall be video recorded and shall be available to any member of the public on payment of copying costs.

(b) The procedure for preliminary enquiry of a complaint shall be such as the Lokpal deems appropriate in the circumstances of the case and in particular, the Lokpal may, if it deems necessary to do so, call for the comments of the public servant concerned:

Provided that the preliminary enquiry should be completed and a decision taken whether to close a case or to proceed with investigations within one month of receipt of any complaint.

(2) Where the Lokpal proposes, either directly or after making preliminary inquiry, to conduct any investigation under this Act, he,

(a) may make such order as to the safe custody of documents relevant to the investigation, as it deems fit.

(b) at appropriate stage of investigations or in the end, it shall forward a copy of the complaint, its findings and copy of the material relied upon to the concerned public servant and the complainant,

(c) shall afford to such public servant and the complainant an opportunity to offer comments and be heard:

Provided that such hearing shall be held in public, except in such rare circumstances, to be recorded in writing, will it be held in camera.

(3) The conduct of an investigation under this Act against a Public servant in respect of any action shall not affect such action, or any power or duty of any other public servant to take further action with respect to any matter subject to the investigation.

(4) If, during the course of preliminary inquiry or investigation under this Act, the Lokpal is *prima facie* satisfied that the allegation or grievance in respect of any action is likely to be sustained either wholly or partly, he may, through an interim order, direct the public servant concerned to stay the implementation or enforcement of the decision or action complained against, or to take such mandatory or preventive action, on such terms and conditions, as he may specify in his order to prevent further harm from taking place.

(5) The Lokpal, either during the course of investigations, if it is satisfied that prosecution is likely to be initiated in that case, or at the end of the investigations at the time of initiating prosecution, shall make a list of moveable and immoveable assets of all the accused in that case and shall notify the same.

No transfer of the same shall be permitted after such notification. In the event of final conviction, the court shall be empowered to recover loss determined under section 19 of this Act from this property, in addition to other measures.

(6) If during the course of investigation or enquiry into a complaint, Lokpal feels that continuance of a public servant in that position could adversely affect the course of investigations or enquiry or that the said person is likely to impact evidence or witnesses, the Lokpal may issue appropriate orders including transfer of that public servant from that position or his suspension:

Provided that such orders shall not be passed against the Prime Minister.

(7) In case of a grievance, the Lokpal may issue interim orders to the appropriate authority recommending grant of interim relief to the complainant if he is satisfied at any stage of preliminary inquiry on investigation that the complainant has sustained injustice or undue hardship in consequence of any decision or action of a public servant.

(8) The Lokpal may, at any stage of inquiry or investigation under this Act, direct through an interim order, appropriate authorities to take such action as is necessary, including suspension of a government servant, pending inquiry or investigation.

(a) to safeguard wastage or damage of public property or public revenue by the administrative acts of the public servant;

(b) to prevent further acts of misconduct by the public servant;

(c) to prevent the public servant from secreting the assets allegedly acquired by him by corrupt means;

(9) Where after investigation into a complaint, the Lokpal is satisfied that the complaint involving an allegation against the public servant is substantiated and that the public servant concerned should not continue to hold the post held by him, the Lokpal shall pass orders to that effect. In case of public servant being a Minister, Lokpal shall make such recommendation to

the President, who shall decide either to accept such recommendation or reject it within a month of its receipt:

Provided that the provisions of this section shall not apply to the Prime Minister.

(10) If, after enquiry into a grievance and after affording reasonable opportunity of being heard to both the complainant and the public authority, the Lokpal is satisfied that such grievance is substantiated either wholly or partly, he shall,

(i) pass appropriate orders directing appropriate authorities to redress the grievance in a manner and within the time prescribed in the order, and

(ii) direct the appropriate authorities to deduct from the salary of the officials mentioned in the order, such penalty amounts as are directed by Lokpal, which shall not be less than ₹ 250 per day of delay calculated from day the time limit mentioned in citizens' charter for redressing that grievance got over, and

(iii) direct the appropriate authorities to compensate the complainant with such amounts as mentioned in the order:

Provided that any grievance shall be disposed within 15 days of its receipt:

Provided further that if it relates to life and liberty of a person or if the matter is such as to warrant immediate attention and the Lokpal is so satisfied, the same shall be disposed within 48 hours.

(11) All records and information of Lokpal shall be public and shall be provided under Right to Information Act, even at the stage of investigation or enquiry, unless release of such information would adversely affect the process of enquiry or investigation:

Provided that no information in any case shall be withheld under Right to Information Act after the completion of enquiry or investigation.

RECOVERY OF LOSS TO THE GOVERNMENT AND PUNISHMENTS

19. Recovery of loss to the Government: If a person is convicted of an offence under Prevention of Corruption Act, then the trial court will also quantify the loss caused to the government and apportion that amount to various convicts from whom this money must be recovered as arrears of land revenue.

19A. Punishments for offences: For offences mentioned in Chapter III of Prevention of Corruption Act, punishment shall not be less than five years which may extend upto life imprisonment:

Provided that if the accused is any officer of the rank of Joint Secretary in the state or above or a Minister, the punishment shall not be less than ten years.

Provided further that if the offence is of the nature mentioned in proviso to section 2(4) of this Act and if the beneficiary is any corporate house, in addition to other punishments mentioned in this Act and under Prevention of Corruption Act, a fine amounting to five times the loss caused to the government shall be recovered from the accused and the recovery may be done from the assets of the company and from the personal assets of all Directors of the company, if the assets of the accused are inadequate.

WHISTLEBLOWER PROTECTION

20. Protection of Whistleblower: (1) A whistleblower may write to Lokpal seeking protection from threat of physical or professional victimization or if he has been subjected to such professional or physical victimization.

(2) On receiving such a complaint, Lokpal shall take following steps:

(a) Threat of professional victimization: Lokpal shall conduct appropriate enquiries and if it feels that there is a real threat to the person and the threat is on account of that person having made an allegation under this Act, then the Lokpal shall pass appropriate orders, as soon as possible but in not more than a month of receipt of such complaint, directing appropriate authorities to take such steps as directed by the Lokpal.

(b) If a person complains that he has already been victimized professionally on account of making an allegation under this Act, Lokpal shall, after conducting enquiries, if he is of the opinion that the victimization is indeed because of that person's having made an allegation under this Act, pass appropriate orders, as soon as possible but in not more than a month, directing appropriate authorities to take such steps as directed by the Lokpal:

Provided that for clause (a) Lokpal may, but for clause (b) the Lokpal shall, also issue orders imposing penalties under CCS Conduct Rules against the officer or officials who issued threats or caused victimization:

Provided further that no such penalties shall be imposed without giving an opportunity of being heard to the affected officials.

(c) Threat of physical victimization: Lokpal shall conduct appropriate enquiries and if it feels that there is a real threat to the person and the threat is on account of that person having made an allegation under this Act or for having filed an RTI application to any public authority covered under this Act, then notwithstanding anything contained in any other law, the Lokpal shall pass appropriate orders, as soon as possible but in not more than a week, directing appropriate authorities, including police, to take such steps as directed by the Lokpal to provide adequate security to that person, to register criminal cases against those who are issuing threats and also to take all such steps necessary to mitigate circumstances leading to such threat:

Provided that if the threat is imminent, Lokpal may decide to act immediately, within a few hours to prevent physical assault on that person.

(d) If a person complains that he has already been physically assaulted on account of making an allegation under this Act and if Lokpal is satisfied after conducting enquiries that the person has been assaulted because of his having made an allegation under this Act or for filing an RTI application in any of the public authorities covered under this Act, then notwithstanding anything else contained in any other law, the Lokpal shall pass such orders, as soon as possible but in not more than 24 hours, directing the concerned authorities to take such steps as directed by the Lokpal to provide adequate security to that person, to register criminal cases and also to ensure that no further harm visits on that person.

(e) If the whistleblower has alleged an act punishable under Prevention of Corruption Act, then for cases under clause (c), Lokpal may and for cases under clause (d), the Lokpal shall, assign the allegations made by that person to a special team, put it on a fast track and complete investigations in that case in not more than a month.

(f) If the whistleblower has alleged an act punishable under any law other than the Prevention of Corruption Act, then for cases under clause (c), Lokpal may and for cases under clause (d), the Lokpal shall, direct the agency which has the powers to enforce that law to assign the allegations made by the whistleblower to a special team, put it on a fast track and complete investigations in that case in such time as directed by the Lokpal.

(g) Lokpal shall have the powers to issue directions to appropriate agencies in the cases covered under clause (f), monitor such investigations and if necessary, issue directions to that agency to do the investigations in the manner as directed by the Lokpal.

(3) If any complainant requests that his identity should be kept secret, Lokpal shall ensure the same. Lokpal shall prescribe detailed procedures on how such complainants shall be dealt with.

(4) Lokpal shall issue orders to the Public Authorities to make necessary changes in their policies and practices to prevent recurrence of victimization.

GRIEVANCE REDRESSAL SYSTEMS

21. Citizens Charters: (1) Each public authority shall be responsible for ensuring the preparation and implementation of Citizens Charter, within a reasonable time, and not exceeding one year from the coming into force of this Act.

(2) Every Citizens Charter shall enumerate the commitments of the respective public authority to the citizens, officer responsible for meeting each such commitment and the time limit within which the commitment shall be met.

(3) Each public authority shall designate an official called Public Grievance Redressal Officer, whom a complainant should approach for any violation of the Citizens Charter.

(4) Every public authority shall review and revise its Citizens Charter at least once every year through a process of public consultation.

(5) Lokpal may direct any public authority to make such changes in their Citizens Charter as are mentioned in that order.

(6) No grievance shall be accepted by Lokpal if 15 days have not elapsed after submission of complaint by the complainant with the Public Grievance Redressal Officer of that Public Authority:

Provided that if Lokpal feels that considering the gravity or urgency of the grievance, it is necessary to do so, the Lokpal may decide to accept such grievance earlier also.

EMPLOYEES AND STAFF AND AUTHORITIES IN LOKPAL

22. Chief Vigilance Officer: (1) There shall be a Chief Vigilance Officer in each public authority to be selected and appointed by Lokpal.

(2) He shall not be from the same public authority.

(3) He shall be a person of impeccable integrity and ability to take proactive measures against corruption.

(4) He shall be responsible for accepting complaints against any public authority and shall transfer the complaints related to other public authorities within two days of receipt.

(5) He shall be responsible for carrying out all such responsibilities as assigned to him from time to time by Lokpal including dealing with complaints in the manner as laid down by Lokpal from time to time:

Provided that the complaints which require investigations under Prevention of Corruption Act, 1988 shall be transferred to the Investigative wing of Lokpal:

Provided further that the complaints, other than grievances, against officers of the level of Joint Secretary or above shall not be dealt by the Chief Vigilance Officer and shall be transferred to the Lokpal, who shall set up a committee of Chief Vigilance Officers of three other public authorities to enquire into such complaint.

(6) All the grievances shall be received and disposed by Chief Vigilance Officer on behalf of Lokpal, if the citizen fails to get satisfactory redressal from Public Grievance Officer under section 21 of this Act.

23. Staff of Lokpal, etc.: (1) There shall be such officers and employees as may be prescribed to assist the Lokpal in the discharge of their functions under this Act.

(2) The number and categories of officers and employees shall be decided by the Lokpal in consultation with the government.

(3) The categories, recruitment and conditions of service of the officers and employees referred in sub-section (1) including such special conditions or special pay as may be necessary for enabling them to act without fear in the discharge of their functions, shall be such as may be prescribed according to the recommendations of Lokpal:

Provided that no official, whose integrity is in doubt, shall be considered for being posted in Lokpal:

Provided further that all officers and employees, who work in Lokpal on deputation or otherwise shall be eligible for the same terms and conditions as prescribed under this clause.

(4) Without prejudice to the provisions of sub-section (1), the Lokpal may for the purpose of conducting investigations under this Act utilize the services of—

(a) any officer or investigating agency of the Central Government; or

(b) any officer or investigating agency of any other Government with the prior concurrence of that Government; or

(c) any person or any other agency.

(5) The officers and other employees referred to in sub-section (1) shall be under the administrative and disciplinary control of the Lokpal.

(6) Lokpal shall have the powers to choose its own officials. Lokpal may enlist officials on deputation from other government agencies for a fixed tenure or it may enlist officials on permanent basis from other government agencies or it may appoint people from outside on permanent basis or on a fixed tenure basis.

(7) The staff and officers shall be entitled to such pay scales and other allowances, which may be different and more than the ordinary pay scales in the Central Government, as are decided by the Lokpal from time to time, in consultation with the Prime Minister, so as to attract honest and efficient people to work in Lokpal.

24. Repeal and savings: (1) The Central Vigilance Commission Act shall stand repealed.

(2) Notwithstanding such repeal, any act or thing done under the said Act shall be deemed to have been done under this Act and may be continued and completed under the corresponding provisions of this Act.

(3) All enquiries and investigations and other disciplinary proceedings pending before the Central Vigilance Commission and which have not been disposed of, shall stand transferred to and be continued by the Lokpal as if they were commenced before him under this Act.

(4) Notwithstanding anything contained in any Act, the posts of the Secretary and other Officers and Employees of the Central Vigilance Commission are hereby abolished and they are hereby appointed as the Secretary and other officers and employees of the Lokpal. The salaries, allowances and other

terms and conditions of services of the said Secretary, officers and other employees shall, until they are varied, be the same as to which they were entitled to immediately before the commencement of this Act.

(5) All vigilance administration under the control of all Departments of Central Government, Ministries of the Central Government, corporations established by or under any Central Act, Government companies, societies and local authorities owned or controlled by the Central Government shall stand transferred, along with its personnel, assets and liabilities to Lokpal for all purposes.

(6) The personnel working in vigilance wings of the agencies mentioned in sub-section (5) shall be deemed to be on deputation to Lokpal for a period of five years from the date they are transferred to Lokpal. However, Lokpal may decide to repatriate any one of them anytime.

(7) That Department from where any personnel have been transferred to Lokpal under sub-section (5), shall cease to have any control over the administration and functions of transferred personnel.

(8) Lokpal shall rotate the personnel and create vigilance wing of each department in such a way that no personnel from the same department get posted for vigilance functions in the same department.

(9) No person shall be employed with Lokpal against whom any vigilance enquiry or any criminal case is pending at the time of being considered.

25. Investigation wing of Lokpal: (1) There shall be an investigation wing at Lokpal.

(2) Notwithstanding anything contained in section 17 of Prevention of Corruption Act, such officers of Investigation wing, upto the level as decided by Lokpal, shall have, in relation to the investigation and arrest of persons throughout India, in connection with investigation of complaints under this Act, all the powers, duties, privileges and liabilities which members of Delhi Special Police Establishment have in connection with the investigation of offences committed therein.

(3) That part of Delhi Special Police Establishment, in so far as it relates to investigation and prosecution of offences alleged to have been committed under the Prevention of Corruption Act, 1988, shall stand transferred, along with its employees, assets and liabilities to Lokpal for all purposes.

(4) That part of Delhi Special Police Establishment, which has been transferred under sub-section (3), shall form part of Investigation wing of Lokpal.

(5) The Central Government shall cease to have any control over the transferred part and its personnel.

(6) The salaries, allowances and other terms and conditions of services of the personnel transferred under sub-section (3) shall be the same as to which they were entitled to immediately before the commencement of this Act.

(7) All cases which were being dealt by that part of Delhi Special Police Establishment, which has been transferred under sub-section (3), shall stand transferred to Lokpal.

(8) After completion of investigation in any case, the investigation wing shall present the case to an appropriate bench of Lokpal, which shall decide whether to grant permission for prosecution or not.

26. Complaints against officers or employees of Lokpal: (1) Complaints against employees or officers of Lokpal shall be dealt with separately and as per provisions of this section.

(2) Such complaint could relate to an allegation of an offence punishable under Prevention of Corruption Act or a misconduct or a dishonest enquiry or investigation.

(3) As soon as such a complaint is received, the same shall be displayed on the website of Lokpal, along with the contents of the complaint.

(4) Investigations into each such complaint shall be completed within a month of its receipt.

(5) In addition to examining the allegations against the said official, the allegations shall especially be examined against sections 107, 166, 167, 177, 182, 191, 192, 196, 199, 200, 201, 202, 204, 217, 218, 219, 463, 464, 468, 469, 470, 471, 474 of Indian Penal Code.

(6) If, during the course of investigations, the Lokpal feels that the charges are likely to be sustained, the Lokpal shall divest such officer of all his responsibilities and powers and shall place him under suspension.

(7) If after completion of enquiry or investigations, Lokpal decides to prosecute that person under Prevention of Corruption Act, 1988 or holds him guilty of any misconduct or of conducting dishonest enquiry or investigations, then that person shall not work with Lokpal anymore. Lokpal shall either dismiss that person from the job, if that person is in the employment of Lokpal, or shall repatriate him, if he is on deputation:

Provided that no order under this clause shall be passed without giving reasonable opportunity of being heard to the accused person:

Provided further that order under this clause shall be passed within 15 days of completion of investigations.

(8) There shall be a separate wing in Lokpal to deal with complaints against officers or staff of Lokpal.

(9) Lokpal shall take all steps to ensure that all enquiries and investigations on complaints against its own staff and officials are conducted in most transparent and honest manner.

27. Protection: (1) No suit, prosecution, or other legal proceedings shall lie against the Chairperson or members or against any officer, employee, agency or person referred to in section 14(4) in respect of anything which is in good faith done while acting or purporting to act in the discharge of his official duties under this Act.

(2) No proceedings of the Lokpal shall be held to be bad for want of form and except on the ground of jurisdiction, no proceedings or decision of the Lokpal shall be liable to be challenged, reviewed, quashed or called in question in any court of ordinary Civil Jurisdiction.

MISCELLANEOUS

28. Public Servants to submit property statements: (1) Every public servant, other than those mentioned in section 2(11)(a) to (c), shall within three months after the commencement of this

Act and thereafter before the 30th June of every year submit to the head of that public authority, in the form prescribed by Lokpal, a statement of his assets and liabilities and those of the members of his family. Public servants mentioned in sections 2(11)(a) to (c) shall submit their returns in a format prescribed by the Lokpal to the Lokpal with the aforesaid time lines.

(2) The Head of each public authority shall ensure that all such statements are put on the website by 31st August of that year.

(3) If no such statement is received by the Head of that public authority from any such public servant within the time specified in sub-section (1), the Head of that public authority shall direct the concerned public servant to do so immediately. If within next one month, the public servant concerned does not submit such statement, the Head shall stop the salary and allowances of that public servant till he submits such statement.

Explanation: In this section "family of a public servant" means the spouse and such children and parents of the public servant as are dependent on him.

(4) The Lokpal may initiate prosecution against such public servant under section 176 IPC.

(5) If any public servant furnishes any statement, which is subsequently found to be incorrect, then Lokpal, in addition to taking action against the said public servant under other sections of this Act, may also impose a penalty upto a maximum of 50 per cent of the value of the additional property subsequently detected. Lokpal shall also intimate such information to the Income Tax Department for appropriate action.

29. Power to delegate and assign functions: (1) Lokpal shall be competent to delegate its powers and assign functions to the officials working in Lokpal.

(2) All functions carried out and powers exercised by such officials shall be deemed to have been so done by the Lokpal:

Provided that the following functions shall be performed by the benches and cannot be delegated:

(i) Granting permission to initiate prosecution in any case.

(ii) Order for dismissal of any government servant under CCS Conduct Rules.

(iii) Passing orders under section 10 on complaints against officials and staff of Lokpal.

(iv) Pass orders in cases of complaints, other than grievances, against officers of the level of Joint Secretary and above.

30. Time limits: (1) Preliminary enquiry under sub-section (1) of section 9 of this Act should be completed within a month of receipt of complaint:

Provided that the enquiry officer shall be liable for an explanation if the enquiry is not completed within this time limit.

(2) Investigation into any allegation shall be completed within six months, and in any case, not more than one year, from the date of receipt of complaint.

(3) Trial in any case filed by Lokpal should be completed within one year. Adjournments should be granted in rarest circumstances.

31. Penalty for false complaint: (1) Notwithstanding anything contained in this Act, if someone makes any false or frivolous complaint under this Act, Lokpal may impose such fines on that complainant as it deems fit:

Provided that no fine can be imposed without giving a reasonable opportunity of being heard.

(2) Such fines shall be recoverable as dues under Land Revenue Act.

(3) A complaint or allegation once made under this Act shall not be allowed to be withdrawn.

31A. Preventive measures: (1) Lokpal shall, at regular intervals, either study itself or cause to be studied the functioning of all public authorities falling within its jurisdiction and in consultation with respective public authority, issue such directions as it deems fit to prevent incidence of corruption in future.

(2) Lokpal shall also be responsible for creating awareness about this Act and involving general public in curbing corruption and maladministration.

32. Power to make rules: (1) The Government may, by notification in the Official Gazette, make rules for the purpose of carrying into effect the provisions of this Act:

Provided that such rules shall be made only in consultation and with the approval of Lokpal.

(2) In particular, and without prejudice to the generality of the foregoing provisions, such rules may provide for—

(i) the allowance and pensions payable to and other conditions of service of the Chairperson and members of Lokpal;

(ii) the powers of a Civil Court which may be exercised by the Lokpal under clause (h) of sub-section (2) of section 11;

(iii) the salary, allowances, recruitment and other conditions of service of the staff and employees of the Lokpal;

(iv) any other matter for which rules have to be made are necessary under this Act.

(3) Any rule made under this Act may be made with retrospective effect and when such a rule is made the reasons for making the rule shall be specified in a Statement laid before both Houses of the Parliament.

33. Removal of difficulties: Notwithstanding anything contained in this Act, the President, in consultation with Lokpal or on request of Lokpal may, by order, make such provision—

(i) for bringing the provisions of this Act into effective operation;

(ii) for continuing the enquiries and investigations pending before the Central Vigilance Commission by the Lokpal.

34. Power to make regulations: Lokpal shall have power to make its own regulations for the smooth functioning of the institution and to effectively implement various provisions of this Act.

35. This Act shall override the provisions of all other laws.

16

Corruption

Despite frequent criticism from those in authority and the Press, corruption has been sanctified and virtually has become a part of life. There are seven sins of public life. Politics without Principles, Wealth without Work, Pleasure without Conscious, Teaching without Knowledge, Commerce without Morality, Science without Humanity and Worship without Sacrifice, all have become a part of our life.

We want neither favours nor stringent measures. We want that everybody does his duty so that everybody gets justice soon and even the most powerful man is punished if he is found guilty. If an officer does not do his duty, he should be punished by the system, otherwise the system would not work. To keep the system affective, severe punishment to corrupt officers is a must.

Morality is too weak to make officers do their duty. Morality has to be of the standard that the government servant must spend public money as a prudent taxpayer. Therefore the punishment to Rathore alone would not break the ice. We would have to strike at the root of corruption, which is stopping our officers do their duty sincerely and honestly and is the root cause of many evils in the country.

The present punishment for corruption is not enough to control or eradicate it. More and more persons are indulging in it. It has grown many folds and has become rampant. Earlier the senior colleagues used to advise that so and so is corrupt, do not mix with him. Now they say that so and so is honest, beware of him. New ways for indulging in corruption are being added daily. It has entered all the spheres of life.

Shri O.P. Verma, the ex-governor and the ex-chief justice of the Kerala High Court, while speaking in the oath taking ceremony of the Bar Association of Ghaziabad, U.P., said that to control the increasing cases of corruption a law should be made to confiscate the property of the corrupt [*Amar Ujala* (Hindi) dated 21 February 2010].

Indians by birth are not corrupt. They are law-abiding citizens. They indulge in corruption when they find that their neighbour is not being punished for the same crime or the punishment is much less than the gain. Otherwise one would not find a chauffeur driving an empty car with a black suitcase on the backseat with millions of rupees in it and delivering it to the place where his master wanted without touching the money. Similarly one would find a servant in Surat delivering a suitcase full of diamonds to someone in Bombay. The servants are generally trustworthy and the masters have trust in them.

The businessmen get valuable land allotted to a school for poor children at throw away price. Then they have it converted into a hospital, then into a working girls' hostel and then they build a palatial house on it for themselves. This is how they are looting the public exchequer with the connivance of the government servants.

The punishment of confiscation of property and death penalty would prevent all government servants from indulging in corruption including politicians and businessmen who do it with their connivance. There would not remain any prize posting. The duty would be without attachment.

Money is behind all evils. The removal of corruption would reduce the difference between the rich and the poor. It will solve the problem of black money, terrorism, narcotics, adulteration, purchase and sale of properties, fake currency, melting of coins, etc. Buildings and roads would last longer being made of standard material. The flow of cash in the market would reduce.

The number of cases of robberies and abduction would go down. Government purchases would not be fake or of sub-standard items. No corruption would remain in the recruitment.

Thus the list of benefits that would flow due to eradication of corruption would be very long.

No amount of meditation, yoga or taking oath of honesty is going to help because our religious teachers are already rolling in wealth. Their ashrams are like forts with all modern facilities like electricity, water, air-conditioned rooms and cars and other luxurious facilities with a large number of servants to attend to them. Some of them are even involved in sex rackets and murders.

Lesser punishment than this would not be able to eradicate corruption. Bribe would let off the government servants caught for taking bribe. Someone in politics or police or judiciary may help them. Ruchikas and Ashu would continue to suffer. The file would not move without pulls and pressures or without payment of illegal money.

The common man would continue to feel the urge to take up arms to get justice and it may lead to anarchy. He is already losing his cool. Delhi witnessed 523 murders in 2009. A sizeable number of the cases were due to petty reasons (*HT* dated 10th January 2010). Justice KG Balakrishnan, the Honourable Chief Justice of India, has said that the patience of the common man may come to end and he may revolt if nothing is done quickly.

The people in the countryside and the tribal areas are starving whereas the rich are rolling in wealth. The Maoists are exploiting the situation. By suppressing those with force would not solve the problem. The problem can only be solved by removing corruption and by undertaking development works to increase the income of the common man. Otherwise they may revolt if nothing is done. The people in Ghaziabad (UP) beat a Sub-Inspector of police, who was drunk (*Amar Ujala* dated 16th January 2010). This was never heard before.

There are Rathores in every society. But they must be punished soon by ordinary courts, which is within the reach of a common man. It is only the collector, SSP and the Session Judge of the district who can help the common man if they perform their duty honestly and sincerely. Ruchika could not get justice because they failed to do their duty.

Measures like calling for details of assets held by a government servant or tough laws that are not going to solve the problem of getting fast justice. It would take years to get justice if corruption is not eradicated. Appointment of more judges may ease the situation for some time to come, but the problem of early justice would not be solved permanently due to rampant corruption in the country. Somebody would still be able to buy justice. Due to corruption even Panchayat system in the villages is failing. A confiscation of the entire property of the corrupt government servant with severe punishment is the only solution to remove this menace. The media can create the necessary atmosphere for a debate in the country on this issue.

Some people say that even in England there was rampant corruption in the beginning and slowly and slowly it was over. But are we going to wait for hundred or two hundred years for removal of corruption? We are already lagging behind the western nations due to corruption. We are wasting 84 paisa in a rupee of public money. If we can control it we would also be ahead. We should not remain one of the most corrupt nations of the world. There are no biological differences among races. But there are differences among people's environment. Let us also create the environments of honesty and hard work. In this respect China has been successful to some extent.

People say that God only knows whether the corruption, which is increasing day by day, would stop or not. Bhagvat Geeta says that whenever there is decline of righteousness, and unrighteousness is in the ascendant, He takes birth (*Chapter IV couplet* 7). Now, He has sent Anna Hazare in the form of another Mahatma Gandhi and let us take advantage of his presence. Otherwise like China, He may send somebody with a gun to put things in order.

Some communist leader, before China became red, had said that the way of communism from Moscow to Paris is via Peking and New Delhi. We may or may not believe in it. But if we want democracy in our country to flourish, we can at least guard against it by improving our system of justice.

The incompetence and inefficiency among some of the officers is also due to corruption. So our first efforts should be to eradicate corruption if we want democracy to function in this country and if we want justice and fair play for everybody irrespective of caste, creed and status in society.

But what corruption is there in government? The government works according to rules and procedures. For awarding a contract, certain rules and procedures are followed. Sometimes it becomes necessary to deviate from the rules and procedures. But then four things have to be observed. First it is in public interest. Secondly, there is no loss to the public exchequer, thirdly, the officer has no personal interest in the transaction including his relatives and friends, fourthly, the officer, including his friends and relatives, has made no money in the transaction.

If these four things are followed, even the biggest decision can be taken by those who are empowered to take a decision. Those who are not empowered to take a decision, can take a decision in emergency and immediately report the matter to the higher ups. But the emergency should be real and not artificial. The money taken by the officer as a bribe or kickback is corruption. The favour done to a friend or relative is also corruption.

In all scams it has been found that the transaction was not in public interest. It has caused a loss to the public exchequer. There is personal interest involved in it either of self or of relatives or friends and the money is taken through bribes and kickbacks. The scams which are taking place one after the other prove that there is no fear in officers of the law and the gain is much more than the punishment.

If the pay of the officers is less than the job they are doing, they should protest against it through their associations instead of indulging in corruption to supplement their income. The pay of the secretary should not be less than twenty times the pay of the peon. This would be though less than the money they are earning by corrupt means, but it would compensate them with respect and praise they would get from the public.

All secretaries must understand that nobody in India respects those who get small pay and go to jail by earning crores through corruption. But unluckily they meekly submit to the political heads to get perks of good posting instead of the pay. The political heads often increase both their pay and perks and still indulge in scams due to heavy expenditure they have to incur on elections every five years. This would stop once the officers do not indulge in corruption and would not allow others to do it.

India is a poor country. It cannot afford a very good salary to its officers. Earlier it was not possible to control the birth of children, which can be done now. Therefore we may enforce the Chinese policy of one child for employment in government, semi government, local bodies and government institutions.

Those who already have one or more children can be asked not to have any more in the interest of the welfare of the State. The policy can be implemented after one year to take into account the present pregnancies. This will cut down the requirement of housing, clothing, food, transport and employment. The expenditure of government servants would reduce and it would appear to them that their pay packet is enough.

Those who do business, even if they earn money by unfair means, the Indian public do not look down upon them because they do it with the connivance of government officers. In fact they respect them if they are kind hearted and charitable. So those who have a desire to earn more money, should try their luck in business instead of becoming government officers where there is less money, but more respect and authority.

Due to corruption all government schemes are spoiled. The money is not reaching the needy. Large-scale irregularities have been detected in the central government's debt waiver and debt relief scheme, 2008, for farmers in UP. In the majority of the cases, the officials concerned did not adhere to the government orders and guidelines pertaining to loan disbursement and waiver.

Farmer Khajan Singh of Bijnore got ₹ 87,000 waiver despite having paid back the loan on 16 January 2008 (Receipt No. 265487). Ranjit Kaur of Kuan Khera village of the same district got ₹ 79,000 waiver. However, the loan had been paid back on 29 February 2008 (Receipt No 65338). But, farmer Joga Singh's case is interesting. He was given ₹ 1,10,578 waiver though his loan was sanctioned on 20 November 2007 after the cut off date of 31 March 2007. Lakha Singh son of Darshan Singh of Kasimpur Garhi had 5 acres of land. He was entitled to a loan of ₹ 50,000. However, he was given ₹ 80,000 and the entire amount was waived.

After a preliminary inquiry, a sum of ₹ 12,01,465.65 was recovered from 16 erring cooperative societies of Bijnor and given back to the UP Cooperative Bank on 10th January 2011. But no action was taken against the erring officials. Out of 189 farmers who were given loan waiver, 45 were not eligible. But they were given relief of ₹ 92,202 under the scheme in Ismailpur cooperative society.

There is a long story of sanctioning loans or waivers to ineligible farmers, recovering the amount from some of them and of not taking any action against the erring officials (*HT* dated 5th May 2011).

But when the government acquires farmers' land they talk of corruption in the government. The government acquires their lands at cheaper rate and gives it to the company by taking bribe. But again it is the farmers who are at fault. They do the registry for sale of their lands at the circle rate of ₹ 400 per meter, but they would have actually sold their land at ₹ 1000 per meter. The collector of the district assesses the land on the basis of sale deeds and awards ₹ 400 per meter for their lands whereas the actual market value of the land is ₹ 1000 per meter. Then they go for violent agitation and demand the actual market value of land.

But how the actual market value of land would be decided? On the basis of sale deeds it comes to ₹ 400 per meter only. Then how to pay them ₹ 1000 per meter, which is the actual market value of land? It becomes a million-dollar question. Therefore all companies want to acquire land for their projects through the government and bribe the government machinery for it. So there is always a dispute between the farmers and the government regarding acquisition of lands for the companies.

Recently the farmers in Noida, UP, went for agitation to press their demand for greater compensation for land being acquired for a toll road and other projects. The farmers have been agitating since 17th January 2011. Talks between them and the government have failed. On 6th May 2011 the farmers became violent. There were clashes between the farmers and the police in which the DM was injured with a bullet in the right knee, the SSP with a brickbat and two police constables were killed on the spot along with two villagers. This is all taking place due to corruption and is a shame for the government and the society. We are injuring those who protect us. Due to corruption no solution of such problems can be found out (*HT* dated 8th May 2011).

Although everybody is against corruption, even then there is rampant corruption in India. Ask any Indian about corruption, he would give a lecture on corruption. He would be able to tell you how it brings down our moral standard and how it is harmful for the society and the nation as a whole. Even the Prime Minister Manmohan Singh in whose government one scam after the other is taking place, gave a full lecture on corruption the other day.

Prime Minister Manmohan Singh while speaking at the annual conference of chief secretaries of states on 4th February 2011 said that the two of the biggest challenges facing his government today are corruption and inflation. Corruption dints India's image, hampers good government, and needs to be tackled boldly and quickly. Corruption strikes at the root of good governance. It is an impediment to faster growth. It dilutes, if not negates our efforts at social inclusion. Mr. Singh gave this lecture two days after ex-telecom minister A. Raja was arrested by the CBI in the 2-G spectrum case. His government has been under attack over a host of scams such as Commonwealth Games, 2-G spectrum, and Adarsh Housing Society.

The Time magazine has written on the telecom scandal and said that in recent months, India's ruling coalition government has been rocked by an epic corruption scandal that has challenged its once unbreakable grip on power.

The report also does not have any kind words for Indian democracy or the judiciary. It says that following the 2008 elections, the telecom ministry was awarded to A. Raja, a relatively green lawmaker from a regional party who won his post as a result of India's usual parliamentary political horse-trading.

The Prime Minister again gave his advice on 10th February 2011 while talking to the IAS probationers. He told them that when the political leadership and the government officers leave their way of honesty, it is the public who suffer. If there is any occasion when they have to leave the way of honesty, it should be remembered that in India millions of people sleep without having their food [*Amar Ujala* (Hindi) dated 11th February 2011].

While replying to the motion of thanks to the President for her address to Parliament on 24th February 2011 the Prime Minister said that nobody involved in Commonwealth Games would be pardoned. He further said that his government is not an incompetent government. He had started getting complaints before the games began. From the Red Fort he had promised that if there was any scandal it would be inquired into. The government is fully co-operating with the inquiries so that the truth may come out of it and the guilty are punished. Whenever there was any proof, action has been taken against the wrong doers. But he did not disclose the number of wrong doers his government has punished [*Amar Ujala* (Hindi) dated 25th February 2011].

He also did not make it clear who is stopping him from taking action against the corrupt ministers and the secretaries. He is the supreme executive. He has all the powers and the machinery at his command. The example of Mrs. Indira Gandhi is there with him who is called the iron lady and the only man in her cabinet. Punish a few erring secretaries and the message would go round to the lowest cadre what he wants. He is an honest man. He has nothing to hide and nothing to fear. An executive, who merely gives advice, cannot stay for long in his chair. The time has come for him to act to remove rampant corruption from the country and earn a name and fame. Once the officer cadre is set right, everything would fall in line.

However, he expresses his helplessness in facing challenges that have come up during his tenure. He is seeking refuge in compulsions in dealing with crucial national matters. He admits the failures of his cabinet colleagues while trying to absolve himself of his total responsibilities. He is trying to correct his image at the cost of his party or coalition partners. No Prime Minister should do it, as he is also a part of his party and his government.

While speaking to the editors of news channels at his residence on 16th February 2011 the Prime Minister said that he had to make some compromises to run a coalition government. His government was dead serious in bringing to book all the wrong doers regardless of the position they occupy. He admitted that there were weaknesses of processes in governance and the quality of governance needed to be improved. He further said that his hands were also tied by coalition politics over the re-induction of A. Raja into the cabinet in 2009 despite complaints against him (*HT* dated 17th February 2011).

All political parties are against corruption. Even the ladies are against corruption. But they do not stop their husbands and sons from indulging in corruption and adulteration. Many of the ladies who are in government job including the officers are indulging in corruption.

All men are against corruption. But they also do not stop or advise their sons and daughters against corruption. When they go to find a bridegroom for their daughters, they even ask the bridegroom not only about his salary but also his extra income. The reason is our greed for wealth. They say that it is God who bestows wealth on us. There is nothing like legal or illegal before God. If we are poor, it is our fate. The day God is pleased with us, He will bestow wealth on us. If the wealth comes to us by illegal means, it is the fault of the government who does not catch and prosecute us.

Ask any government officer why he is indulging in corruption. His answer is his low salary with which he cannot maintain his status. The government in the name of socialism does not increase his salary. The principal of equal work for equal pay and equal pay for equal work is not being followed. The Law Minister Shanti Bhushan in Janta government did not increase the salary of the Delhi judiciary saying that whatever salary government may give them they would still take bribe. But he could neither stop corruption among the judiciary nor increase their salary. Let us hope that he would propose a reasonable salary for the Jan Lokpal whose bill is being drafted with his cooperation.

The government officer not only takes bribe because his salary is low, but sometimes his seniors compel him to do that by harassing him by frequent postings and transfers and by superseding him in promotion. Once he starts taking money, he gets so much money that he does not know where to keep it. If he stops taking bribe people say that he is behaving like a cat that has become a saint after eating 100 rats.

People bring approaches and are prepared to pay money to get their illegal jobs done. If their jobs are still not done, they say that a corrupt officer is better than an honest officer. At least he would do the job after taking money. They call an honest officer an honest fool or Satyavadi Harischandra who had to leave his throne for the sake of truth. But his fame has not vanished or reduced after thousands of years.

One may give hundred reasons for corruption, but the main reason is the man's greed. The inequality prevalent in society is also responsible for it. But the biggest worry is that corruption has become a part of our habit. In such an atmosphere it becomes difficult for a government servant to save his honesty. For this he has to bear the taunts of his friends, relatives and his family. He is taken as a big obstacle and a challenge in the way of the corrupt people. Then by a conspiracy he is posted to such a corner, which is generally called a punishment posting. The first IPS lady Kiran Bedi is an example of it.

If such a treatment can be meted out to such a high lady officer, what would happen to a junior officer can be well imagined? In such an environment to keep oneself honest against all the corrupt persons is very difficult. From here starts the process of an honest government officer becoming dishonest. If he is forced to leave his honesty how he would behave afterwards can also be imagined. In the hierarchy the share of the high officer in corruption also attract him to become corrupt. Due to family responsibility and his career it is difficult for a junior officer to displease his seniors [By Niraj, *Amar Ujala* (Hindi) dated 23rd February 2011].

If the government officer does not stop taking bribe, the money accumulates and it has to be invested in purchasing properties and gold and other securities. A sizeable amount is kept in cash. During raids the CBI has found it in lockers, pillows, quilts and even in commodes and mattresses. This is given as bribe when caught by income tax authorities or by the police. Thus they are caught for taking a bribe and are let off by giving bribe. So their condition is also miserable whether they take bribe or not. If they take bribe they are all the time worried about its consequences. If they do not take bribe their financial position remains weak. Sometimes they also start getting threat for being honest and are killed. In UP an honest Executive Engineer was killed by the BSP MLA and his associates for not allowing corruption to the contractors executing the works under him. Recently in U.P. two Chief Medical Officers have been killed for the same reasons by the Mafia.

The CBI arrested the president of National Aluminium Company Ltd. (NALCO) who used to receive gold bricks in bribe because, first they cover less space and, secondly, their price goes on increasing. It has now increased to ₹ 23,000 per 10 gms. He kept the bricks in other person's locker operated by his wife. A total of ten bricks were found with him.

The Attorney General of India, while defending P.J. Thomas, the new CVC, said that if the competence of officers is inquired sincerely, no vacant post could be filled in India. It means that honesty has disappeared from India like Dinosaurs from the world (*HT* dated 9th February 2011).

Ask any minister why he indulges in corruption. His answer usually is that he cannot win any election without spending millions of rupees. Sometimes even the people demand money for giving them votes. If they do not spend money they may lose the election. The chairman of a local body said that every member has to spend about ₹ 5 lakh to 10 lakh to win an election. Then about ₹ 50 lakh are to be spent to be elected the chairman. Even a Pradhan (chief) of the village has to spend ₹ 5 lakh in his election.

The expenditure on the election of MLAs and MPs is in crores. To make money they have to do it with the connivance of government officers. Wherever there is an honest government officer, he becomes an obstruction. The telecom minister A. Raja has been caught with his secretary for indulging in corruption to the tune of ₹ 1.76 lakh crore. Perhaps he could not have done it without the connivance of his secretary and his staff. But they are all against corruption because politicians have lost their respect in the public eye due to corruption.

Ask any businessman why he indulges in corruption and adulteration. His answer is that since his competitor indulges in corruption he has also to do it otherwise he would be out of business. He also says that it is the government officers who compel him to be guilty of corruption. Otherwise they put so many impediments in his work that he can't do his business or run his factory. But he is also against corruption and calls it a sin. The proof that all of them are against corruption is that all the above-mentioned classes joined Anna Hazare's movement and took part in the candle march in support of drafting the stringent Lokpal bill against corruption.

Even a poor man is against corruption. But he takes a grant from the government on false grounds and pays a bribe of 40 per cent out of it. He pays bribe for getting a job. When he is cheated he makes a complaint to the police that so and so cheated him for getting him a job, although it is a crime both to give and take bribe. But the police prosecute only the taker. He is also critical about the corruption being done by higher ups.

The wave of anti graft protests possibly reflects the sense among many Indians that the corruption problem is becoming worse, according to a new Gallup poll.

In 2010, almost half (47%) said that the level of corruption in India is higher than it was five years earlier, while 27 per cent said that it is about the same, the poll released by the noted US public opinion agency revealed. The groundswell of public support for socialist activists Anna Hazare and the anti-corruption movement shows Indians recognize that the problem is endemic, the poll suggested (*HT* dated 18th May 2011).

So in India everybody is against corruption and most of the people do it under one compulsion or the other. In fact all Asians and Africans are against corruption. So there is no necessity to create an atmosphere for it. It is already there. What is required is to make the necessary law.

Corruption is one of the causes of revolution. If the corruption is not eradicated or controlled it may lead to revolution. After the revolution becomes successful, the type of government that would be formed would depend upon the leaders of the revolution and the ideology they believe in. If they believe in communism and have been following Maoism, then the chances are that the country may become a communist or a socialist communist, etc. So those who want the democracy to continue in this country should strike at the root of the corruption.

17

Remedy (Lokpal)

Faced with the malady of corruption, we can approach the following organizations in the country:

1. The Central Vigilance Commission: This is the main agency to deal the cases of corruption and misuse of public office. While the CVC deals with disciplinary proceedings, the CBI deals with the criminal aspect of a corruption case.
2. The Central Bureau of Investigation: The CBI can investigate any case related to a central government department or the one referred to it by a state government or by the court.
3. The Police: In most cases, the police department has special anti-corruption cells. The police are also empowered to register an FIR if a corruption complaint seems genuine. It can lodge FIRs regarding corruption against members of Parliament and members of the legislative assemblies too, though they are required to notify the presiding officer of the House.
4. The State Vigilance Department: Each state has a vigilance wing that deals with corruption complaints against government officials.
5. The Lok Ayuktas: This state-level anti-corruption authority deals with corruption complaints against legislators, state ministers and government officials. Currently there are Lok Ayuktas in 17 states.

But in spite of the vigilance department in the Centre and in the States, there is rampant corruption in the country. The reason is that they are not autonomous and independent bodies to perform their duties. The punishment that is given is not exemplary.

The punishment provided in the anti-corruption laws, viz. The Indian Penal Code 1860, Prevention of Corruption Act 1988, Un-authorized Sale and Purchase of Property Act 1988 and Anti Money Laundering Act 2002, is too little to create a fear among the public and the government servants to deter them from indulging in corruption.

In Democracy there is only one way to eradicate corruption and that is by appointing a Lokpal with draconian powers and secondly, by providing exemplary punishment against corruption. Less than this will not create any fear among the public and the government servants to reduce the number of persons to be punished.

Lokpal Bill: The government drafted a Bill called 'Lokpal 2010'. It was completely toothless. It excluded bureaucrats. It is with their connivance only that politicians and businessmen indulge in corruption. Complaint against minister can be entertained only with the sanction of the speaker of the Lok Sabha or the chairman of the Rajya Sabha. Therefore the Civil Society drafted its own bill called 'Jan Lokpal' Bill 2010 with strong teeth.

What does the Jan Lokpal Bill 2010 provide for?—

1. It envisages creating an independent body, a Lokpal, at the Centre to probe corruption cases and complete the investigation within a year.
2. Whereas the government's draft gives it the power only to probe complaints forwarded by the Speaker of the Lok Sabha or the Chairman of the Rajya Sabha, the Jan Lokpal Bill gives the powers to initiate action on its own or on the basis of complaints from the public. It does not have to obtain the government's permission.
3. It will have police powers.

4. It has to ensure that the guilty are punished within two years of the filing of the complaint.
5. Those found guilty will have to compensate the government for the losses caused by the corrupt practice.
6. Judges, citizens and constitutional authorities, but not politicians will select the Lokpal's members through a transparent and participatory process.
7. Existing anti-corruption agencies such as the Central Vigilance Commission and the CBI's anti-corruption branch will be merged into the Lokpal office.

Corruption poses a serious challenge. In the political realm, it undermines democracy and good government by flouting or even subverting formal processes. Corruption in elections and in legislative bodies reduces accountability and distorts representation in policy-making.

Corruption in the judiciary compromises the rule of law. Corruption in public administration results in the inefficient provision of services. More generally, corruption erodes the institutional capacity of government as procedures are disregarded, resources are siphoned off, and public offices are bought and sold. At the same time, corruption undermines the legitimacy of government and such democratic values as trust and tolerance.

Morality is too weak to make the officers do their duty. Morality has to be of the standard that the government servant spends public money as a prudent taxpayer or otherwise he is punished for wasting public money. We must strike at the root of the corruption, which is hindering our officers from doing their duties. It is the root cause of many evils in the country. For this if the pay of the officers is increased there should be no objection to it. Equal pay for equal work and equal work for equal pay should be the rule.

The present punishment for corruption not being enough to control or eradicate it, more and more persons are indulging in it. It has grown many folds and has become rampant. New items are being added daily. It has entered those spheres where it could not have been imagined earlier.

Activists against graft have often pointed out that even the threat of jail hardly serves as a deterrent for a corrupt person, as he can enjoy his ill-gotten gains after he completes his sentence. Assets amassed through corrupt means by a public servant should be frozen during investigation and liquidated on his being proved guilty.

The FBI has charged further 14 people, including two Indians and Wall Street professionals, in a widening $ 53 million insider trading scam, the largest ever such case in the United States. The latest action brings the number of people who have been charged in the case to 20, including four Indians (*The Times of India* dated 7th November 2009).

If corruption can be there in USA where there is self-discipline among the public, then it cannot be eradicated in India where it has gone to our blood without exemplary punishment. In old good days whenever the kings gave a stern warning it was announced that if anyone did this job, his skin would be taken out and filled with husk. It had its effect. Nobody dared to do it.

Pandit Jawahar Lal Nehru, the first Prime Minister of India, said before independence that in free India every corrupt and black marketeer would be hanged by the nearest lamp post. Perhaps he did not do it because corruption had not become so rampant at that time. Pure milk and ghee (oil) were available. Today milk is adulterated with urea and ghee with animal fat.

There was a rampant corruption in Egypt. Colonel Nasser was the President of Egypt. He issued orders that anyone found indulging in corruption would be shot dead. After this there was no corruption in Egypt. When a foreign correspondent asked President Nasser how many people he had to shoot, he said, "None". The people knew that Colonel Nasser would do it if anyone were found indulging in corruption.

In Arab countries the penalty for theft is the cutting off a hand. This is the punishment in all theft cases. The result is that there are no thefts in Arab countries. Moreover, one does not find a person with a hand cut off from the wrist for theft. That means no more thefts cases are taking place in the Arab countries.

In Singapore there is no corruption. The people are hanged for corruption.

After the Commonwealth Games scams came to light, Prime Minister Manmohan Singh said that the corrupt officials would be given exemplary punishment. Thus no body is recommending a lesser punishment for corruption. The public also would not recommend a lesser punishment than the exemplary.

We only want that everybody is made to do his duty so that everybody may get justice soon and even the most powerful man is punished if he is found guilty. If the officer does not do his duty, he should be punished automatically by the system, otherwise the system of government would fail.

Thus the aim of the bill should be to act as a deterrent and instill fear against corruption. This frankly is the best way to eradicate corruption effectively.

What is provided u/s 19 and 19A of the Jan Lokpal Bill, 2010 is the punishment of five years, which may be extended up to life imprisonment with recovery of loss to the government. It is not a sufficient punishment for a person who misappropriated ₹ 8000 crore in the scam. This would not create a fear among the public and the government servants for not indulging in corruption.

That is possible only when the punishment provided is exemplary like the penalty of death with the confiscation of the property of the culprit. The punishment for corruption should be such that it may stop corruption forever. It is not necessary to punish many people for corruption. We want the snake to die without breaking the stick.

Those who are indulging in corruption are cruel. Even for a death certificate they charge money. They produce synthetic milk made from urea and shampoo. In ghee they mix animal fat. They have made the life of the entire society miserable. Every year due to adulteration hundreds of people lose their lives and equal number of people lose their eyesight.

Therefore, there is no need to be kind hearted towards them while awarding death penalty and in confiscating their property.

In a few years hardly any one would be left to punish for corruption.

It may take a long time before the committee drafts the bill, it is passed by the Parliament and the Lokpal and his office begin to function. So all efforts at all levels are necessary to expedite it.

Let us not be rigid. If some people want that the posts of the Prime Minister and the Chief Justice of India be kept outside the jurisdiction of Lokpal, let us agree to it and make a beginning. But let the job be done fast lest the things go out of control.

18

Killing a Snake Without Breaking the Stick

We do not want to prosecute lakhs of people for indulging in corruption. After the law of confiscation of both movable and immovable property for taking a bribe or holding unaccounted money is passed, it may be made applicable from a prospective date of one year in order to establish the infrastructure for its execution. During this one year:

The people who are not government servants and are having unaccounted money, may be allowed to deposit 30 per cent of their unaccounted money as Income tax because that is their hard earned money on which no tax has been paid. The deposit would be in cash only. For depositing the tax if somebody is holding immovable property that he may have to sell. Government may not take the liability of holding the immovable property and other problems connected with it. This should be for a period of one year only and no extension should be provided for in the law. The Income Tax Department can recover the additional tax if their assessments are found to be low. If they are found to be hiding any wealth/property, they can be dealt with under the new law.

The government servants who are holding unaccounted money and want to continue in service may be allowed to deposit the entire money in the government treasury in cash as the money is not their hard earned money, but has been taken as bribe from the public. Thus they may be pardoned for their misdeeds in the past. If they hide any property they can also be dealt with under the new law.

The government servants, who do not want to continue in service, may be allowed to deposit 70 per cent of their illegal money with the resignation letter from the service. They will not get any benefit of past service. This would be like the handshake for leaving the government job voluntarily. Again for hiding any property they can also be dealt with under the new law.

Thus within one year the unaccounted money in the country would be normalized. There would remain a warning that if any one indulges in corruption or adulteration or black money in future he would be dealt with a heavy hand by the administration in the country and no one may be able to help him.

The black money is used in election expenses. Once the black money is no more the election expenses would become so nominal that even a common man would be able to fight an election. Due to deposit of unaccounted money in the treasury, the prices also may come down. Those who had to indulge in corruption due to circumstances beyond their control would heave a sigh of relief.

19

Baba Ramdev's Anti-Corruption Campaign

Baba Ramdev addressing his supporters before hunger strike

Baba Ramdev is a yogacharya. He has his ashrama in Haridwar, UP. He has organized yoga camps throughout India and abroad. He has become very famous not only in India but also in the world. He has also taken up the issue of eradicating corruption in India. He organized a big yoga camp at Ramlila Maidan in Delhi on 3 June 2011 and converted it into a hunger strike against corruption.

On 3 June 2011 the Ramlila Maidan at old Delhi was set to behold a jamboree similar to that witnessed during Gandhian Anna Hazare-led protest at Jantar Mantar with songs, dances, slogans, and live painting. Painter Tabreez Alam, who was also present at Hazare's camp two months ago, created his artistic impression of the protest and depicting the 'monster of corruption' grinding innocent people in poverty. He also drew paintings with the message of bringing back black money stashed abroad.

Citing a difference between the two protests, he said that Anna's fight was only for the Lokpal Bill, but Baba Ramdev's task was bigger of fighting corruption as a whole. Some sadhus conducted a 'yagna' at the site while a group from Rajasthan wearing colourful turbans burst into an impromptu folk dance and music performance. A group of women volunteers displayed their solidarity to Ramdev by raising slogans against corruption.

Leaders from different religious sects also shared the stage with the yoga guru, who said that the Ravana of corruption would be killed at Ramlila Maidan. The President of Imam Parishad Mufti Shamoon Qasmi said that the people in our country were amazed to see Hindus and Muslims protesting together. We all are citizens of the country first and we must get together to fight this great evil of corruption and black money irrespective of religion.

A separate tent had been put up at the ground for serving food to the people. Rice, chapaties, dal and vegetables were served while lemon water was kept for those fasting from Saturday. Perhaps fasting included taking fruits and lemon water.

On 1 June 2011 the Prime Minister Manmohan Singh sent four of his top ministers to meet Ramdev at the Delhi airport where he arrived from Ujjain. The six-hour long meeting between government representatives and Baba Ramdev ended inconclusively on 3 June 2011. The yoga guru said that he was going ahead with his fast-unto-death against corruption from 4 June 2011. Emerging from the meeting with ministers Kapil Sibal and Subodh Kant Sahai at a five star hotel in Delhi, Ramdev further said that he had not yet reached a compromise and he would sit on fast. They would continue their satyagraha till their demands were completely met.

Sibal said that the dialogue was constructive. They had constructive dialogue on several issues and the government had agreed to all the issues Baba had raised. Most of these issues were of national concern and the government was already acting on many of them. However, the minister said that these were issues that could not be resolved in a day as they have long-term implications. He said that the government hoped that Baba Ramdev would do what was right. Prime Minister Manmohan Singh briefed President Pratibha Patil on the deliberations.

Medha Patkar, a social activist, said that such expensive agitation shows a different face of protest. She was also against corruption, but such an expensive agitation by spending crores was never seen by her. Anna Hazare said that they would have to think about the welfare of the people.

Ramdev's fast against corruption and black money started at 7 a.m. at the Ramlila Maidan, where a huge tent was set up. Thousands of supporters started gathering at the venue on 3rd June. They came from various corners of the country. Many came with huge suitcases with clothes enough to last several weeks. Some arrived from Madhya Pradesh and would stay till Baba needed them, even if it meant months. They supported Baba and his cause and wanted the country clean.

They were there from morning and the crowd was just swelling a thousand every hour. Surendra Rana, sitting at one of the many registration tables, had a thousand registration forms with him in the morning and only a handful was left. The Delhi government was to provide basic amenities at the venue.

Chief minister Sheila Dikshit said that she was approached for certain civic amenities like water, power and cleaning facilities for the congregation. She had given the required permission and had directed the department concerned to look into the matter (*HT* dated 4th June 2011).

The Congress on Saturday (4th June) targeted Ramdev's fast alleging that it had been 'hijacked' by the BJP and RSS to destabilize the government through the campaign. Ramdev, however, said that his protest had no political colour and his only intention was to fight against corruption. During her address, Ritambhara lavished praise on the yoga guru and said that if there were more Vallabhbhai Patels, then there was no need for a sanyasi to sit on satyagraha. Senior Congress leader Digvijay

Singh alleged that Ramdev's protest was totally engineered by RSS and VHP. VHP had announced that its president Giriraj Kishore would share dais with Ramdev at Ramlila Maidan.

Anna Hazare, who had announced plans of joining the fast on 5th June, appeared non-committal about it. He told reporters that he would go to Delhi on 5th June and would discuss what should be the form and direction of the Satyagraha. Speculations were rife whether Hazare would participate in the protest as his camp had indicated that it would be uncomfortable to join ranks with communal groups. Lokpal member justice Santosh Hegde told reporters that so far as the presence of Sadhvi Ritambhara was concerned she might be an accused in Ayodhya case. They were not supporting that cause. They were supporting only the fight against corruption.

Baba Ramdev addressing his supporters

Despite the Congress criticism, Ramdev refused to go back on his demand on black money. The yoga guru took a two-hour break from the protest and prayer session to discuss with government representatives his demands for bringing back black money stashed away abroad. Ramdev alleged that there were attempt to threaten him and said that he would not sit back if attacks were unleashed on him. Some people were making irresponsible remarks that Baba wanted to create instability. Baba said that he did not bring discord between Hindus and Muslims or between the castes or regions. He said this in an obvious reference to Congress targeting him. In this fight for truth he would not attack first, but he would not sit back if they were attacked. He would give a proper reply (*HT* dated 5th June 2011).

A political decision was taken to end the protest of Baba Ramdev. The police withdrew the permission for his yoga camp and imposed prohibitory orders. On Saturday night (4th June), the Centre and Ramdev indulged in a blame game. Union Minister Kapil Sibal, who had negotiated with Ramdev, made public a letter written by his aide that the fast would be called off on Saturday evening if Centre gave written assurances on a legislation to bring back the black money from abroad and stringent punishment to offenders.

Ramdev hit back saying that the government had indulged in betrayal and cheating and vowed not to talk to Sibal ever in his life. He said that he would go by the word of the PM. After mutual accusations, the Centre on late Saturday sent a fresh letter of assurances on his demands and appealed to him to withdraw his fast. But Baba Ramdev did not do it.

The talks broke down and the police arrived at the venue along with Rapid Action Force. The police swooped down on Baba Ramdev a little past Saturday (4th June) midnight and fired tear gas shells and resorted to lathicharge on his supporters to end his day old indefinite hunger strike on black money issue. The dramatic police action came after government and yoga guru accused each other.

As the men in Khaki in large numbers marched in at the Ramlila Maidan at around one a.m., the saffron-robbed yoga guru rushed to the microphone and shouted 'Vande Matram' to wake up most of his followers who had by then fallen asleep. The Police approached Baba Ramdev. A large number of lathi and gun-toting policemen tried to climb the dais. Ramdev sought five minutes from them to gather his articles, but leaped from the three-metre high podium and ran towards the enclosure where women were seated.

Ramdev's supporters, who were woken up from their sleep, rose in protest against the police action. Some elderly people swooned due to the impact of tear gas shelling resorted to by the police. Thirty of Baba's supporters were admitted to a nearby government hospital for treatment of injuries suffered during the police action.

Baba Ramdev in Salwar Kameej

In order to dupe them, Baba Ramdev clad himself in a woman's attire (salwar and kameej) and covered his beard with a 'dupatta'. At 2.10 a.m. Ramdev appealed to his followers to keep calm. At 2.30 a.m. his followers carried him on their shoulders. A little later he could not be seen at the venue. It took almost an hour for the police to locate the yoga guru. Delhi Police spokesman said that Baba Ramdev was detained when he was leaving the site. Later sources said that he was allowed to go out of Delhi and he headed to Haridwar. He was alleged to have gone to Dehradun by air and then to Haridwar by taxi. The Home Secretary maintained that he was not arrested or detained.

After daybreak, the police cleared all the remnants of Baba's support by evicting his followers from the protest site amidst stiff resistance. The Delhi Police Commissioner said that there were some security concerns and that the permission for the yoga camp had been cancelled. Ramdev's supporters indulged in stone throwing. The police did not use force except some tear gas, he added. Tijarawala, Ramdev's key aide, alleged that the police kidnapped him and he feared for his life. The spokesman of Baba Ramdev appealed to the Chief Justice of India to intervene and ensure Baba's safety.

Hours after police broke up Baba Ramdev's protest against corruption, both the Centre and the yoga guru hardened their stand. The government on Sunday (5th June) ruled out further talks with the yoga guru on his demands to bring back black money from abroad. Ramdev said that his stir was on and he would return to Delhi. Union Minister Subodh Kant Sahai, involved in negotiations with the yoga guru told reporters in New Delhi that there was nothing left to discuss with Ramdev. He asked on what issue they would talk then? Whatever talks had to take place had already taken place. His colleague Kapil Sibal made it clear that the police's early morning swoop, which took the yoga guru and his followers by surprise, had the backing of the government and the party.

To a question whether the action had the endorsement of the party, he said "absolutely, 100 per cent. No such action takes place without 100 per cent unity in the government and the party." Ramdev, who reached his ashram in Haridwar after being forcefully evicted from Delhi's Ramlila Maidan, told media that they wanted to kidnap him and kill him or send him somewhere. He termed the police action inhuman and barbaric.

About the hunger strike Baba Ramdev said that one lakh people had gathered at the Ramlila Maidan. About 5000 policemen in Khaki uniform surrounded them. The scenario was shameful and barbaric. Nursing a sore throat and at times tear-eyed Ramdev said that despite his pleadings, the police did not spare women and children but attacked them. He also accused the government of cheating him. The government had said that by the end of June 6, all their demands would be accepted. They were forced to write the said letter and were told that it would be presented to the Prime Minister.

Ramdev further said that Kapil Sibal was a liar and a cunning person. He cheated and mislead them. He was forced into signing the letter Sibal had made public, a handwritten note in which Ramdev had agreed to end his stir in two days. Ramdev also attacked Congress president Sonia Gandhi saying that she was not born in this country but was the daughter-in-law of this country. By ordering attack on one lakh people, she proved that she has no love for the people of this country.

Rejecting BJP's allegation that the police action against Ramdev was reminiscent of the Emergency, Union Parliamentary Affairs Minister Pawan Kumar Bansal said in Chandigarh that the government had to act as the yoga guru did not see reason. He refuted the allegations that the Delhi Police charged thousands of Ramdev's followers to evict them from the Ramlila ground. The Delhi Police said that the yoga guru's supporters were responsible for the entire chaos. They used tear gas after Ramdev's supporters pelted stones and when they attacked them with iron rods, fire extinguishers and what appeared to be baseball bats. This all was due to Baba Ramdev (*HT* dated 6th June 2011).

Claiming the support of all major parties barring the Congress to his agitation, yoga guru Baba Ramdev said on Monday (6th June) that the Centre would not be able to bear the consequences of the satyagraha. He had the respect for the Prime Minister on a personal level. But he did not discharge his national duty. When pointed out that he flew from the site dressed like a woman, he said that it was not a weakness to be in woman's dress (*HT* dated 7th June 2011).

Swabhiman Trust of Baba Ramdev had booked the Ramlila ground for 20 days for organizing yoga shivir (camp). After the police crackdown on Baba Ramdev's anti-graft fast on Saturday, the ground resembled a fortress as entry was restricted and the police officials manned the area that was bustling with protestors a few days ago.

Whatever may be the reasons for Baba Ramdev's leaving the stage in Ramlila Maidan in a woman's attire or leaving one-lakh supporters at the mercy of Delhi Police on Saturday night, he lost a golden opportunity to succeed in his anti-corruption campaign. He should have fought in Ramlila Maidan with one-lakh supporters with the weapon of 'Ahinsa' given by Mahatma Gandhi. The end of corruption might have come nearer.

20

Black Money

Black money refers to funds earned in the black market, on which income and other taxes have not been paid. The total amount of black money deposited in foreign banks by Indians is unknown, but shri R. Vaidyanathan, a Professor of Finance, has estimated that the total amount may be over ₹ 72,80,000 crores ($1.4 trillion).

In January 2011 the Supreme Court of India asked why the names of those who have stashed money in the Liechtenstein Bank have not been disclosed. The court argued that the government should be more forthcoming in releasing all available information on what it called a "mind-boggling" amount of money that is believed to be held illegally in foreign banks. While official figure of black money in Swiss banks is not available, Swiss banking officials have said that the largest depositors of illegal foreign money in Switzerland are Indians.

In August 2010, the government revised the Double Taxation Avoidance Agreement to provide means for investigations of black money in Swiss banks. This revision expected to become active by January 2012. It will allow the government to make inquiries from Swiss banks in cases where they have specific information about possible black money being stored in Switzerland.

Although the Swiss Parliament has ratified a treaty allowing Indian authorities to get information on illegal funds stashed in Swiss banks, the government cannot glean much data as the pact is applicable with prospective effect, a top tax official said on

5 April 2011. "As far as I can remember, it is prospective...I think it is prospective date, from the date the treaty comes into effect." The Central Board of Direct Taxes chairman Prakash Chandra told reporters when asked about the prospects of getting data from the Swiss banks.

This means that accounts opened in the secretive Swiss banks before ratification of the treaty would not be liable to scrutiny by Indian authorities. Finance Minister Pranab Mukherjee and Swiss Federal Councilor Micheline Calmy-Rey had in August last year signed a protocol to amend the double taxation agreement (DTA) in the area of taxes, which was ratified by the Swiss Parliament's upper house on August 17. Chandra said that although the Swiss Parliament has ratified the treaty, under the Swiss law around 90-100 days are required to make the law take effect. Once the treaty takes effect, "The understanding is that yes, if we ask specific information with regard to a tax payer giving details as asked for, then they are willing to part with that (information) which earlier was not the case," Chandra said. Meanwhile Chandra said that a government-constituted committee on black money has received more than 2,500 suggestions from across the country in the last 10 days to deal with the issue.

When asked about efforts to re-negotiate DTAA with Mauritius, news on which had led to a sharp fall in equity markets earlier this month, Chandra said that both the countries have decided to take the negotiations—stuck since 2008—forward and will be meeting to discuss the modalities. He, however, refused to give any timeframe for the same. The BSE Sensex had tanked by 550 points in intra-day trade on June 20 on fears that the Government might impose capital gains tax on investments routed via Mauritius once the DTAA is through. Chandra said that the quarterly tax numbers will have to grow at a "sustained" 20-24 per cent in the coming quarters in order to achieve the tax collection target of ₹ 5,32,000 crore announced in the Budget.

In order to check the illegal fund flows, the government had decided to place Indian tax officers abroad and two such officials have already been posted in Singapore and Mauritius. Plans are afoot to operationalise similar officers in Japan, UAE, Germany, UK, USA, France and Canada, he said.

(http://www.hindustantimes.com/News-Feed/mumbai/Swiss-treaty-won-t-allow-India-to-glean-data-on-olde) (*HT* West India Mumbai dated 7th April 2011)

To curb the black money, India has signed the Tax Information Exchange Agreement (TIEA) with 10 countries. They are Bahamas, Bermuda, the British Virgin Islands, the Isle of Man, the Cayman Island, the British Island of Jersey, Monaco, St. Kitts and Nevis, Argentina and the Marshal Islands where money is believed to have been stashed away. The Prominent case has been of Hasan Ali Khan who was arrested in April 2011 on charges of stashing over 36,000 crore in foreign banks.

On March 16, the Communist Party of India (Marxist) is said to have issued its manifesto, which said that, if it came to power, it would "launch a drive to unearth black money, especially those stashed in Swiss banks. Sharad Yadav of Janata Dal (United) said on March 27 that there were 1.47 trillion dollars hidden by Indians in Swiss banks.

If the money is brought back, it can repay the entire foreign debt of India and leave enough to abolish all taxes for many years. He further said that the reasons why the UPA government has not put pressure on Switzerland to send the money back is that many of its own politicians may be having Swiss accounts.

Then Shri L.K. Advani took up the issue in his press conference on March 29. He said that illicit money lodged in Swiss banks totalled $2.6 trillion (₹ 130 lakh crore in today's exchange rate) in 2001 and $5.7 trillion (₹ 285 lakh crore) in 2007. The illicit money deposited by rich Indians in Swiss banks and elsewhere was between $0.5-1.4 trillion (₹ 25-70 lakh crore).

Even the lower amount was enough to relieve the debt of all farmers and landless workers. It can build roads all over the country and take electricity to every rural home. It can provide drinking water in all villages and towns, construct good houses for 10 crore families, provide ₹ 4 crore to every village to build a school, a health centre, a veterinary clinic, a playground with gymnasium, and more. Advani referred to Hasan Ali Khan whom the income tax department has found having unaccounted wealth worth ₹ 35,000 crore including the wealth in the accounts abroad.

Secret bank accounts can destroy our financial system and support terror networks, which increased their attacks on India. If elected, a BJP-led NDA government will join global efforts to put an end to banking secrecy and try its best to get hold of money held abroad. Meanwhile, the BJP is making intense propaganda on the issue.

Hasan Ali Khan, whom Advani refers to as a typical tax evader and holder of Swiss bank accounts, was a bon voyeur who bought racehorses and flaunted his money in Pune. But there is no independent confirmation of his wealth because no documents have so far been filed in the court.

The United States of America has been successful in getting details of assets of US citizens from Swiss banks. Till now, the US Justice Department has succeeded against only one bank. On February 19, UBS agreed to pay the US $780 million and give details of assets amounting to $20 billion and names of 250 clients.

The US is asking for details of 52,000 clients, but Swiss banks are resisting and have the support of the Swiss government. Compared to that $20 billion, Shri Advani hopes to bring back $1,400 billion. The US Internal Revenue Service is not seeking to expropriate Americans' deposits in Switzerland. It is asking for 20 per cent of the highest balance held abroad, plus six years' back taxes plus interest.

The US makes those demands because it taxes the world income of Americans wherever they are (they get rebates for other countries' income taxes they pay). India makes such demands only from the residents of India and there are simply not so many Indians who reside in India and leave their money in Switzerland. Those who wanted to keep their assets abroad long ago went to live abroad and are beyond the Indian tax net.

Last of all the US can succeed in pressuring Swiss banks because business in the US is indispensable for them. Their business in India is not even 5 per cent of their total business. So the complete success in bringing back the black money may not be possible. However, the evil can certainly be reduced. So continuous efforts to bring back black money from Swiss banks and other foreign banks need to be made.

But unfortunately we have still not succeeded in drafting a strong anti-corruption law, which can eradicate the rampant corruption in the country. So such demands of the political parties in the opposition appear to be only a slogan to please the voters.

On 4th July 2011 the Supreme Court set up a Special Investigation Team (SIT) to probe black money stashed in foreign banks by Indian citizens. The former apex court judge BP Jeevan Ready is the Chairman of the committee. The court also has directed the central government to disclose the names of people holding accounts in LGT bank in Liechtenstein, a principality in Europe bordering Switzerland and Austria as disclosed to it by German authorities. However, the names of people holding the accounts but not involved in any wrong acts, may not be made public.

The court converted the existing high level committee constituted by the central government into the SIT. Justice M.B. Shah is the vice-chairman of the committee. In its lengthy order the apex court repeatedly pulled up the Central government for dragging its feet and delaying the investigation into the black money stashed abroad. The court also mocked the Central government for using double-taxation avoidance agreement with Germany in holding back the names of the money launderers who were not even remotely covered under the India-German treaty.

The Finance Minister Pranab Mukerjee told reporters when asked to comment on the order that the government would decide the future course of action on black money after studying the Supreme Court order. The Opposition, however, welcomed the move, saying that it came as a slap on the face of the UPA government for consistently failing to bring back the money stashed in foreign banks. This has fully exposed the government and the Congress. The government does not want to do anything in this matter (*HT* dated 5th July 2011).

The country's highest court has, on the face of it, taken upon itself to cleanse the economy of black money. This incursion by the judiciary into the executive's preserve, whatever the provocation might be, is a trespass. The courts have every right to rule on individual instances of regulatory failure, but the job of systemic overhaul is beyond their capabilities.

The Supreme Court has often in the past refused to judge the merits of policy. There is little to recommend upturning this restraint over black money. After all, a gamut of statecraft, from foreign policy to law enforcement and to economic management, is responsible for its generation. The court is correct in its diagnosis that unaccounted cash is an economy wise phenomenon that calls for an economy wise cure. However, it is in no position to administer that medicine.

In India the issue of black money has acquired endemic proportions. As a beginning, the government needs to introspect on the shortages that create black markets in the first place, the regulatory mechanism that nudges resources underground, and the lack of policing that allows the parallel economy unfettered growth. The courts are well within their jurisdiction to act as keepers of a society's conscience. But the courts must remember that there is a thin line between activism and moral policing (*HT* dated 7th July 2011).

Here is an article about the judiciary doing the duty of the executive by Anil Dharker, who is a Mumbai based writer. He asks that if the Supreme Court of India wants to be the Government of India? Or do the judges of the apex court want to assert their right to be considered as ordinary citizens?

Today's buzz phrase is 'civil society'. It occurs everywhere, in print, on TV, in everyday conversation. The context is the same. The civil society is always pitted in an adversarial position vis-à-vis government. It's a recent development, probably beginning with 26/11 when the terrorist attacks in Mumbai showed up government's unpreparedness and incompetence as never before.

In the last couple of years the focus of antagonism has shifted from securing almost completely to corruption and with good reasons too. The scams that have been unearthed in the last few years are of such staggering proportions that all earlier cases appear to deal in small changes. The government's obvious inability and, worse, seeming unwillingness to deal with these cases, has taken us the members of civil society, beyond a point of no return. We are no longer willing to be passive bystanders.

Has the Supreme Court reached that stage too? Its recent order stemming from the Hasan Ali income tax-hawala case seems to suggest that. Not content to rebuke the government for moving too slowly in the matter, it has taken over the role of the executive by appointing a Special Investigation Team (SIT) under two retired Supreme Court judges to look into the issue of black money.

Astonishingly, the court order goes beyond the specific case of Ali. The SIT is reporting directly to the court and has been asked to prepare a comprehensive action plan, including creation of necessary institutional structures, that can enable and strengthen the country's battle against generations of unaccounted monies, and their stashing away in foreign banks or in various forms domestically.

If Anna Hazare and his team had made such sweeping demands, we would have dismissed them as good intentions overcoming good sense, perhaps caused by a failure to see the different roles assigned by the Constitution to the 'three estates'. But these are not vague social reformers talking, this is an order of the Supreme Court.

The order you see above is one that should have come from the ministry of finance. The apex court, in effect, takes over the government function of very many executive agencies such as the Reserve Bank, the Enforcement Directorate, the Central Bureau of Investigation, and the Central Board of Direct Taxes. Incidentally, by an amazing coincidence, on the very day the court issued this order, the finance ministry came out with the proposal of making the Central Economic Intelligence Bureau as the nodal agency for all economic offences, with all enforcement agencies compulsorily reporting to it. Is not that the correct way of going about it, rather than the judiciary's approach of taking over the case completely?

This, of course is not the first time that the Supreme Court has intervened in this way. The 2G probe, for example, is now being conducted solely under its directions. A look at the daily newspaper will tell you how our courts seem to be overstepping the constitutionally assigned role for the judiciary in different fields. There is the recent Supreme Court judgement that virtually tells the government how to fight the war against the Maoists in Chhattisgarh.

Local issues are not exempt either. These are examples picked up at random on a single day. High Court probe into pollution near Taloja jail and the Court raps BMC for squatters near water pipelines. Where are the questions of law that are being resolved here? Aren't these matters for the executive alone.

Apart from the question of propriety, these interventions also take up the court's time. In the meantime the arrears of pending cases mount daily, denying justice to lakhs of people. Should clearing the backlog not be a greater priority for the courts? And without meaning any disrespect to the Supreme Court, why not set up an SIT to look into cases of corruption in the judiciary that have been alleged from an ex-Chief Justice downwards to the lower courts? If the government did that, how would the judiciary react? (*The Hindustan Times* dated 9th July 2011).

As mentioned above the apex court has taken upon itself the duties of the executive and thousands of writ petitions are pending for disposal in their own courts for the last 5-10 years. No committee has been constituted to suggest ways and means for their early disposal. On the other hand government officers are forcing the citizens, employees and pensioners to go to court even on small matters by passing unreasoned orders or by not giving the decisions for months or years together. The government officer knows it fully well that if one goes to the court it would take 10 years before the court finally decides the case. By that time the government officer would retire.

Even if the whole 1.47 trillion dollars of black money in Swiss banks is brought back, its 84 per cent will go in the pockets of the politicians, government officers and the middlemen due to rampant corruption in the country. Shri Rajiv Gandhi, the ex-Prime Minister of India, had said that only 16 paisa in a rupee reaches the common man.

Therefore our first job should be to set at right the conditions at home by drafting a strong anti-corruption law which may create so much fear in the public that before indulging in corruption they may think twice about its consequences.

APPENDIX-I

Supreme Court Judgement on Black Money

Item No. 63(ph) Court No. 9 Section Pil

SUPREMECOURTOFINDIA

Record of Proceedings

Writ Petition (Civil) No(s). 176 of 2009

Ram Jethmalani & Ors. Petitioner(s)

Versus

Union Of India & Ors. Respondent(s)

(With appln(s) for directions and permission to file additional documents)

WITH SLP(C) No. 11032 of 2009 (PH)

(With prayer for interim relief)

W.P.(C) No. 37 of 2010 (PH)

W.P.(C) No. 136 of 2011

(With office report)

Date: 04/07/2011 These Petitions were called on for hearing today.

CORAM:

Hon'ble Mr. Justice B. Sudershan Reddy

Hon'ble Mr. Justice Surinder Singh Nijjar

For the appearing parties:
Mr. Anil Divan, Sr. Adv.
Ms. Lata Krishnamurthi, Adv.
Mr. R.N. Karanjawala, Adv.
Ms. Manik Karanjawala, Adv.
Mr. Sandeep Kapur, Adv.
Mr. Ranvir Singh, Adv.
Mr. Ravi Sharma, Adv.
Mr. Pranav Diesh, Adv.
Mr. Karan Kalia, Adv.
Mr. Arjun Mahajan, Adv.
for M/S. Karanjawala & Co., Adv.
Mr. Rajindra Sachchar, Sr. Adv.
Mr. Gaurav Jain, Adv.
Ms. Abha Jain, Adv.
For Intervenor:
K.V.M.PAI Mr. Krishnan Venugopal, Sr. Adv.
Mrs. Anuradha Mutatkar, Adv.
Mrs. Anagha S. Desai, Adv.
Mr. Shyamohan, Adv.
Ms. Meenakshi Arora, Adv.
For UOI Mr. Gopal Subramanium, SG
Mr. H.P. Raval, ASG
Mr. Devansh Mohta, Adv.
Mr. T.A. Khan, Adv.
Mr. Arijit Prasad, Adv.
Mr. Kunal Bahri, Adv.
Mr. B.V. Balaram Das, Adv.
Mr. B. Krishna Prasad, Adv.
Mr. Mukul Rohatgi, Sr. Adv.
Mr. Rajiv Nanda, Adv.

For RR-3 (SEBI) Mr. Pratap Venugopal, Adv.
Ms. Surekha Raman, Adv.
Mr. Dileep Poolakkit, Adv.
Ms. Namrata Sood, Adv.
Mr. Anuj Sarma, Adv.
for M/S. K.J. John & Co., Adv.
Mr. Kuldeep S. Parihar, Adv.
Mr. H.S. Parihar, Adv.
Mr. Sanjay Kharde, Adv.
Ms. Asha Gopalan Nair, Adv.
Mr. P.P. Malhotra, ASG
Mr. J.S. Attri, Sr. Adv.
Ms. Sadhana Sandhu, Adv.
Ms. Anil Katiyar, Adv.
Mr. Samir Ali Khan, Adv.
Mr. Rajiv Mohiti, Sr. Adv.
Mr. I.P. Bagadia, Sr. Adv.
Mr. Santosh Paul, Adv.
Mr. B.V. Reddy, Adv.
Mr. Arvind Gupta, Adv.
Ms. Arti Singh, Adv.
Ms. Mohita Bagati, Adv.
Mr. Ashok Kumar Gupta-I, Adv.
UPON hearing counsel the Court made the following

ORDER

W.P.(C) No. 176 of 2009

For the reasons given in the reportable order compliance report shall be filed by the respondents with respect of all the orders issued by this Court today. List this matter for further directions in the week following the Independence Day, August 15, 2011.

The status reports and other documents furnished from time to time shall be kept in the safe custody of the Registrar (Judicial).

The Registry is directed to forthwith dispatch copies of this order to the Chief Secretaries of all the State Governments and the Union Territories for compliance.

I.A. No. 7 – application for intervention is dismissed.

SLP(C) No. 11032 of 2009

W.P.(C) No. 37 of 2010

W.P.(C) No. 136 of 2011

List these matters on 5th July, 2011 at the end of the Board.

REPORTABLE

IN THE SUPREME COURT OF INDIA CIVIL ORIGINAL JURISDICTION WRIT PETITION (CIVIL) NO. 176 OF 2009 RAM JETHMALANI & ORS. ...PETITIONERS VERSUS UNION OF INDIA & ORS. ...RESPONDENTS WITH I.A.NO.1 OF 2009

O R D E R

I

"Follow the money" was the short and simple advice given by the secret informant, within the American Government, to Bob Woodward, the journalist from Washington Post, in aid of his investigations of the Watergate Hotel break in. Money has often been claimed, by economists, to only be a veil that covers the real value and the economy. As a medium of exchange, money is vital for the smooth functioning of exchange in the market place. However, increasing monetization of most social transactions has been viewed as potentially problematic for the social order, in as much as it signifies a move to evaluating value, and ethical desirability, of most areas of social interaction only in terms of price obtained in the market place. Price based notions of value and values, as propounded by some extreme neo-liberal doctrines, implies that the values that ought to be promoted, in societies, are the ones for which people are willing to pay a price for. Values, and social actions, for which an effective demand is not expressed in the market, are neglected, even if lip service is paid to their essentiality. However, it cannot be denied that not everything that can be, and is transacted, in the market for a price is necessarily good, and enhances social welfare. Moreover, some activities, even if costly and without being directly measurable in terms of exchange value, are to be rightly viewed as essential. It is a well established proposition, of political economy, and of statecraft, that the State has a necessary interest in determining, and influencing, the kinds of transactions, and social actions, that occur within a legal order. From prevention of certain kinds of harmful activities, that may range from outright crimes, to regulating or controlling, and consequently mitigating, socially harmful modes of social and economic production, to promotion of activities that are deemed to be of higher priority, than other activities which may have a lower priority, howsoever evaluated in terms of social utility, are all the responsibilities of the State. Whether such activities by the State result in directly measurable benefits or not is often not the most important factor in determining their desirability; their absence, or their substantial evisceration, are to be viewed as socially destructive.

The scrutiny, and control, of activities, whether in the economic, social or political contexts, by the State, in the public interest as posited by modern constitutionalism, is substantially effectuated by the State "following the money". In modern societies very little gets accomplished without transfer of money. The incidence of crime, petty and grand, like any other social phenomena is often linked to transfers of monies, small or large. Money, in that sense, can both power, and also reward, crime. As noted by many scholars, with increasing globalization, an ideological and social construct, in which transactions across borders are accomplished with little or no control over the quantum, and mode of transfers of money in exchange for various services and value rendered, both legal and illegal, nation-states also have begun to confront complex problems of cross-border crimes of all kinds. Whether this complex web of flows of funds, instantaneously, and in large sums is good or bad, from the perspective of lawful and desired transactions is not at issue in the context of the matters before this Court.

4. The worries of this Court that arise, in the context of the matters placed before us, are with respect to transfers of monies, and accumulation of monies, which are unaccounted for by many individuals and other legal entities in the country, in foreign banks. The worries of this Court relate not merely to the quantum of monies said to have been secreted away in foreign banks, but also the manner in which they may have been taken away from the country, and with the nature of activities that may have engendered the accumulation of such monies. The worries of this Court are also with regard to the nature of activities that such monies may engender, both in terms of the concentration of economic power, and also the fact that such monies may be transferred to groups and individuals who may use them for unlawful activities that are extremely dangerous to the nation, including actions against the State. The worries of this Court also relate to whether the activities of engendering such unaccounted monies, transferring them abroad, and the routing them back to India may not actually be creating a culture that extols the virtue of such cycles, and the activities that engender such cycles are viewed as desirable modes of individual and group action. The worries of this Court also relate to the manner, and the extent to which such cycles are damaging to both national and international attempts to combat the extent, nature and intensity of cross-border criminal activity. Finally, the worries of this Court are also with respect to the extent of incapacities, system wide, in terms of institutional resources, skills, and knowledge, as well as about incapacities of ethical nature, in keeping an account of the monies generated by various facets of social action in the country, and thereby developing effective mechanisms of control. These incapacities go to the very heart of constitutional imperatives of governance. Whether such incapacities are on account of not having devoted enough resources towards building such capacities, or on account of a broader culture of venality in the wider spheres of social and political action, they run afoul of constitutional imperatives.

5. Large amounts of unaccounted monies, stashed away in banks located in jurisdictions that thrive on strong privacy laws protecting bearers of those accounts to avoid scrutiny, raise each

and every worry delineated above. First and foremost, such large monies stashed abroad, and unaccounted for by individuals and entities of a country, would suggest the necessity of suspecting that they have been generated in activities that have been deemed to be unlawful. In addition, such large amounts of unaccounted monies would also lead to a natural suspicion that they have been transferred out of the country in order to evade payment of taxes, thereby depleting the capacity of the nation to undertake many tasks that are in public interest.

6. Many schools of thought exist with regard to the primary functions of the State, and the normative expectations of what the role of the State ought to be. The questions regarding which of those schools provide the absolutely correct view cannot be the criteria to choose or reject any specific school of thought as an aid in constitutional adjudication. Charged with the responsibility of having to make decisions in the present, within the constraints of epistemic frailties of human knowledge, constitutional adjudicators willy-nilly are compelled to choose those that seem to provide a reasoned basis for framing of questions relevant, both with respect to law, and to facts. Institutional economics gives one such perspective which may be a useful guide for us here. Viewed from a functional perspective, the State, and governments, may be seen as coming into existence in order to solve, what institutional economists have come to refer to as, the coordination problems in providing public goods, and prevent the disutility that emerges from the moral hazard of a short run utility maximizer, who may desire the benefits of goods and services that are to be provided in common to the public, and yet have the interest of not paying for their production.

7. Security of the nation, infrastructure of governance, including those that relate to law making and law keeping functions, crime prevention, detection and punishment, coordination of the economy, and ensuring minimal levels of material, and cultural goods for those who may not be in a position to fend for themselves or who have been left by the wayside by the operation of the economy and society, may all be cited as some examples of the kinds of public goods that the State is expected to provide for, or enable the provision of. In as

much as the market is primarily expected to cater to purely self centered activities of individuals and groups, markets and the domain of purely private social action significantly fail to provide such goods. Consequently, the State, and government, emerges to rectify the coordination problem, and provide the public goods.

8. Unaccounted monies, especially large sums held by nationals and entities with a legal presence in the nation, in banks abroad, especially in tax havens or in jurisdictions with a known history of silence about sources of monies, clearly indicate a compromise of the ability of the State to manage its affairs in consonance with what is required from a constitutional perspective. This is so in two respects. The quantum of such monies by itself, along with the numbers of individuals or other legal entities who hold such monies, may indicate in the first instance that a large volume of activities, in the social and the economic spheres within the country are unlawful and causing great social damage, both at the individual and the collective levels. Secondly, large quanta of monies stashed abroad, would also indicate a substantial weakness in the capacity of the State in collection of taxes on incomes generated by individuals and other legal entities within the country. The generation of such revenues is essential for the State to undertake the various public goods and services that it is constitutionally mandated, and normatively expected by its citizenry, to provide. A substantial degree of incapacity, in the above respect, would be an indicia of the degree of failure of the State; and beyond a particular point, the State may spin into a vicious cycle of declining moral authority, thereby causing the incidence of unlawful activities in which wealth is sought to be generated, as well as instances of tax evasion, to increase in volume and in intensity.

9. Consequently, the issue of unaccounted monies held by nationals, and other legal entities, in foreign banks, is of primordial importance to the welfare of the citizens. The quantum of such monies may be rough indicators of the weakness of the State, in terms of both crime prevention, and also of tax collection. Depending on the volume of such monies, and the number of incidents through which such monies are generated and secreted

away, it may very well reveal the degree of "softness of the State."

10. The concept of a "soft state" was famously articulated by the Nobel Laureate, Gunnar Myrdal. It is a broad based assessment of the degree to which the State, and its machinery, is equipped to deal with its responsibilities of governance. The more soft the State is, greater the likelihood that there is an unholy nexus between the law maker, the law keeper, and the law breaker.

11. When a catchall word like "crimes" is used, it is common for people, and the popular culture to assume that it is "petty crime," or crimes of passion committed by individuals. That would be a gross mischaracterization of the seriousness of the issues involved. Far more dangerous are the crimes that threaten national security, and national interest. For instance, with globalization, nation states are also confronted by the dark worlds of international arms dealers, drug peddlers, and various kinds of criminal networks, including networks of terror. International criminal networks that extend support to home-grown terror or extremist groups, or those that have been nurtured and sustained in hostile countries, depend on networks of formal and informal, lawful and unlawful mechanisms of transfer of monies across boundaries of nation states. They work in the interstices of the microstructures of financial transfers across the globe, and thrive in the lacunae, the gaps in law and of effort. The loosening of control over those mechanisms of transfers, guided by an extreme neoliberal thirst to create a global market that is free of the friction of law and its enforcement, by nation-states, may have also contributed to an increase in the volume, extent and intensity of activities by criminal and terror networks across the globe.

12. Increasingly, on account of "greed is good" culture that has been promoted by neo-liberal ideologues, many countries face the situation where the model of capitalism that the State is compelled to institute, and the markets it spawns, is predatory in nature. From mining mafias to political operators who, all too willingly, bend policies of the State to suit particular individuals

or groups in the social and economic sphere, the raison d'etre for weakening the capacities and intent to enforce the laws is the lure of the lucre. Even as the State provides violent support to those who benefit from such predatory capitalism, often violating the human rights of its citizens, particularly it's poor, the market begins to function like a bureaucratic machine dominated by big business; and the State begins to function like the market, where everything is available for sale at a price.

13. The paradigm of governance that has emerged, over the past three decades, prioritizes the market, and its natural course, over any degree of control of it by the State. The role for the State is visualized by votaries of the neoliberal paradigm as that of a night watchman; and moreover it is also expected to take its hands out of the till of the wealth generating machinery. Based on the theories of Arthur Laffer, and pushed by the Washington Consensus, the prevailing wisdom of the elite, and of the policy makers, is that reduction of tax rates, thereby making tax regimes regressive, would incentivise the supposed genius of entrepreneurial souls of individuals, actuated by pursuit of self-interest and desire to accumulate great economic power. It was expected that this would enable the generation of more wealth, at a more rapid pace, thereby enabling the State to generate appropriate tax revenues even with lowered tax rates. Further, benefits were also expected in moral terms—that the lowering of tax rates would reduce the incentives of wealth generators to hide their monies, thereby saving them from the guilt of tax evasion. Whether that is an appropriate model of social organization or not, and from the perspective of constitutional adjudication, whether it meets the requirements of constitutionalism as embedded in the texts of various constitutions, is not a question that we want to enter in this matter.

14. Nevertheless, it would be necessary to note that there is a fly in the ointment of the above story of friction free markets that would always clear, and always work to the benefit of the society. The strength of tax collection machinery can, and ought to be, expected to have a direct bearing on the revenues collected by the State. If the machinery is weak, understaffed, ideologically

motivated to look the other way, or the agents motivated by not so salubrious motives, the amount of revenue collected by the State would decline, stagnate, or may not generate the revenue for the State that is consonant with its responsibilities. From within the neoliberal paradigm, also emerged the under-girding current of thought that revenues for the State implies a big government, and hence a strong tax collecting machinery itself would be undesirable. Where the elite lose out in democratic politics of achieving ever decreasing tax rates, it would appear that state machineries in the hands of the executive, all too willing to promote the extreme versions of the neoliberal paradigm and co-opt itself in the enterprises of the elite, may also become all too willing to not develop substantial capacities to monitor and follow the money, collect the lawfully mandated taxes, and even look the other way. The results, as may be expected, have been disastrous across many nations.

15. In addition, it would also appear that in this miasmic cultural environment in which greed is extolled, conspicuous consumption viewed as both necessary and socially valuable, and the wealthy viewed as demi-gods, the agents of the State may have also succumbed to the notions of the neoliberal paradigm that the role of the State ought to only be an enabling one, and not exercise significant control. This attitude would have a significant impact on exercise of discretion, especially in the context of regulating economic activities, including keeping an account of the monies generated in various activities, both legal and illegal. Carried away by the ideology of neoliberalism, it is entirely possible that the agents of the State entrusted with the task of supervising the economic and social activities may err more on the side of extreme caution, whereby signals of wrong doing may be ignored even when they are strong. Instances of the powers that be ignoring publicly visible stock market scams, or turning a blind eye to large scale illegal mining have become all too familiar, and may be readily cited. That such activities are allowed to continue to occur, with weak, or non-existent, responses from the State may, at best, be charitably ascribed to this broader culture of permissibility of all manner of private activities in search of ever more lucre. Ethical compromises, by

the elite—those who wield the powers of the state, and those who fatten themselves in an ever more exploitative economic sphere—can be expected to thrive in an environment marked by such a permissive attitude, of weakened laws, and of weakened law enforcement machineries and attitudes.

16. To the above, we must also add the fragmentation of administration. Even as the range of economic, and social activities have expanded, and their sophistication increased by leaps and bounds, the response in terms of administration by the State has been to create ever more specialized agencies, and departments. To some degree this has been unavoidable. Nevertheless, it would also appear that there is a need to build internal capacities to share information across such departments, lessen the informational asymmetries between, and friction to flow of information across the boundaries of departments and agencies, and reduce the levels of consequent problems in achieving coordination. Life, and social action within which human life becomes possible, do not proceed on the basis of specialized fiefdoms of expertise. They cut across the boundaries erected as a consequence of an inherent tendency of experts to specialize. The result, often, is a system wide blindness, while yet being lured by the dazzle of ever greater specialization. Many dots of information, now collected in ever increasing volume by development of sophisticated information technologies, get ignored on account of lack of coordination across agencies, and departments, and tendency within bureaucracy to jealously guard their own turfs. In some instances, the failure to properly investigate, or to prevent, unlawful activities could be the result of such over-specialization, frictions in sharing of information, and coordination across departmental and specialized agency boundaries.

17. If the State is soft to a large extent, especially in terms of the unholy nexus between the law makers, the law keepers, and the law breakers, the moral authority, and also the moral incentives, to exercise suitable control over the economy and the society would vanish. Large unaccounted monies are generally an indication of that. In a recent book, Prof. Rotberg states, after

evaluating many failed and collapsed states over the past few decades:

> Failed states offer unparalleled economic opportunity—but only for a privileged few. Those around the ruler or ruling oligarchy grow richer while their less fortunate brethren starve. Immense profits are available from an awareness of regulatory advantages and currency speculation and arbitrage. But the privilege of making real money when everything else is deteriorating is confined to clients of the ruling elite.... The nation-state's responsibility to maximize the well-being and prosperity of all its citizens is conspicuously absent, if it ever existed.... Corruption flourishes in many states, but in failed states it often does so on an unusually destructive scale. There is widespread petty or lubricating corruption as a matter of course, but escalating levels of venal corruption mark failed states ("The Failure and Collapse of Nation-States—Breakdown, Prevention and Repair" in *When States Fail: Causes and Consequences*, Rotberg, Robert I., Ed. Princeton University Press, 2004).

18. India finds itself in a peculiar situation. Often celebrated, in popular culture, as an emerging economy that is rapidly growing, and expected to be a future economic and political giant on the global stage, it is also popularly perceived, and apparently even in some responsible and scholarly circles, and official quarters, that some of its nationals and other legal entities have stashed the largest quantum of unaccounted monies in foreign banks, especially in tax havens, and in other jurisdictions with strong laws of secrecy. There are also apparently reports, and analyses, generated by Government of India itself, which place the amounts of such unaccounted monies at astronomical levels.

19. We do not wish to engage in any speculation as to what such analyses, reports, and factuality imply with respect to the state of the nation. The citizens of our country can make, and ought to be making, rational assessments of the situation. We fervently hope that it leads to responsible, reasoned and reasonable debate, thereby exerting the appropriate democratic pressure on

the State, and its agents, within the constitutional framework, to bring about the necessary changes without sacrificing cherished, and inherently invaluable social goals and values enshrined in the Constitution. The failures are discernible when viewed against the vision of the constitutional project, and as forewarned by Dr. Ambedkar, have been on account of the fact that man has been vile, and not the defects of a Constitution forged in the fires of wisdom gathered over eons of human experience. If the politico-bureaucratic, power wielding, and business classes bear a large part of the blame, at least some part of blame ought to be apportioned to those portions of the citizenry that is well informed, or is expected to be informed. Much of that citizenry has disengaged itself with the political process, and with the masses. Informed by contempt for the poor and the downtrodden, the elite classes that have benefited the most, or expects to benefit substantially from the neoliberal policies that would wish away the hordes, has also chosen to forget that constitutional mandate is as much the responsibility of the citizenry, and through their constant vigilance, of all the organs of the state, and national institutions including political parties. To not be engaged in the process, is to ensure the evisceration of constitutional content. Knee jerk reactions, and ill advised tinkering with the constitutional framework are not the solutions. The road is always long, and needs the constant march of the citizenry on it. There is no other way. To expect instant solutions, because this law or that body is formed, without striving to solve system wide, and systemic, problems that have emerged is to not understand the demands of a responsible citizenry in modern constitutional republican democracies.

20. These matters before us relate to issues of large sums of unaccounted monies, allegedly held by certain named individuals, and loose associations of them; consequently we have to express our serious concerns from a constitutional perspective. The amount of unaccounted monies, as alleged by the Government of India itself is massive. The show cause notices were issued a substantial length of time ago. The named individuals were very much present in the country. Yet, for unknown, and possibly unknowable, though easily surmisable, reasons the investigations

into the matter proceeded at a laggardly pace. Even the named individuals had not yet been questioned with any degree of seriousness. These are serious lapses, especially when viewed from the perspective of larger issues of security, both internal and external, of the country.

21. It is in light of the above, that we heard some significant elements of the instant writ petitions filed in this Court, and at this stage it is necessary that appropriate orders be issued. There are two issues we deal with below:

(i) the appointment of a Special Investigation Team; and

(ii) disclosure, to the Petitioners, of certain documents relied upon by the Union of India in its response.

II

22. The instant writ petition was filed, in 2009, by Shri Ram Jethmalani, Shri Gopal Sharman, Smt. Jalbala Vaidya, Shri K.P.S. Gill, Prof. B.B. Dutta, and Shri Subhash Kashyap, all well known professionals, social activists, former bureaucrats or those who have held responsible positions in the society. They have also formed an organization called Citizen India, the stated objective of which is said to be to bring about changes and betterment in the quality of governance, and functioning of all public institutions.

23. The Petitioners state that there have been a slew of reports, in the media, and also in scholarly publications that various individuals, mostly citizens, but may also include noncitizens, and other entities with presence in India, have generated, and secreted away large sums of monies, through their activities in India or relating to India, in various foreign banks, especially in tax havens, and jurisdictions that have strong secrecy laws with respect to the contents of bank accounts and the identities of individuals holding such accounts. The Petitioners allege that most of such monies are unaccounted, and in all probability have been generated through unlawful activities, whether in India or outside India, but relating to India. Further, the Petitioners also allege that a large part of such monies may have been generated within India, and have been taken away

from India, breaking various laws, including but not limited to evasion of taxes.

24. The Petitioners contend: (i) that the sheer volume of such monies points to grave weaknesses in the governance of the nation, because they indicate a significant lack of control over unlawful activities through which such monies are generated, evasion of taxes, and use of unlawful means of transfer of funds; (ii) that these funds are then laundered and brought back into India, to be used in both legal and illegal activities; (iii) that the use of various unlawful modes of transfer of funds across borders, gives support to such unlawful networks of international finance; and (iv) that in as much as such unlawful networks are widely acknowledged to also effectuate transfer of funds across borders in aid of various crimes committed against persons and the State, including but not limited to activities that may be classifiable as terrorist, extremist, or unlawful narcotic trade, the prevailing situation also has very serious connotations for the security and integrity of India.

25. The Petitioners also further contend that a significant part of such large unaccounted monies include the monies of powerful persons in India, including leaders of many political parties. It was also contended that the Government of India, and its agencies, have been very lax in terms of keeping an eye on the various unlawful activities generating unaccounted monies, the consequent tax evasion; and that such laxity extends to efforts to curtail the flow of such funds out, and into, India. Further, the Petitioners also contend that the efforts to prosecute the individuals, and other entities, who have secreted such monies in foreign banks, have been weak or non-existent. It was strongly argued that the efforts at identification of such monies in various bank accounts in many jurisdictions across the globe, attempts to bring back such monies, and efforts to strengthen the governance framework to prevent further outflows of such funds, have been sorely lacking.

26. The Petitioners also made allegations about certain specific incidents and patterns of dereliction of duty, wherein the Government of India, and its various agencies, even though in

possession of specific knowledge about the monies in certain bank accounts, and having estimated that such monies run into many scores of thousands of crores, and upon issuance of show cause notices to the said individual, surprisingly have not proceeded to initiate, and carry out suitable investigations, and prosecute the individuals. The individual specifically named is one Hassan Ali Khan. The Petitioners also contended that Kashinath Tapuria, and his wife Chandrika Tapuria, are also party to the illegal activities of Hassan Ali Khan.

27. Specifically, it was alleged that Hassan Ali Khan was served with an income tax demand for ₹ 40,000.00 Crores (Rupees Forty Thousand Crores), and that the Tapurias were served an income tax demand notice of ₹ 20,580.00 Crores (Rupees Twenty Thousand Five Hundred and Eighty Crores). The Enforcement Directorate, in 2007, disclosed that Hassan Ali Khan had "dealings amounting to 1.6 billion US dollars" in the period 2001-05. In January 2007, upon raiding Hassan Ali's residence in Pune, certain documents and evidence had been discovered regarding deposits of 8.04 billion dollars with UBS bank in Zurich. It is the contention of the Petitioners that, even though such evidence was secured nearly four and half years ago, (i) a proper investigation had not been launched to obtain the right facts from abroad; (ii) the individuals concerned, though present in India, and subject to its jurisdiction, and easily available for its exercise, had not even been interrogated appropriately; (iii) that the Union of India, and its various departments, had even been refusing to divulge the details and information that would reveal the actual status of the investigation, whether in fact it was being conducted at all, or with any degree of seriousness; (iv) given the magnitude of amounts in question, especially of the demand notice of income tax, the laxity of investigation indicates multiple problems of serious non-governance, and weaknesses in the system, including pressure from political quarters to hinder, or scuttle, the investigation, prosecution, and ultimately securing the return of such monies; and (v) given the broadly accepted fact that within the political class corruption is rampant, illbegotten wealth has begun to be amassed in massive quantities by many members in that class, it

may be reasonable to suspect, or even conclude, that investigation was being deliberately hindered because Hassan Ali Khan, and the Tapurias, had or were continuing to handle the monies of such a class. The fact that both Income Tax department, and the Enforcement Directorate routinely, and with alacrity, seek the powers for long stretches of custodial interrogation of even those suspected of having engaged in money laundering, or evaded taxes, with respect to very small amounts, ought to raise the reasonable suspicion that inaction in the matters concerning Hassan Ali Khan, and Tapurias, was deliberately engineered, for nefarious reasons.

28. In addition, the Petitioners also state that in as much as the bank in which the monies had been stashed by Hassan Ali Khan was UBS Zurich, the needle of suspicion has to inexorably turn to high level political interference and hindrance to the investigations. The said bank, it was submitted, is the biggest or one of the biggest wealth management companies in the world. The Petitioners also narrated the mode, and the manner, in which the United States had dealt with UBS, with respect to monies of American citizens secreted away with the said bank. It was also alleged that UBS had not cooperated with the U.S. authorities. Contrasting the relative alacrity, and vigour, with which the United States government had pursued the matters, the Petitioners contend the inaction of Union of India is shocking.

29. The Petitioners further allege that in 2007, the Reserve Bank of India had obtained some "knowledge of the dubious character" of UBS Security India Private Limited, a branch of UBS, and consequently stopped this bank from extending its business in India by refusing to approve its takeover of Standard Chartered Mutual Funds business in India. It was also claimed by the Petitioners that the SEBI had alleged that UBS played a role in the stock market crash of 2004. The said UBS Bank has apparently applied for a retail banking license in India, which was approved in principle by RBI initially. In 2008, this license was withheld on the ground that "investigation of its unsavoury role in the Hassan Ali Khan case was pending investigation in the Enforcement Directorate." However, it seems that the RBI

reversed its decision in 2009, and no good reasons seem to be forthcoming for the reversal of the decision of 2008.

30. The Petitioners contend that such a reversal of decision could only have been accomplished through high level intervention, and that it is further evidence of linkages between members of the political class, and possibly even members of the bureaucracy, and such banking operations, and the illegal activities of Hassan Ali Khan and the Tapurias. Hence, the Petitioners argued, in the circumstances it would have to be necessarily concluded that the investigations into the affairs of Hassan Ali Khan, and the Tapurias, would be severely compromised if the Court does not intervene, and monitor the investigative processes by appointing a special investigation team reporting directly to the Court.

31. The learned senior counsel for the Petitioners sought that this Court intervene, order proper investigations, and monitor continuously, the actions of the Union of India, and any and all governmental departments and agencies, in these matters. It was submitted that their filing of this Writ Petition under Article 32 is proper, as the inaction of the Union of India, as described above, violates the fundamental rights—to proper governance, in as much as Article 14 provides for equality before the law and equal protection of the law, and Article 21 promises dignity of life to all citizens.

32. We have heard the learned senior counsel for the Petitioners, Shri Anil B. Divan, the learned senior counsel for interveners, Shri K.K. Venugopal, and the learned senior counsel for the petitioners in the connected Writ Petition, Shri Shanti Bhushan. We have also heard the learned Solicitor General, Shri Gopal Subramaniam, on behalf of the respondents.

33. Shri Divan, specifically argued that, having regard to the nature of the investigation, its slow pace so far, and the non-seriousness on the part of the respondents, there is a need to constitute a Special Investigation Team ("SIT") headed by a former judge or two of this court. However, this particular plea has been vociferously resisted by the Solicitor General. Relying on the status reports submitted from time to time, the learned

Solicitor General stated that all possible steps were being taken to bring back the monies stashed in foreign banks, and that the investigations in cases registered were proceeding in an appropriate manner. He expressed his willingness for a Court monitored investigation. He also further submitted that the Respondents, in principle, have no objections whatsoever against the main submissions of the Petitioners.

34. The real point of controversy is, given above, as to whether there is a need to constitute a SIT to be headed by a judge or two, of this court, to supervise the investigation.

35. We must express our serious reservations about the responses of the Union of India. In the first instance, during the earlier phases of hearing before us, the attempts were clearly evasive, confused, or originating in the denial mode. It was only upon being repeatedly pressed by us did the Union of India begin to admit that indeed the investigation was proceeding very slowly. It also became clear to us that in fact the investigation had completely stalled, in as much as custodial interrogation of Hassan Ali Khan had not even been sought for, even though he was very much resident in India. Further, it also now appears that even though his passport had been impounded, he was able to secure another passport from the RPO in Patna, possibly with the help or aid of a politician.

36. During the course of the hearings the Union of India repeatedly insisted that the matter involves many jurisdictions, across the globe, and a proper investigation could be accomplished only through the concerted efforts by different law enforcement agencies, both within the Central Government, and also various State governments. However, the absence of any satisfactory explanation of the slowness of the pace of investigation, and lack of any credible answers as to why the respondents did not act with respect to those actions that were feasible, and within the ambit of powers of the Enforcement Directorate itself, such as custodial investigation, leads us to conclude that the lack of seriousness in the efforts of the respondents are contrary to the requirements of laws and constitutional obligations of the Union of India. It was only upon the insistence and intervention of this

Court has the Enforcement Directorate initiated and secured custodial interrogation over Hassan Ali Khan. The Union of India has explicitly acknowledged that there was much to be desired with the manner in which the investigation had proceeded prior to the intervention of this court. From the more recent reports, it would appear that the Union of India, on account of its more recent efforts to conduct the investigation with seriousness, on account of the gravitas brought by this Court, has led to the securing of additional information, and leads, which could aid in further investigation. For instance, during the continuing interrogation of Hassan Ali Khan and the Tapurias, undertaken for the first time at the behest of this Court, many names of important persons, including leaders of some corporate giants, politically powerful people, and international arms dealers have cropped up. So far, no significant attempt has been made to investigate and verify the same. This is a further cause for the grave concerns of this Court, and points to the need for continued, effective and day to day monitoring by a SIT constituted by this Court, and acting on behalf, behest and direction of this Court.

37. In light of the fact that the issues are complex, requiring expertise and knowledge of different departments, and the necessity of coordination of efforts across various agencies and departments, it was submitted to us that the Union of India has recently formed a High Level Committee, under the aegis of the Department of Revenue in the Ministry of Finance, which is the nodal agency responsible for all economic offences. The composition of the High Level Committee ("HLC") is said to be as follows: (i) Secretary, Department of Revenue, as the Chairman; (ii) Deputy Governor, Reserve Bank of India; (iii) Director (IB); (iv) Director, Enforcement; (v) Director, CBI; (vi) Chairman, CBDT; (vii) DG, Narcotics Control Bureau; (viii) DG, Revenue Intelligence; (ix) Director, Financial Intelligence Unit; and (x) JS (FT & TR-I), CBDT. It was also submitted that the HLC may co-opt, as necessary, representation not below the rank of Joint Secretary from the Home Secretary, Foreign Secretary, Defense Secretary and the Secretary, Cabinet Secretariat. The Union of India claims that such a multi-disciplinary group and committee would now enable the conducting of an efficient and a systematic

investigation into the matters concerning allegations against Hassan Ali Khan and the Tapurias; and further that such a committee would also enable the taking of appropriate steps to bring back the monies stashed in foreign banks, for which purposes a need may arise to register further cases. The Union of India also claims that the formation of such a committee indicates the seriousness with which it is viewing the entire matter.

38. While it would appear, from the Status Reports submitted to this Court, that the Enforcement Directorate has moved in some small measure, the actual facts are not comforting to an appropriate extent. In fact we are not convinced that the situation has changed to the extent that it ought to so as to accept that the investigation would now be conducted with the degree of seriousness that is warranted. According to the Union of India the HLC was formed in order to take charge of and direct the entire investigation, and subsequently, the prosecution. In the meanwhile a chargesheet has been filed against Hassan Ali Khan. Upon inquiry by us as to whether the chargesheet had been vetted by the HLC, and its inputs secured, the counsel for Union of India were flummoxed. The fact was that the chargesheet had not been given even for the perusal of the HLC, let alone securing its inputs, guidance and direction. We are not satisfied by the explanation offered by the Directorate of Enforcement by way of affidavit after the orders were reserved. Be it noted that a nodal agency was set up, pursuant to directions of this Court in Vineet Narain case given many years ago. Yet the same was not involved and these matters were never placed before it. Why?

39. From the status reports, it is clear that the problem is extremely complex, and many agencies and departments spread across the country have not responded with the alacrity, and urgency, that one would desire. Moreover, the Union of India has been unable to answer any of the questions regarding its past actions, and their implications, such as the slowness of the investigation, or about grant of license to conduct retail banking by UBS, by reversing the decision taken earlier to withhold such a license on the grounds that the said bank's credentials were suspect. To this latter query, the stance of the Union of India has

been that entry of UBS would facilitate flow of foreign investments into India. The question that arises is whether the task of bringing foreign funds into India override all other constitutional concerns and obligations?

40. The predominant theme in the responses of Union of India before this court has been that it is doing all that it can to bring back the unaccounted monies stashed in various banks abroad. To this is added the qualifier that it is an extremely complex problem, requiring the cooperation of many different jurisdictions, and an internationally coordinated effort. Indeed they are complex. We do not wish to go into the details of arguments about whether the Union of India is, or is not, doing necessary things to achieve such goals. That is not necessary for the matters at hand.

41. What is important is that the Union of India had obtained knowledge, documents and information that indicated possible connections between Hassan Ali Khan, and his alleged co-conspirators and known international arms dealers. Further, the Union of India was also in possession of information that suggested that because the international arms dealing network, and a very prominent dealer in it, could not open a bank account even in a jurisdiction that is generally acknowledged to lay great emphasis on not asking sources of money being deposited into its banks, Hassan Ali Khan may have played a crucial role in opening an account with the branch of the same bank in another jurisdiction. The volume of alleged income taxes owed to the country, as demanded by the Union of India itself, and the volume of monies, by some accounts US $8.04 billion, and some other accounts in excess of ₹ 70,000 crores, that are said to have been routed through various bank accounts of Hassan Ali Khan, and Tapurias. Further, from all accounts it has been acknowledged that none of the named individuals have any known and lawful sources for such huge quantities of monies. All of these factors, either individually or combined, ought to have immediately raised questions regarding the sources being unlawful activities, national security, and transfer of funds into India for other illegal activities, including acts against the State. It was only at the repeated insistence by us that such matters have equal, if not

even greater importance than issues of tax collection, has the Union of India belatedly concluded that such aspects also ought to be investigated with thoroughness. However, there is still no evidence of a really serious investigation into these other matters from the national security perspective.

42. The fact remains that the Union of India has struggled in conducting a proper investigation into the affairs of Hassan Ali Khan and the Tapurias. While some individuals, whose names have come to the adverse knowledge of the Union of India, through the more recent investigations, have been interrogated, many more are yet to be investigated. This highly complex investigation has in fact just begun. It is still too early to conclude that the Union of India has indeed placed all the necessary machinery to conduct a proper investigation. The formation of the HLC was a necessary step, and may even be characterized as a welcome step. Nevertheless, it is an insufficient step.

43. In light of the above, we had proposed to the Union of India that the same HLC constituted by it be converted into a Special Investigation Team, headed by two retired judges of the Supreme Court of India. The Union of India opposes the same, but provides no principle as to why that would be undesirable, especially in light of the many lapses and lacunae in its actions in these matters spread over the past four years.

44. We are of the firm opinion that in these matters fragmentation of government, and expertise and knowledge, across many departments, agencies and across various jurisdictions, both within the country, and across the globe, is a serious impediment to the conduct of a proper investigation. We hold that it is in fact necessary to create a body that coordinates, directs, and where necessary orders timely and urgent action by various institutions of the State. We also hold that the continued involvement of this Court in these matters, in a broad oversight capacity, is necessary for upholding the rule of law, and achievement of constitutional values. However, it would be impossible for this Court to be involved in day to day investigations, or to constantly monitor each and every aspect of the investigation.

45. The resources of this Court are scarce, and it is overburdened with the task of rendering justice in well over a lakh of cases every year. Nevertheless, this Court is bound to uphold the Constitution, and its own burdens, excessive as they already are, cannot become an excuse for it to not perform that task. In a country where most of its people are uneducated and illiterate, suffering from hunger and squalor, the retraction of the monitoring of these matters by this Court would be unconscionable.

46. The issue is not merely whether the Union of India is making the necessary effort to bring back all or some significant part of the alleged monies. The fact that there is some information and knowledge that such vast amounts may have been stashed away in foreign banks, implies that the State has the primordial responsibility, under the Constitution, to make every effort to trace the sources of such monies, punish the guilty where such monies have been generated and/or taken abroad through unlawful activities, and bring back the monies owed to the Country. We do recognize that the degree of success, measured in terms of the amounts of monies brought back, is dependent on a number of factors, including aspects that relate to international political economy and relations, which may or may not be under our control. The fact remains that with respect to those factors that were within the powers of the Union of India, such as investigation of possible criminal nexus, threats to national security, etc., were not even attempted. Fealty to the Constitution is not a matter of mere material success; but, and probably more importantly from the perspective of the moral authority of the State, a matter of integrity of effort on all the dimensions that inform a problem that threatens the constitutional projects. Further, the degree of seriousness with which efforts are made with respect to those various dimensions can also be expected to bear fruit in terms of building capacities, and the development of necessary attitudes to take the law enforcement part of accounting or following the money seriously in the future.

47. The merits of vigour of investigations, and attempts at law enforcement, cannot be measured merely on the scale of what we accomplish with respect to what has happened in the

past. It would necessarily also have to be appreciated from the benefits that are likely to accrue to the country in preventing such activities in the future. Our people may be poor, and may be suffering from all manner of deprivation. However, the same poor and suffering masses are rich, morally and from a humanistic point of view. Their forbearance of the many foibles and failures of those who wield power, no less in their name and behalf than of the rich and the empowered, is itself indicative of their great qualities, of humanity, trust and tolerance. That greatness can only be matched by exercise of every sinew, and every resource, in the broad goal of our constitutional project of bringing to their lives dignity. The efforts that this Court makes in this regard, and will make in this respect and these matters, can only be conceived as a small and minor, though nevertheless necessary, part. Ultimately the protection of the Constitution and striving to promote its vision and values is an elemental mode of service to our people.

48. We note that in many instances, in the past, when issues referred to the Court have been very complex in nature, and yet required the intervention of the Court, Special Investigation Teams have been ordered and constituted in order to enable the Court, and the Union of India and/or other organs of the State, to fulfill their constitutional obligations. The following instances may be noted: Vineet Narain v Union of India1, NHRC v State of Gujarat2, Sanjiv Kumar v State of Haryana3, and Centre for PIL v Union of India 4. [1 (1996) 2 SCC 199; 2 (2004) 8 SCC 610; 3 (2005) 5 SCC 517; 4 (2011) 1 SCC 560].

49. In light of the above we herewith order:

(i) That the High Level Committee constituted by the Union of India, comprising of (i) Secretary, Department of Revenue; (ii) Deputy Governor, Reserve Bank of India; (iii) Director (IB); (iv) Director, Enforcement; (v) Director, CBI; (vi) Chairman, CBDT; (vii) DG, Narcotics Control Bureau; (viii) DG, Revenue Intelligence; (ix) Director, Financial Intelligence Unit; and (x) JS (FT & TR-I), CBDT be forthwith appointed with immediate effect as a Special Investigation Team;

(ii) That the Special Investigation Team, so constituted, also include Director, Research and Analysis Wing;

(iii) That the above Special Investigation Team, so constituted, be headed by and include the following former eminent judges of this Court: (a) Hon'ble Mr. Justice B.P. Jeevan Reddy as Chairman; and (b) Hon'ble Mr. Justice M.B. Shah as Vice-Chairman; and that the Special Investigation Team function under their guidance and direction;

(iv) That the Special Investigation Team, so constituted, shall be charged with the responsibilities and duties of investigation, initiation of proceedings, and prosecution, whether in the context of appropriate criminal or civil proceedings of: (a) all issues relating to the matters concerning and arising from unaccounted monies of Hassan Ali Khan and the Tapurias; (b) all other investigations already commenced and are pending, or awaiting to be initiated, with respect to any other known instances of the stashing of unaccounted monies in foreign bank accounts by Indians or other entities operating in India; and (c) all other matters with respect to unaccounted monies being stashed in foreign banks by Indians or other entities operating in India that may arise in the course of such investigations and proceedings. It is clarified here that within the ambit of responsibilities described above, also lie the responsibilities to ensure that the matters are also investigated, proceedings initiated and prosecutions conducted with regard to criminality and/or unlawfulness of activities that may have been the source for such monies, as well as the criminal and/or unlawful means that are used to take such unaccounted monies out of and/or bring such monies back into the country, and use of such monies in India or abroad. The Special Investigation Team shall also be charged with the responsibility of preparing a comprehensive action plan, including the creation of necessary institutional structures that can enable and strengthen the country's battle against generation of unaccounted monies, and their stashing away in foreign banks or in various forms domestically.

(v) That the Special Investigation Team so constituted report and be responsible to this Court, and that it shall be charged with the duty to keep this Court informed of all major developments by the filing of periodic status reports, and following of any special orders that this Court may issue from time to time;

(vi) That all organs, agencies, departments and agents of the State, whether at the level of the Union of India, or the State Government, including but not limited to all statutorily formed individual bodies, and other constitutional bodies, extend all the cooperation necessary for the Special Investigation Team so constituted and functioning;

(vii) That the Union of India, and where needed even the State Governments, are directed to facilitate the conduct of the investigations, in their fullest measure, by the Special Investigation Team so constituted and functioning, by extending all the necessary financial, material, legal, diplomatic and intelligence resources, whether such investigations or portions of such investigations occur inside the country or abroad.

(viii) That the Special Investigation Team also be empowered to further investigate even where chargesheets have been previously filed; and that the Special Investigation Team may register further cases, and conduct appropriate investigations and initiate proceedings, for the purpose of bringing back unaccounted monies unlawfully kept in bank accounts abroad.

50. We accordingly direct the Union of India to issue appropriate notification and publish the same forthwith. It is needless to clarify that the former judges of this Court so appointed to supervise the Special Investigation Team are entitled to their remuneration, allowances, perks, facilities as that of the judges of the Supreme Court. The Ministry of Finance, Union of India, shall be responsible for creating the appropriate infrastructure and other facilities for proper and effective functioning of the Special Investigation Team at once.

III

51. We now turn our attention to the matter of disclosure of various documents referenced by the Union of India, as sought by the Petitioners. These documents, including names and bank particulars, relate to various bank accounts, of Indian citizens, in the Principality of Liechtenstein ("Liechtenstein"), a small landlocked sovereign nation-state in Europe. It is generally acknowledged that Liechtenstein is a tax haven.

52. Apparently, as alleged by the Petitioners, a former employee of a bank or banks in Liechtenstein secured the names of some 1400 bank account holders, along with the particulars of such accounts, and offered the information to various entities. The same was secured by the Federal Republic of Germany ("Germany"), which in turn, apart from initiating tax proceedings against some 600 individuals, also offered the information regarding nationals and citizens of other countries to such countries. It is the contention of the Petitioners that even though the Union of India was informed about the presence of the names of a large number of Indian citizens in the list of names revealed by the former bank employee, the Union of India never made a serious attempt to secure such information and proceed to investigate such individuals. It is the contention of the Petitioners that such names include the identities of prominent and powerful Indians, or the identities of individuals, who may or may not be Indian citizens, but who could lead to information about various powerful Indians holding unaccounted monies in bank accounts abroad. It is also the contention of the Petitioners that, even though they had sought the information under the Right to Information Act (2005), the Respondents had not revealed the names nor divulged the relevant documents. The Petitioners argue that such a reluctance is only on account of the Union of India not having initiated suitable steps to recover such monies, and punish the named individuals, and also because revelation of names of individuals on the list would lead to discovery of powerful persons engaged in various unlawful activities, both in generation of unlawful and unaccounted monies, and their stashing away in banks abroad.

53. It was also alleged by the Petitioners that in fact Germany had offered such information, freely and generally to any country that requests the same, and did not specify that the names and other information pertaining to such names ought to be requested only pursuant to any double taxation agreements it has with other countries. The Petitioners also alleged that Union of India has chosen to proceed under the assumption that it could have requested such information only pursuant to the double taxation agreement it has with Germany. The Petitioners contend that the

Government of India took such a step primarily to conceal the information from public gaze.

54. The response of the Union of India may be summed up briefly: (i) that they secured the names of individuals with bank accounts in banks in Liechtenstein, and other details with respect to such bank accounts, pursuant to an agreement of India with Germany for avoidance of double taxation and prevention of fiscal evasion; (ii) that the said agreement proscribes the Union of India from disclosing such names, and other documents and information with respect to such bank accounts, to the Petitioners, even in the context of these ongoing proceedings before this court; (iii) that the disclosure of such names, and other documents and information, secured from Germany, would jeopardize the relations of India with a foreign state; (iv) that the disclosure of such names, and other documents and information, would violate the right to privacy of those individuals who may have only deposited monies in a lawful manner; (v) that disclosure of names, and other documents and information can be made with respect to those individuals with regard to whom investigations are completed, and proceedings initiated; and (vi) that contrary to assertions by the Petitioners, it was Germany which had asked the Union of India to seek the information under double taxation agreement, and that this was in response to an earlier request by Union of India for the said information.

55. For the purposes of the instant order, the issue of whether the Union of India could have sought and secured the names, and other documents and information, without having to take recourse to the double taxation agreement is not relevant. For the purposes of determining whether Union of India is obligated to disclose the information that it obtained, from Germany, with respect to accounts of Indian citizens in a bank in the Principality of Liechtenstein, we need only examine the claims of the Union of India as to whether it is proscribed by the double taxation agreement with Germany from disclosing such information. Further, and most importantly, we would also have to examine whether in the context of Article 32 proceedings before this court, wherein this court has exercised jurisdiction, the Union of India can claim exemption from providing such

information to the Petitioners, and also with respect to issues of right to privacy of individuals who hold such accounts, and with respect of whom no investigations have yet been commenced, or only partially conducted, so that the State has not yet issued a show cause and initiated proceedings.

56. We have perused the said agreement with Germany. We are convinced that the said agreement, by itself, does not proscribe the disclosure of the relevant documents and details of the same, including the names of various bank account holders in Liechtenstein. In the first instance, we note that the names of the individuals are with respect to bank accounts in the Liechtenstein, which though populated by largely German speaking people, is an independent and sovereign nationstate. The agreement between Germany and India is with regard to various issues that crop up with respect to German and Indian citizens' liability to pay taxes to Germany and/or India. It does not even remotely touch upon information regarding Indian citizens' bank accounts in Liechtenstein that Germany secures and shares that have no bearing upon the matters that are covered by the double taxation agreement between the two countries. In fact, the "information" that is referred to in Article 26 is that which is "necessary for carrying out the purposes of this agreement", i.e. the Indo-German DTAA. Therefore, the information sought does not fall within the ambit of this provision. It is disingenuous for the Union of India, under these circumstances, to repeatedly claim that it is unable to reveal the documents and names as sought by the Petitioners on the ground that the same is proscribed by the said agreement. It does not matter that Germany itself may have asked India to treat the information shared as being subject to the confidentiality and secrecy clause of the double taxation agreement. It is for the Union of India, and the courts, in appropriate proceedings, to determine whether such information concerns matters that are covered by the double taxation agreement or not. In any event, we also proceed to examine the provisions of the double taxation agreement below, to also examine whether they proscribe the disclosure of such names, and other documents and information, even in the context of these instant proceedings.

57. Relevant portions of Article 26 of the double taxation agreement with Germany, a copy of which was submitted by Union of India, reads as follows:

> 1. The competent authorities of the Contracting States shall exchange such information as is necessary for carrying out the purposes of this Agreement. Any information received by a Contracting State shall be treated as secret in the same manner as information obtained under the domestic laws of that State and shall be disclosed only to persons or authorities (including courts and administrative bodies) involved in the assessment or collection of, the enforcement or prosecution in respect of, or the determination of appeals in relation to, the taxes covered by this Agreement. They may disclose the information in public court proceedings or in judicial proceedings.
>
> 2. In no case shall the provisions of paragraph 1 be construed so as to impose on a Contracting State the obligation:
>
> (a) to carry out administrative measures at variance with the laws and administrative practice of that or of the other Contracting State;
>
> (b) to supply information which is not obtainable under the laws or in the normal course of the administration of that or of the other Contracting State;
>
> (c) to supply information which would disclose any trade, business, industrial, commercial or professional secret or trade process, or information, the disclosure of which would be contrary to public policy (order public).

58. The above clause in the relevant agreement with Germany would indicate that, contrary to the assertions of Union of India, there is no absolute bar of secrecy. Instead the agreement specifically provides that the information may be disclosed in public court proceedings, which the instant proceedings are. The proceedings in this matter before this court, relate both to the issue of tax collection with respect to unaccounted monies deposited into foreign bank accounts, as well as with issues relating to the manner in which such monies were generated, which may include activities that are criminal in nature also.

Comity of nations cannot be predicated upon clauses of secrecy that could hinder constitutional proceedings such as these, or criminal proceedings.

59. The claim of Union of India is that the phrase "public court proceedings", in the last sentence in Article 26(1) of the double taxation agreement only relates to proceedings relating to tax matters. The Union of India claims that such an understanding comports with how it is understood internationally. In this regard Union of India cites a few treatises. However, the Union of India did not provide any evidence that Germany specifically requested it to not reveal the details with respect to accounts in the Liechtenstein even in the context of proceedings before this court.

60. Article 31, "General Rule of Interpretation", of the Vienna Convention of the Law of Treaties, 1969 provides that a "treaty shall be interpreted in good faith in accordance with the ordinary meaning to be given to the terms of the treaty in their context and in the light of its object and purpose." While India is not a party to the Vienna Convention, it contains many principles of customary international law, and the principle of interpretation, of Article 31 of the Vienna Convention, provides a broad guideline as to what could be an appropriate manner of interpreting a treaty in the Indian context also.

61. This Court in Union of India v. Azadi Bachao Andolan, (2004) 10 SCC 1 approvingly noted Frank Bennion's observations that a treaty is really an indirect enactment, instead of a substantive legislation, and that drafting of treaties is notoriously sloppy, whereby inconveniences obtain. In this regard this Court further noted the dictum of Lord Widgery, C.J. that the words "are to be given their general meaning, general to lawyer and layman alike.... The meaning of the diplomat rather than the lawyer." The broad principle of interpretation, with respect to treaties, and provisions therein, would be that ordinary meanings of words be given effect to, unless the context requires or otherwise. However, the fact that such treaties are drafted by diplomats, and not lawyers, leading to sloppiness in drafting also implies that care has to be taken to not render any word, phrase, or sentence redundant, especially where rendering of

such word, phrase or sentence redundant would lead to a manifestly absurd situation, particularly from a constitutional perspective. The government cannot bind India in a manner that derogates from Constitutional provisions, values and imperatives.

62. The last sentence of Article 26(1) of the double taxation agreement with Germany, "[T]hey may disclose this information in public court proceedings or in judicial decisions," is revelatory in this regard. It stands out as an additional aspect or provision, and an exception, to the preceding portion of the said article. It is located after the specification that information shared between contracting parties may be revealed only to "persons or authorities (including courts and administrative bodies) involved in the assessment or collection of, the enforcement or prosecution in respect of, or the determination of appeals in relation to taxes covered by this Agreement." Consequently, it has to be understood that the phrase "public court proceedings" specified in the last sentence in Article 26(1) of the double taxation agreement with Germany refers to court proceedings other than those in connection with tax assessment, enforcement, prosecution, etc., with respect to tax matters. If it were otherwise, as argued by Union of India, then there would have been no need to have that last sentence in Article 26(1) of the double taxation agreement at all. The last sentence would become redundant if the interpretation pressed by Union of India is accepted. Thus, notwithstanding the alleged convention of interpreting the last sentence only as referring to proceedings in tax matters, the rubric of common law jurisprudence, and fealty to its principles, leads us inexorably to the conclusion that the language in this specific treaty, and under these circumstances cannot be interpreted in the manner sought by Union of India.

63. While we agree that the language could have been tighter, and may be deemed to be sloppy, to use Frank Bennion's characterization, negotiation of such treaties are conducted and secured at very high levels of government, with awareness of general principles of interpretation used in various jurisdictions. It is fairly well known, at least in Common Law jurisdictions, that legal instruments and statutes are interpreted in amanner

whereby redundancy of expressions and phrases is sought to be avoided. Germany would have been well aware of it.

64. The redundancy that would have to be ascribed to the said last sentence of Article 26(1) of the double taxation agreement with Germany, if the position of Union of India were to be accepted, also leads to a manifest absurdity, in the context of the Indian Constitution. Such a redundancy would mean that constitutional imperatives themselves are to be set aside. Modern constitutionalism, to which Germany is a major contributor too, especially in terms of the basic structure doctrine, specifies that powers vested in any organ of the State have to be exercised within the four corners of the Constitution, and further that organs created by a Constitution cannot change the identity of the Constitution itself.

65. The basic structure of the Constitution cannot be amended even by the amending power of the legislature. Our Constitution guarantees the right, pursuant to Clause (1) of Article 32, to petition this Court on the ground that the rights guaranteed under Part III of the Constitution have been violated. This provision is a part of the basic structure of the Constitution. Clause (2) of Article 32 empowers this Court to issue "directions or orders or writs, including writs in the nature of *habeas corpus, mandamus, prohibition, quo warranto and certiorari*, whichever may be appropriate for the enforcement of any of the rights conferred by" Part III. This is also a part of the basic structure of the Constitution.

66. In order that the right guaranteed by Clause (1) of Article 32 be meaningful, and particularly because such petitions seek the protection of fundamental rights, it is imperative that in such proceedings the petitioners are not denied the information necessary for them to properly articulate the case and be heard, especially where such information is in the possession of the State. To deny access to such information, without citing any constitutional principle or enumerated grounds of constitutional prohibition, would be to thwart the right granted by Clause (1) of Article 32.

67. Further, in as much as, by history and tradition of common law, judicial proceedings are substantively, though not necessarily fully, adversarial, both parties bear the responsibility of placing all the relevant information, analyses, and facts before this court as completely as possible. In most situations, it is the State which may have more comprehensive information that is relevant to the matters at hand in such proceedings. However, some agents of the State may perceive that because these proceedings are adversarial in nature, the duty and burden to furnish all the necessary information rests upon the Petitioners, and hence the State has no obligation to fully furnish such information. Some agents of the State may also seek to cast the events and facts in a light that is favourable to the government in the immediate context of the proceedings, even though such actions do not lead to rendering of complete justice in the task of protection of fundamental rights. To that extent, both the petitioners and this Court would be handicapped in proceedings under Clause (1) of Article 32.

68. It is necessary for us to note that the burden of asserting, and proving, by relevant evidence a claim in judicial proceedings would ordinarily be placed upon the proponent of such a claim; however, the burden of protection of fundamental rights is primarily the duty of the State. Consequently, unless constitutional grounds exist, the State may not act in a manner that hinders this Court from rendering complete justice in such proceedings. Withholding of information from the petitioners, or seeking to cast the relevant events and facts in a light favourable to the State in the context of the proceedings, even though ultimately detrimental to the essential task of protecting fundamental rights, would be destructive to the guarantee in Clause (1) of Article 32, and substantially eviscerate the capacity of this Court in exercising its powers contained in Clause (2) of Article 32, and those traceable to other provisions of the Constitution and broader jurisprudence of constitutionalism, in upholding fundamental rights enshrined in Part III. In the task of upholding of fundamental rights, the State cannot be an adversary. The State has the duty, generally, to reveal all the facts and information in its possession to the Court, and also provide the same to the

petitioners. This is so, because the petitioners would also then be enabled to bring to light facts and the law that may be relevant for the Court in rendering its decision. In proceedings such as those under Article 32, both the petitioner and the State, have to necessarily be the eyes and ears of the Court. Blinding the petitioner would substantially detract from the integrity of the process of judicial decision making in Article 32 proceedings, especially where the issue is of upholding of fundamental rights.

69. Furthermore, we hold that there is a special relationship between Clause (1) of Article 32 and Sub-Clause (a) of Clause (1) of Article 19, which guarantees citizens the freedom of speech and expression. The very genesis, and the normative desirability of such a freedom, lies in historical experiences of the entire humanity: unless accountable, the State would turn tyrannical. A proceeding under Clause (1) of Article 32, and invocation of the powers granted by Clause (2) of Article 32, is a primordial constitutional feature of ensuring such accountability. The very promise, and existence, of a constitutional democracy rests substantially on such proceedings.

70. Withholding of information from the petitioners by the State, thereby constraining their freedom of speech and expression before this Court, may be premised only on the exceptions carved out, in Clause (2) of Article 19, "in the interests of sovereignty and integrity of India, security of the State, friendly relations with foreign States, public order, decency or morality, or in relation to contempt of court, defamation or incitement to an offence" or by law that demarcate exceptions, provided that such a law comports with the enumerated grounds in Clause (2) of Article 19, or that may be provided for elsewhere in the Constitution.

71. It is now a well recognized proposition that we are increasingly being entwined in a global network of events and social action. Considerable care has to be exercised in this process, particularly where governments which come into being on account of a constitutive document, enter into treaties. The actions of governments can only be lawful when exercised within the four corners of constitutional permissibility. No treaty can

be entered into, or interpreted, such that constitutional fealty is derogated from. The redundancy, that the Union of India presses, with respect to the last sentence of Article 26(1) of the double taxation agreement with Germany, necessarily transgresses upon the boundaries erected by our Constitution. It cannot be permitted.

72. We have perused the documents in question, and heard the arguments of Union of India with respect to the double taxation agreement with Germany as an obstacle to disclosure. We do not find merit in its arguments flowing from the provisions of double taxation agreement with Germany. However, one major constitutional issue, and concern remains. This is with regard to whether the names of individuals, and details of their bank accounts, with respect to whom there has been no completed investigations that reveal wrong doing and proceedings initiated, and there is no other credible information and evidence currently available with the Petitioners that there has been any wrong doing, may be disclosed to the Petitioners.

73. Right to privacy is an integral part of right to life. This is a cherished constitutional value, and it is important that human beings be allowed domains of freedom that are free of public scrutiny unless they act in an unlawful manner. We understand and appreciate the fact that the situation with respect to unaccounted monies is extremely grave. Nevertheless, as constitutional adjudicators we always have to be mindful of preserving the sanctity of constitutional values, and hasty steps that derogate from fundamental rights, whether urged by governments or private citizens, howsoever well meaning they may be, have to be necessarily very carefully scrutinised. The solution for the problem of abrogation of one zone of constitutional values cannot be the creation of another zone of abrogation of constitutional values. The rights of citizens, to effectively seek the protection of fundamental rights, under Clause (1) of Article 32 have to be balanced against the rights of citizens and persons under Article 21. The latter cannot be sacrificed on the anvil of fervid desire to find instantaneous solutions to systemic problems such as unaccounted monies, for it would lead to dangerous circumstances, in which vigilante

investigations, inquisitions and rabble rousing, by masses of other citizens could become the order of the day. The right of citizens to petition this Court for upholding of fundamental rights is granted in order that citizens, inter-alia, are ever vigilant about the functioning of the State in order to protect the constitutional project. That right cannot be extended to being inquisitors of fellow citizens. An inquisitorial order, where citizens' fundamental right to privacy is breached by fellow citizens is destructive of social order. The notion of fundamental rights, such as a right to privacy as part of right to life, is not merely that the State is enjoined from derogating from them. It also includes the responsibility of the State to uphold them against the actions of others in the society, even in the context of exercise of fundamental rights by those others.

74. An argument can be made that this Court can make exceptions under the peculiar circumstances of this case, wherein the State has acknowledged that it has not acted with the requisite speed and vigour in the case of large volumes of suspected unaccounted monies of certain individuals. There is an inherent danger in making exceptions to fundamental principles and rights on the fly.

Those exceptions, bit by bit, would then eviscerate the content of the main right itself. Undesirable lapses in upholding of fundamental rights by the legislature, or the executive, can be rectified by assertion of constitutional principles by this Court. However, a decision by this Court that an exception could be carved out remains permanently as a part of judicial canon, and becomes a part of the constitutional interpretation itself. It can be used in the future in a manner and form that may far exceed what this Court intended or what the Constitutional text and values can bear. We are not proposing that Constitutions cannot be interpreted in a manner that allows the nation state to tackle the problems it faces. The principle is that exceptions cannot be carved out willy-nilly, and without forethought as to the damage they may cause.

75. One of the chief dangers of making exceptions to principles that have become a part of constitutional law, through

aeons of human experience, is that the logic, and ease of seeing exceptions, would become entrenched as a part of the constitutional order. Such logic would then lead to seeking exceptions, from protective walls of all fundamental rights, on grounds of expediency and claims that there are no solutions to problems that the society is confronting without the evisceration of fundamental rights. That same logic could then be used by the State in demanding exceptions to a slew of other fundamental rights, leading to violation of human rights of citizens on a massive scale.

76. It is indeed true that the information shared by Germany, with regard to certain bank accounts in Liechtenstein, also contains names of individuals who appear to be Indians. The Petitioners have also claimed that names of all the individuals have been made public by certain segments of the media. However, while some of the accounts, and the individuals holding those accounts, are claimed to have been investigated, others have not been. No conclusion can be drawn as to whether those who have not been investigated, or only partially investigated and proceedings not initiated have committed any wrong doing. There is no presumption that every account holder in banks of Liechtenstein has acted unlawfully. In these circumstances, it would be inappropriate for this Court to order the disclosure of such names, even in the context of proceedings under Clause (1) of Article 32.

77. The revelation of details of bank accounts of individuals, without establishment of prima facie grounds to accuse them of wrong doing, would be a violation of their rights to privacy. Details of bank accounts can be used by those who want to harass, or otherwise cause damage, to individuals. We cannot remain blind to such possibilities, and indeed experience reveals that public dissemination of banking details, or availability to unauthorized persons, has led to abuse. The mere fact that a citizen has a bank account in a bank located in a particular jurisdiction cannot be a ground for revelation of details of his or her account that the State has acquired. Innocent citizens, including those actively working towards the betterment of the society and the nation, could fall prey to the machinations of

those who might wish to damage the prospects of smooth functioning of society. Whether the State itself can access details of citizens bank accounts is a separate matter. However, the State cannot compel citizens to reveal, or itself reveal details of their bank accounts to the public at large, either to receive benefits from the State or to facilitate investigations, and prosecutions of such individuals, unless the State itself has, through properly conducted investigations, within the four corners of constitutional permissibility, been able to establish prima facie grounds to accuse the individuals of wrong doing. It is only after the State has been able to arrive at a prima facie conclusion of wrong doing, based on material evidence, would the rights of others in the nation to be informed, enter the picture. In the event citizens, other persons and entities have credible information that a wrong doing could be associated with a bank account, it is needless to state that they have the right, and in fact the moral duty, to inform the State, and consequently the State would have the obligation to investigate the same, within the boundaries of constitutional permissibility. If the State fails to do so, the appropriate courts can always intervene.

78. The major problem, in the matters before us, has been the inaction of the State. This is so, both with regard to the specific instances of Hassan Ali Khan and the Tapurias, and also with respect to the issues regarding parallel economy, generation of black money, etc. The failure is not of the Constitutional values or of the powers available to the State; the failure has been of human agency. The response cannot be the promotion of vigilantism, and thereby violate other constitutional values. The response has to necessarily be a more emphatic assertion of those values, both in terms of protection of an individual's right to privacy and also the protection of individual's right to petition this Court, under Clause (1) of Article 32, to protect fundamental rights from evisceration of content because of failures of the State. The balancing leads only to one conclusion: strengthening of the machinery of investigations, and vigil by broader citizenry in ensuring that the agents of State do not weaken such machinery.

79. In light of the above we order that:

(i) The Union of India shall forthwith disclose to the Petitioners all those documents and information which they have secured from Germany, in connection with the matters discussed above, subject to the conditions specified in (ii) below;

(ii) That the Union of India is exempted from revealing the names of those individuals who have accounts in banks of Liechtenstein, and revealed to it by Germany, with respect of who investigations/enquiries are still in progress and no information or evidence of wrongdoing is yet available;

(iii) That the names of those individuals with bank accounts in Liechtenstein, as revealed by Germany, with respect of whom investigations have been concluded, either partially or wholly, and show cause notices issued and proceedings initiated may be disclosed; and

(iv) That the Special Investigation Team, constituted pursuant to the orders of today by this Court, shall take over the matter of investigation of the individuals whose names have been disclosed by Germany as having accounts in banks in Liechtenstein, and expeditiously conduct the same. The Special Investigation Team shall review the concluded matters also in this regard to assess whether investigations have been thoroughly and properly conducted or not, and on coming to the conclusion that there is a need for further investigation shall proceed further in the matter. After conclusion of such investigations by the Special Investigation Team, the Respondents may disclose the names with regard to whom show cause notices have been issued and proceedings initiated.

80. Compliance reports shall be filed by Respondents, with respect of all the orders issued by this Court today. List for further directions in the week following the Independence Day, August 15, of 2011.

Ordered accordingly.

...

APPENDIX-II

The Prevention of Corruption Act, 1988

PRELIMINARY

1. Short title and extent

(1) This Act may be called the Prevention of Corruption Act, 1988.

(2) It extends to the whole of India except the State of Jammu and Kashmir and it applies also to all citizens of India outside India.

2. Definitions

In this Act, unless the context otherwise requires—

(a) "election" means any election, by whatever means held under any law for the purpose of selecting members of Parliament or of any Legislature, local authority or other public authority;

(b) "public duty" means a duty in the discharge of which the State, the public or the community at large has an interest;

Explanation—In this clause "State" includes a corporation established by or under a Central, Provincial or State Act, or an authority or a body owned or controlled or aided by the Government or a Government company as defined in section 617 of the Companies Act, 1956.

(c) "public servant" means—

(i) any person in the service or pay of the Government or remunerated by the Government by fees or commission for the performance of any public duty;

(ii) any person in the service or pay of a local authority;

(iii) any person in the service or pay of a corporation established by or under a Central, Provincial or State Act, or an authority or a body owned or controlled or aided by the Government or a Government company as defined in section 617 of the Companies Act, 1956;

(iv) any Judge, including any person empowered by law to discharge, whether by himself or as a member of any body of persons, any adjudicatory functions;

(v) any person authorised by a court of justice to perform any duty, in connection with the administration of justice, including a liquidator, receiver or commissioner appointed by such court;

(vi) any arbitrator or other person to whom any cause or matter has been referred for decision or report by a court of justice or by a competent public authority;

(vii) any person who holds an office by virtue of which he is empowered to prepare, publish, maintain or revise an electoral roll or to conduct an election or part of an election;

(viii) any person who holds an office by virtue of which he is authorised or required to perform any public duty;

(ix) any person who is the president, secretary or other office-bearer of a registered co-operative society engaged in agriculture, industry, trade or banking, receiving or having received any financial aid from the Central Government or a State Government or from any corporation established by or under a Central, Provincial or State Act, or any authority or body owned or controlled or aided by the Government or a Government company as defined in section 617 of the Companies Act, 1956;

(x) any person who is a chairman, member or employee of any Service Commission or Board, by whatever name called, or a member of any selection committee appointed by such Commission or Board for the conduct of any examination or making any selection on behalf of such Commission or Board;

(xi) any person who is a Vice-Chancellor or member of any governing body, professor, reader, lecturer or any other teacher or employee, by whatever designation called, of any University and any person whose services have been availed of by a University or any other public authority in connection with holding or conducting examinations;

(xii) any person who is an office-bearer or an employee of an educational, scientific, social, cultural or other institution, in whatever manner established, receiving or having received any financial assistance from the Central Government or any State Government, or local or other public authority.

Explanation 1. Persons falling under any of the above sub-clauses are public servants, whether appointed by the Government or not.

Explanation 2. Wherever the words "public servant" occur, they shall be understood of every person who is in actual possession of the situation of a public servant, whatever legal defect there may be in his right to hold that situation.

3. Power to appoint special Judges

(1) The Central Government or the State Government may, by notification in the. Official Gazette, appoint as many special Judges as may be necessary for such area or areas or for such case or group of cases as may be specified in the notification to try the following offences, namely:

(a) any offence punishable under this Act; and

(b) any conspiracy to commit or any attempt to commit or any abetment of any of the offences specified in clause (a).

(2) A person shall not be qualified for appointment as a special Judge under this Act unless he is or has been a Sessions

Judge or an Additional Sessions Judge or an Assistant Sessions Judge under the Code of Criminal Procedure, 1973.

4. Cases triable by special Judges

(1) Notwithstanding anything contained in the Code of Criminal Procedure, 1973, or in any other law for the time being in force, the offences specified in sub-section (1) of section 3 shall be tried by special Judges only.

(2) Every offence specified in sub-section (1) of section 3 shall be tried by the special Judge for the area within which it was committed, or, as the case may be, by the special Judge appointed for the case, or where there are more special Judges than one for such area, by such one of them as may be specified in this behalf by the Central Government.

(3) When trying any case, a special Judge may also try any offence, other than an offence specified in section 3, with which the accused may, under the Code of Criminal Procedure, 1973, be charged at the same trial.

(4) Notwithstanding anything contained in the Code of Criminal Procedure, 1973, a special Judge shall, as far as practicable, hold the trial of an offence on day-to-day basis.

5. Procedure and powers of special Judge

(1) A special Judge may take cognizance of offences without the accused being committed to him for trial and, in trying the accused persons, shall follow the procedure prescribed by the Code of Criminal Procedure, 1973 for the trial of warrant cases by Magistrates.

(2) A special Judge may, with a view to obtaining the evidence of any person supposed to have been directly or indirectly concerned in or privy to, an offence, tender a pardon to such person on condition of his making a full and true disclosure of the whole circumstances within his knowledge, relating to the offence and to every other person concerned, whether as principal or abettor, in the commission thereof and any pardon so tendered shall, for the purposes of sub-sections (1) to (5) of section 308 of the Code of Criminal Procedure, 1973, be deemed to have been tendered under section 307 of that Code.

(3) Save as provided in sub-sections (1) or sub-section (2), the provisions of the Code of Criminal Procedure, 1973, shall, so far as they are not inconsistent with this Act, apply to the proceedings before a special Judge; and for the purposes of the said provisions, the Court of the special Judge shall be deemed to be a Court of Session and the person conducting a prosecution before a special Judge shall be deemed to be a public prosecutor.

(4) In particular and without prejudice to the generality of the provisions contained in sub-section (3), the provisions of sections 326 and 475 of the Code of Criminal Procedure, 1973, shall, so for as may be, apply to the proceedings before a special Judge and for the purposes of the said provisions, a special Judge shall be deemed to be a Magistrate.

(5) A special Judge may pass upon any person convicted by him any sentence authorised by law for the punishment of the offence of which such person is convicted.

(6) A special Judge, while trying an offence punishable under this Act, shall exercise all the powers and functions exercisable by a District Judge under the Criminal Law Amendment Ordinance, 1944.

6. Power to try summarily

(1) Where a special Judge tries any offence specified in sub-section (1) of section 3, alleged to have been committed by a public servant in relation to the contravention of any special order referred to in sub-section (1) of section 12A of the Essential Commodities Act, 1955 or of an order referred to in clause (a) of sub-section (2) of that section, then, notwithstanding anything contained in sub-section (1) of section 5 of this Act or section 260 of the Code of Criminal Procedure, 1973, the special Judge shall try the offence in a summary way, and the provisions of sections 262 to 265 (both inclusive) of the said Code shall, as far as may be, apply to such trial:

Provided that, in the case of any conviction in a summary trial under this section, it shall be lawful for the special Judge to pass a sentence of imprisonment for a term not exceeding one year:

Provided further that when at the commencement of, or in the course of, a summary trial under this section, it appears to the special Judge that the nature of the case is such that a sentence of imprisonment for a term exceeding one year may have to be passed or that it is, for any other reason, undesirable to try the case summarily, the special Judge shall, after hearing the parties, record an order to that effect and thereafter recall any witnesses who may have been examined and proceed to hear or re-hear the case in accordance with the procedure prescribed by the said Code for the trial of warrant cases by Magistrates.

(2) Notwithstanding anything to the contrary contained in this Act or in the code of Criminal Procedure, 1973, there shall be no appeal by a convicted person in any case tried summarily under this section in which the special Judge passes a sentence of imprisonment not exceeding one month, and of fine not exceeding two thousand rupees whether or not any order under section 452 of the said Code is made in addition to such sentence, but an appeal shall lie where any sentence in excess of the aforesaid limits is passed by the special Judge.

OFFENCES AND PENALTIES

7. Public servant taking gratification other than legal remuneration in respect of an official act

Whoever, being, or expecting to be a public servant, accepts or obtains or agrees to accept or attempts to obtain from any person, for himself or for any other person, any gratification whatever, other than legal remuneration, as a motive or reward for doing or forbearing to do any official act or for showing or forbearing to show, in the exercise of his official functions, favour or disfavour to any person or for rendering or attempting to render any service or disservice to any person, with the Central Government or any State Government or Parliament or the Legislature of any State or with any local authority, corporation or Government company referred to in clause (c) of section 2, or with any public servant, whether named or otherwise, shall be punishable with imprisonment which shall be not less than six months but which may extend to five years and shall also be liable to fine.

Explanations

(a) "Expecting to be a public servant." If a person not expecting to be in office obtains a gratification by deceiving others into a belief that he is about to be in office, and that he will then serve them, he may be guilty of cheating, but he is not guilty of the offence defined in this section.

(b) "Gratification." The word "gratification" is not restricted to pecuniary gratifications or to gratifications estimable in money.

(c) "Legal remuneration." The words "legal remuneration" are not restricted to remuneration which a public servant can lawfully demand, but include all remuneration which he is permitted by the Government or the organisation, which he serves, to accept.

(d) "A motive or reward for doing." A person who receives a gratification as a motive or reward for doing what he does not intend or is not in a position to do, or has not done, comes within this expression.

(e) Where a public servant induces a person erroneously to believe that his influence with the Government has obtained a title for that person and thus induces that person to give the public servant, money or any other gratification as a reward for this service, the public servant has committed an offence under this section.

8. Taking gratification, in order, by corrupt or illegal means, to influence public servant

Whoever accepts or obtains, or agrees to accept, or attempts to obtain, from any person, for himself or for any other person, any gratification whatever as a motive or reward for inducing, by corrupt or illegal means, any public servant, whether named or otherwise, to do or to forbear to do any official act, or in the exercise of the official functions of such public servant to show favour or disfavour to any person, or to render or attempt to render any service or disservice to any person with the Central Government or any State Government or Parliament or the Legislature of any State or with any local authority, corporation or Government company referred to in clause (c) of section 2, or with any public servant, whether named or otherwise, shall be punishable with imprisonment for a term which shall be not less than six months but which may extend to five years and shall also be liable to fine.

9. Taking gratification, for exercise of personal influence with public servant

Whoever accepts or obtains or agrees to accept or attempts to obtain, from any person, for himself or for any other person, any gratification whatever, as a motive or reward for inducing, by the exercise of personal influence, any public servant whether named or otherwise to do or to forbear to do any official act, or in the exercise of the official functions of such public servant to show favour or disfavour to any person, or to render or attempt to render any service or disservice to any person with the Central Government or any State Government or Parliament or the Legislature of any State or with any local authority, corporation or Government company referred to in clause (c) of section 2, or with any public servant, whether named or otherwise, shall be punishable with imprisonment for a term which shall be not less than six months but which may extend to five years and shall also be liable to fine.

10. Punishment for abetment by public servant of offences defined in section 8 or 9

Whoever, being a public servant, in respect of whom either of the offences defined in section 8 or 9 is committed, abets the offence, whether or not that offence is committed in consequence of that abetment, shall be punishable with imprisonment for a term which shall be not less than six months but which may extend to five years and shall also be liable to fine.

11. Public servant obtaining valuable thing, without consideration from person concerned in proceeding or business transacted by such public servant

Whoever, being a public servant, accepts or obtains or agrees to accept or attempts to obtain for himself, or for any other person, any valuable thing without consideration, or for a consideration which he knows to be inadequate, from any person whom he knows to have been, or to be, or to be likely to be concerned in any proceeding or business transacted or about to be transacted by such public servant, or having any connection with the official functions of himself or of any public servant to whom he is subordinate, or from any person whom he knows to be interested in or related to the person so concerned, shall be punishable with imprisonment for a term which shall be not less than six months but which may extend to five years and shall also be liable to fine.

12. Punishment for abetment of offences defined in section 7 or 11

Whoever abets any offence punishable under section 7 or 11 whether or not that offence is committed in consequence of that abetment, shall be punishable with imprisonment for a term which shall be not less than six months but which may extend to five years and shall also be liable to fine.

13. Criminal misconduct by a public servant

(1) A public servant is said to commit the offence of criminal misconduct,

(a) if he habitually accepts or obtains or agrees to accept or attempts to obtain from any person for himself or for any other person any gratification other than legal remuneration as a motive or reward such as is mentioned in section 7; or

(b) if he habitually accepts or obtains or agrees to accept or attempts to obtain for himself or for any other person, any valuable thing without consideration or for a consideration which he knows to be inadequate from any person whom he knows to have been, or to be, or to be likely to be concerned in any proceeding or business transacted or about to be transacted by him, or having any connection with the official functions of himself or of any public servant to whom he is subordinate, or from any person whom he knows to be interested in or related to the person so concerned; or

(c) if he dishonestly or fraudulently misappropriates or otherwise converts for his own use any property entrusted to him or under his control as a public servant or allows any other person so to do; or

(d) if he,

(i) by corrupt or illegal means, obtains for himself or for any other person any valuable thing or pecuniary advantage; or

(ii) by abusing his position as a public servant, obtains for himself or for any other person any valuable thing or pecuniary advantage; or

(iii) while holding office as a public servant, obtains for any person any valuable thing or pecuniary advantage without any public interest; or

(e) if he or any person on his behalf, is in possession or has, at any time during the period of his office, been in possession for which the public servant cannot satisfactorily account, of pecuniary resources or property disproportionate to his known sources of income.

Explanation. For the purposes of this section, "known sources of income" means income received from any lawful source and such receipt has been intimated in accordance with the provisions of any law, rules or orders for the time being applicable to a public servant.

(2) Any public servant who commits criminal misconduct shall be punishable with imprisonment for a term which shall be not less than one year but which may extend to seven years and shall also be liable to fine.

14. Habitual committing of offence under sections 8, 9 and 12

Whoever habitually commits—

(a) an offence punishable under section 8 or 9; or

(b) an offence punishable under section 12, shall be punishable with imprisonment for a term which shall be not less than two years but which may extend to seven years and shall also be liable to fine.

15. Punishment for attempt

Whoever attempts to commit an offence referred to in clause (c) or clause (d) of sub-section (1) of section 13 shall be punishable with imprisonment for a term which may extend to three years and with fine.

16. Matters to be taken into consideration for fixing fine

Where a sentence of fine is imposed under sub-section (2) of section 13 or 14, the court in fixing the amount of the fine shall taken into consideration the amount or the value of the property, if any, which the accused person has obtained by committing the offence or where the conviction is for an offence referred to in clause (e) of sub-section (1) of section 13, the pecuniary resources or property referred to in that clause for which the accused person is unable to account satisfactorily.

INVESTIGATION INTO CASES UNDER THE ACT

17. Persons authorised to investigate

Notwithstanding anything contained in the Code of Criminal Procedure, 1973, no police officer below the rank,

(a) in the case of the Delhi Special Police Establishment, of an Inspector of Police;

(b) in the metropolitan areas of Bombay, Calcutta, Madras and Ahmedabad and in any other metropolitan area notified as such under sub-section (1) of section 8 of the Code of Criminal Procedure, 1973, of an Assistant Commissioner of Police;

(c) elsewhere, of a Deputy Superintendent of Police or a police officer of equivalent rank, shall investigate any offence punishable under this Act without the order of a Metropolitan Magistrate or a Magistrate of the first class, as the case may be, or make any arrest therefor without a warrant:

Provided that if a police officer not below the rank of an Inspector of Police is authorised by the State Government in this behalf by general or special order, he may also investigate any such offence without the order of a

Metropolitan Magistrate or a Magistrate of the first class, as the case may be, or make arrest therefor without a warrant:

Provided further that an offence referred to in clause (e) of sub-section (1) of section 13 shall not be investigated without the older of a police officer not below the rank of a Superintendent of Police.

18. Power to inspect bankers' books

If from information received or otherwise, a police officer has reason to suspect the commission of an offence which he is empowered to investigate under section 17 and considers that for the purpose of investigation or inquiry into such offence, it is necessary to inspect any bankers' books, then, notwithstanding anything contained in any law for the time being in force, he may inspect any bankers' books in so far as they relate to the accounts of the persons suspected to have committed that offence or of any other person suspected to be holding money on behalf of such person, and take or cause to be taken certified copies of the relevant entries therefrom, and the bank concerned shall be bound to assist the police officer in the exercise of his powers under this section:

Provided that no power under this section in relation to the accounts of any person shall be exercised by a police officer below the rank of a Superintendent of Police, unless he is specially authorised in this behalf by a police officer of or above the rank of a Superintendent of Police.

Explanation. In this section, the expressions "bank" and "bankers' books" shall have the meanings respectively assigned to them in the Bankers' Books Evidence Act, 1891.

19. Previous sanction necessary for prosecution

(1) No court shall take cognizance of an offence punishable under sections 7, 10, 11, 13 and 15 alleged to have been committed by a public servant, except with the previous sanction,

(a) in the case of a person who is employed in connection with the affairs of the Union and is not removable from his office save by or with the sanction of the Central Government, of that Government;

(b) in the case of a person who is employed in connection with the affairs of a State and is not removable from his office save by or with the sanction of the State Government, of that Government;

(c) in the case of any other person, of the authority competent to remove him from his office.

(2) Where for any reason whatsoever any doubt arises as to whether the previous sanction as required under sub-section (1) should be given by the Central Government or the State Government or any other authority, such sanction shall be given by that Government or authority which would have been competent to remove the public servant from his office at the time when the offence was alleged to have been committed.

(3) Notwithstanding anything contained in the code of Criminal Procedure, 1973,

(a) no finding, sentence or order passed by a special Judge shall be reversed or altered by a Court in appeal, confirmation or revision on the ground of the absence of, or any error, omission or irregularity in, the sanction required under sub-section (1), unless in the opinion of that court, a failure of justice has in fact been occasioned thereby;

(b) no court shall stay the proceedings under this Act on the ground of any error, omission or irregularity in the sanction granted by the authority, unless it is satisfied that such error, omission or irregularity has resulted in a failure of justice;

(c) no court shall stay the proceedings under this Act on any other ground and no court shall exercise the powers of revision in relation to any interlocutory order passed in any inquiry, trial, appeal or other proceedings.

(4) In determining under sub-section (3) whether the absence of, or any error, omission or irregularity in, such sanction has occasioned or resulted in a failure of justice the court shall have

regard to the fact whether the objection could and should have been raised at any earlier stage in the proceedings.

Explanation. For the purposes of this section,

(a) error includes competency of the authority to grant sanction;

(b) a sanction required for prosecution includes reference to any requirement that the prosecution shall be at the instance of a specified authority or with the sanction of a specified person or any requirement of a similar nature.

20. Presumption where public servant accepts gratification other than legal remuneration

(1) Where, in any trial of an offence punishable under section 7 or 11 or clause (a) or (b) of sub-section (1) of section 13 it is proved that an accused person has accepted or obtained or has agreed to accept or attempted to obtain for himself, or for any other person, any gratification (other than legal remuneration) or any valuable thing from any person, it shall be presumed, unless the contrary is proved, that he accepted or obtained or agreed to accept or attempted to obtain that gratification or that valuable thing, as the case may be, as a motive or reward such as is mentioned in section 7 or, as the case may be, without consideration or for a consideration which he knows to be Inadequate.

(2) Where in any trial of an offence punishable under section 12 or under clause (b) of section 14, it is proved that any gratification (other than legal remuneration) or any valuable thing has been given or offered to be given or attempted to be given by an accused person, it shall be presumed, unless the contrary is proved, that he gave or offered to give or attempted to give that gratification or that valuable thing, as the case may be, as a motive or reward such as is mentioned in section 7, or, as the case may be, without consideration or for a consideration which he knows to be inadequate.

(3) Notwithstanding anything contained in sub-sections (1) and (2), the court may decline to draw the presumption referred to in either of the said sub-sections, if the gratification or thing

aforesaid is, in its opinion, so trivial that no inference of corruption may fairly be drawn.

21. Accused person to be a competent witness

Any person charged with an offence punishable under this Act, shall be a competent witness for the defence and may give evidence on oath in disproof of the charges made against him or any person charged together with him at the same trial:

Provided that

(a) he shall not be called as a witness except at his own request;

(b) his failure to give evidence shall not be made the subject of any comment by the prosecution or give rise to any presumption against himself or any person charged together with him at the same trial;

(c) he shall not be asked, and if asked shall not be required to answer, any question tending to show that he has committed or been convicted of any offence other than the offence with which he is charged, or is of bad character, unless—

(i) the proof that he has committed or been convicted of such offence is admissible evidence to that he is guilty of the offence with which he is charged, or

(ii) he has personally or by his pleader asked any question of any witness for the prosecution with a view to establish his own good character, or has given evidence of his good character, or the nature or conduct of the defence is such as to involve imputations on the character of the prosecutor or of any witness for the prosecution, or

(iii) he has given evidence against any other person charged with the same offence.

22. The Code of Criminal Procedure, 1973 to apply subject to certain modifications

The provisions of the Code of Criminal Procedure, 1973, shall in their application to any proceeding in relation to an offence punishable under this Act have effect as if,

(a) in sub-section (1) of section 243, for the words "The accused shall then be called upon", the words "The accused shall then be required to give in writing at once or within such time as the Court may allow, a list of the persons (if any) whom he proposes to examine as his witnesses and of the documents (if any) on which he proposes to rely and he shall then be called upon" had been substituted;

(b) in sub-section (2) of section 309, after the 'third proviso, the following proviso had been inserted, namely:

"Provided also that the proceeding shall not be adjourned or postponed merely on the ground that an application under section 397 has been made by a party to the proceeding.";

(c) after sub-section (2) of section 317, the following sub-section had been inserted, namely:

"(3) Notwithstanding anything contained in sub-section (1) or sub-section (2), the Judge may, if he thinks fit and for reasons to be recorded by him, proceed with inquiry or trial in the absence of the accused or his pleader and record the evidence of any witness subject to the right of the accused to recall the witness for cross-examination";

(d) in sub-section (1) of section 397, before the Explanation, the following proviso had been inserted, namely:

"Provided that where the powers under this section are exercised by a Court on an application made by a party to such proceedings, the Court shall not ordinarily call for the record of the proceedings:

(a) without giving the other party an opportunity of showing cause why the record should not be called for; or

(b) if it is satisfied that an examination of the record of the proceedings may be made from the certified copies."

23. Particulars in a charge in relation to an offence under section 13(1) (c).

Notwithstanding anything contained in the Code of Criminal Procedure, 1973, when an accused is charged with an offence under clause (c) of sub-section (1) of section 13, it shall be sufficient to describe in the charge the property in respect of which the offence is alleged to have been committed, and the dates between which the offence is alleged to have been committed, without specifying particular items or exact dates, and the charge so framed shall be deemed to be a charge of one offence within the meaning of section 219 of the said Code:

Provided that the time included between the first and last of such dates shall not exceed one year.

24. Statement by bribe giver not to subject him to prosecution

Notwithstanding anything contained in any law for the time being in force, a statement made by a person in any proceeding against a public servant for an offence under sections 7 to 11 or under section 13 or section 15, that he offered or agreed to offer any gratification (other than legal remuneration) or any valuable thing to the public servant, shall not subject such person to a prosecution under section 12.

25. Military, Naval and Air Force or other law not to be affected

(1) Nothing in this Act shall affect the jurisdiction exercisable by, or the procedure applicable to, any court or other authority under the Army Act, 1950, the Air Force Act, 1950, the Navy Act, 1957, the Border Security Force Act, 1968, the Coast Guard Act, 1978 and the National Security Guard Act, 1986.

(2) For the removal of doubts, it is hereby declared that for the purposes of any such law as is referred to in sub-section (1), the court of a special Judge shall be deemed to be a court of ordinary criminal justice.

26. Special Judges appointed under Act 46 of 1952 to be special Judges appointed under this Act

Every special Judge appointed under the Criminal Law Amendment Act, 1952, for any area or areas and is holding office on the commencement of this Act shall be deemed to be a special Judge appointed under section 3 of this Act for that area or areas and, accordingly, on and from such commencement, every such Judge shall continue to deal with all the proceedings pending before him on such commencement in accordance with the provisions of this Act.

27. Appeal and revision

Subject to the provisions of this Act, the High Court may exercise, so far as they may be applicable, all the powers of appeal and revision conferred by the Code of Criminal Procedure, 1973 on a High Court as if the court of special Judge were a court of Session trying cases within the local limits of the High Court.

28. Act to be in addition to any other law

The provisions of this Act shall be in addition to, and not in derogation of, any other law for the time being in force, and nothing contained herein shall exempt any public servant from any proceeding which might, apart from this Act, be instituted against him.

29. Amendment of the Ordinance 38 of 1944

In the Criminal Law Amendment Ordinance, 1944,

(a) in sub-section (1) of section 3, sub-section (1) of section 9, clause (a) of section 10, sub-section (1) of section 11 and sub-section (1) of section 13, for the words "State Government", wherever they occur, the words "State Government or, as the case may be, the Central Government" shall be substituted;

(b) in section 10, in clause (a), for the words "three months", the words "one year" shall be substituted;

(c) in the Schedule,

 (i) paragraph 1 shall be omitted;

 (ii) in paragraphs 2 and 4,

(a) after the words "a local authority", the words and figures "or a corporation established by or under a Central, Provincial or State Act, or an authority or a body owned or controlled or aided by Government or a Government company as defined in section 617 of the Companies Act, 1956 or a society aided by such corporation, authority, body or Government company" shall be inserted;

(b) after the words "or authority", the words "or corporation or body or Government company or society" shall be inserted;

(iii) for paragraph 4A, the following paragraph shall be substituted, namely:

"4A. An offence punishable under the Prevention of Corruption Act, 1988.";

(iv) in paragraph 5, for the words and figures "items 2, 3 and 4", the words, figures and letter "items 2, 3, 4 and 4A" shall be substituted.

30. Repeal and saving

(1) The Prevention of Corruption Act, 1947 and the Criminal Law Amendment Act, 1952 are hereby repealed.

(2) Notwithstanding such repeal, but without prejudice to the application of section 6 of the General Clauses Act, 1897, anything done or any action taken or purported to 'have been done or taken under or in pursuance of the Acts so repealed shall, in so far as it is not inconsistent with the provisions of this Act, be deemed to have been done or taken, under or in pursuance of the corresponding provision of this Act.

31. Omission of certain sections of Act 45 of 1860

Sections 161 to 165A (both inclusive) of the Indian Penal Code shall be omitted, and section 6 of the General Clauses Act, 1897, shall apply to such omission as if the said sections had been repealed by a Central Act.